60 Hikes Within 60 Miles: Tampa

60 Hikes Within 60 Miles:

TAMPA

Carolee Boyles   1st Edition

MENASHA RIDGE PRESS
Birmingham, Alabama

DEDICATION

For my parents, who gave me both roots and wings, and taught me to dream.

Copyright © 2001 Carolee Boyles
All rights reserved
Manufactured in the United States of America
Published by Menasha Ridge Press
Distributed by The Globe Pequot Press
First edition, first printing

Library of Congress Cataloging-in-Publication Data

Boyles, Carolee 1953–
  60 hikes within 60 miles, Tampa/by Carolee Boyles
  p. cm.
  Includes index
  ISBN 0-89732-366-1 (alk. paper)
  1. Hiking—Florida—Tampa Region—Guidebooks. 2. Tampa Region (Fl.)—
Guidebooks. I. Title: Sixty hikes within sixty miles, Tampa. II. Title
GV199.42.F62 T363 2001
917.59'650464—dc21

00-068368
CIP

Cover and text design by Grant M. Tatum
Cover photo by Carolee Boyles
Maps by Steve Jones and Susanna Fillingham
Author photo by Faye Boyles
All other photos by Carolee Boyles

Menasha Ridge Press
P.O. Box 43673
Birmingham, AL 35243
www.menasharidge.com

Table of Contents

Table of Contents (continued)

APPENDICES

MAP LEGEND

Main Trail

Alternate Trail

Interstate Highway

U.S. Highway

State Highway

County Road

Forest Service Road

Local Road

Unpaved Road

Direction of Travel

Board Walk

State Border

County Border

Power Line

NATIONAL OR STATE
FOREST/PARK

Park-Forest Boundary
and Label

Trailhead
Locator Map

Water Features
Lake/Pond, Creek/River,
and Waterfall

capitol, city, and town

Peaks and Mountains

Footbridge/Dam,
Footbridge, and Dam

Tunnel

Swamp/Marsh

35: Name of Hike

Map Scale

Compass, Map Number,
Name and Scale

Off map or pinpoint
indication arrow

Caution/Warning

Trailhead
for specific Maps

Ranger Station/
Rest Room Facilities

Ranger Station

Rest Room Facilities

Shelter

Structure
or Feature

Monument/
Sculpture

Parking

Recreation Area

Campgrounds

Picnic Area

Gate

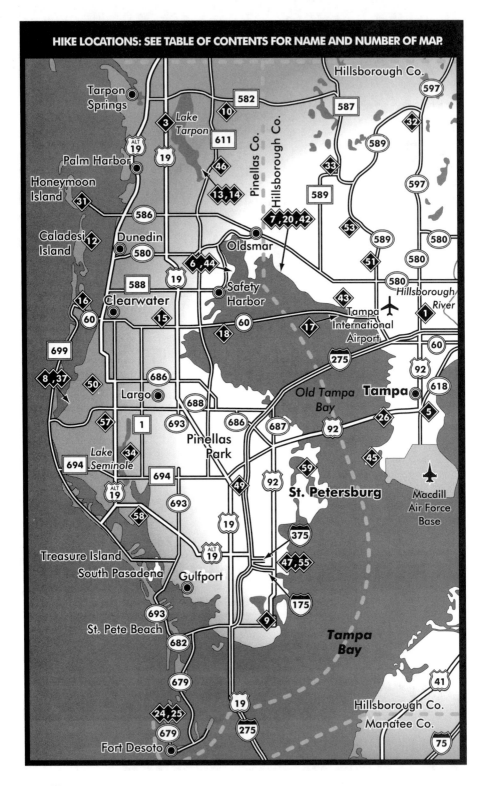

HIKE LOCATIONS: SEE TABLE OF CONTENTS FOR NAME AND NUMBER OF MAP.

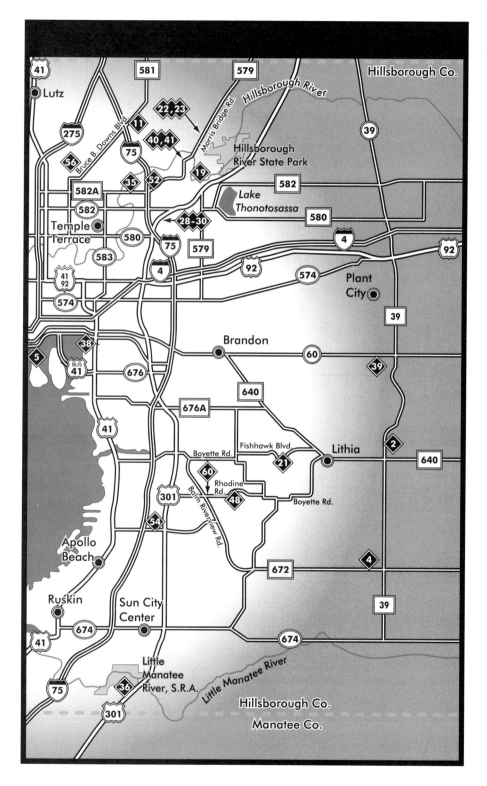

Acknowledgments

A book like this doesn't happen because of the efforts of just one person; I'm grateful to many people who helped me with this project.

First and foremost is Laura Diss, without whose dedication and persistence many of the ELAPP trails would not have been included, and who also found several Hillsborough County park trails of which I was unaware. Laura, thank you.

Bud Zehmer, who allowed me to take on this wonderful project, should get a special award for his patience. This turned into a much bigger undertaking than I ever imagined it would, and Bud's calm perseverance kept me on track.

Russell Helms, my editor at Menasha Ridge Press, must be one of the world's master list-makers. His lists of maps and trail descriptions kept all of us in the loop about what still needed to be done.

Melissa Mathis typed reams of my recorded trail notes, and did yeoman's service in the phonetic spelling of many names and terms with which she was unfamiliar.

And to the guys in the Phalanx Media Group office who hiked with me and helped me with maps—thank you.

Foreword

Welcome to Menasha Ridge Press's *60 Hikes Within 60 Miles,* a series designed to provide hikers with information needed to find and hike the very best trails surrounding cities that are usually underserved by good guidebooks.

Our goal was simple: First, find a hiker who knows the area and loves to hike. Second, ask that person to spend a year researching the most popular and very best trails around. And third, have that person describe each trail in terms of difficulty, scenery, condition, elevation change, and all other categories of information that are important to hikers. "Pretend you've just completed a hike and met up with other hikers at the trailhead," we tell each author. "Imagine their questions; be clear in your answers."

An experienced hiker and writer, author Carolee Boyles has selected 60 of her favorite hikes in and around the Tampa region. From the civilized greenways of downtown Tampa to the historic walks of Fort De Soto, Boyles provides hikers (and walkers) with a great variety of trails—and all within 60 miles of Tampa.

You'll get more out of this book if you take a moment to read the Introduction explaining how to read the trail listings. The "Maps" section will help you understand how useful topos can be on a hike, and also will tell you where to get them. And since this is a "where-to," not a "how-to" guide, even those of you who have hiked extensively will find the Introduction of particular value.

As much for the opportunity to free the mind as well as to free the body, let Carolee Boyle's hikes elevate you above the urban hurry.

All the best.
The editors at Menasha Ridge Press

Preface

When I began the research for this book, I was skeptical—where would I find 60 hikes within 60 miles of Tampa? At that time, I had lived in Tampa for only three years, and it seemed to me that all of Tampa and surrounding Hillsborough County was nothing but a blur of city, with very little green space anywhere.

What I learned is that there's plenty of green space out there. As soon as I took out the map and started looking, I found green spaces, both large and small, everywhere. There had been wilderness right under my nose for three years, but because I assumed it wasn't there and didn't look for it, I hadn't found it.

Hillsborough and Pinellas counties have simply done an excellent job of conserving green space—including a few wild areas—right in the shadows of their cities. Just go outside, and right around the corner you'll find everything from highly developed parks to hidden wildernesses. Many of these areas have the potential for many more hikes, some short, some long. I found so many hikes close to home that I never ventured anywhere near the theoretical 60-mile boundary of this book—the hikes

Hikers can relax in the shade at Fred C. Bonner Park.

You may see alligators from the trail at Lake Seminole Park.

profiled here are from Hillsborough and Pinellas counties. In fact, there are a number of hikes within these two counties that I've been unable to include.

At the same time, Tampa and Hillsborough County are aggressively pushing forward with plans for new trails and greenways throughout the area. In February of 2001, the Tampa City Council approved a plan by the Tampa Parks Department to develop a greenways and trails system. Under their plan an extensive network of bike paths, roadside trails, and green space corridors will link existing trails and parks. Some of the proposed trails' routes will follow major highways and thoroughfares, but others will traverse quiet residential areas and green spaces.

A plan of this magnitude will take years to complete. In the meantime, though, a number of groups are proceeding with plans to build and extend trails in their own jurisdictions.

And that brings up an important caveat to this book: there are a few trails where, when you get out to the trail site, what you find there may be significantly longer or more developed than the trail description indicates. I know of two trails scheduled for major changes in the near future. An extension to Upper Tampa Bay Trail is due to open any day, and the Fishhawk Trail—which was sand when we were there—is slated to open as a paved trail. You may find other changes as well as you hike some of these areas.

With all of these trails and hikes available, you'd think that they'd be quite busy, particularly on weekends. And you'd be right. The urban trails—particularly Bayshore Boulevard and the Friendship Trail Bridge—are busy every day of the week. And although many other trails are quiet or even deserted during the week, some of them have quite a lot of traffic on weekends. As you'll notice in the individual descriptions, however, some of the trails continue to be very quiet and almost undiscovered, even right in town.

A swampy, wet view from a boardwalk on the Lettuce Lake Trail

One other thing I learned while profiling these hikes is that central Florida has an abundance of poison ivy. Fortunately, I seem to be in the 20 percent of the population that's not sensitive to its toxin, since I've never had a rash from it. But before you go out on the trail, learn what poison ivy looks like so you don't walk through it. Remember the old saying, "Leaves of three, leave them be."

A few other hazards to be aware of: mosquitoes, ticks, and snakes. Under the right conditions, a local mosquito population can explode virtually overnight, and can make your hike miserable. Walking through grass and brush, you're also at risk to pick up ticks. With the potential that both have to transmit disease, always apply insect repellent. If you can, tuck your pant legs into your boots to keep out the ticks.

As far as snakes are concerned, you are likely to see some. While doing the research for this book, we saw several species of non-venomous snakes on a number of hikes. Although we didn't see

any rattlesnakes or other venomous snakes, they're certainly out there. The best advice we can give you is this: Watch where you put your hands and feet. Carry a cell phone with you—we didn't find any place on any of these hikes where our cell phone service did not work. If you are bitten, sit down, remain still, and call for help.

ABOUT THE HIKES

The hikes in this book can be divided into several general categories according to the type of facility in which they're located: city, county, and regional parks; urban hikes; greenways; state parks; causeway hikes; and ELAPP sites. Each group of trails is distinctly different, and each individual trail within those groups has its own unique personality.

CITY, COUNTY, AND REGIONAL PARKS

This is by far the largest category of hikes in the book, and also the most diverse. Some of the parks are highly developed, with playgrounds, recreation areas, boat ramps, and full facilities. Most of the Pinellas County parks, and some of the Hillsborough County parks, fall into this group. Others, particularly in Hillsborough County, are still very quiet and have minimal development—Lake Rogers Park comes to mind. A few of these hikes are quite short, and are good "starter" hikes for families with small children. Others, such as the Medard Park Trail, are harder hikes appropriate for more serious hikers. Among the parks are several with many miles of trails, of which we profiled only a few. Medard Park is one of these, along with Flatwoods Park, Trout Creek, and Alderman's Ford Park.

URBAN HIKES

There are only a handful of hikes that I'd classify as truly urban. Most of the urban hikes in this book follow greenways or causeways and I've categorized all of them that way. However three trails—Bruce B. Downs Trail, Friendship Trail Bridge, and the Pinellas Trail Expansion—parallel major highways. One trail in this category that we chose not to classify as urban is the Pinellas Trail. This 47-mile-long trail connects a number of parks in Pinellas County; information on it is available from the Pinellas County Parks Department.

GREENWAYS

Both Pinellas and Hillsborough counties have done an excellent job of creating linear greenway spaces with sidewalks and trails. The best known is Bayshore Boulevard in Tampa, but quite a few others exist. Although most of these are quite urban and have a lot of traffic on them, one of the advantages to hiking greenways is that you can take a multi-mile walk without having to drive a long way to get there. My favorite in this category is definitely

the Clearwater East-West Trail, but I'm also quite fond of Bayshore Boulevard and the entire area from Pioneer Park to Flora Wylie Park in St. Petersburg.

STATE PARKS

The Florida state park system is extensive and well developed, with trails in many of the state parks. The one that's closest to Tampa—Hillsborough River State Park—has a large network of trails that's well worth the trip. If you go out to Honeymoon Island State Park, plan to spend the day and allow time to go over to Caladesi Island. These two trail areas have a lot of "Wow!" in them.

CAUSEWAY HIKES

I stumbled onto the idea of hiking the causeways entirely by accident. I happened to be driving across the Courtney Campbell Causeway one day to take my son to a doctor's appointment and glanced over to the side of the road to see someone walking a dog. The following weekend I went back and discovered that the Courtney Campbell Causeway has an access road right along the water that makes a great hike/bicycle ride/place to fish. As I drove around the area and looked, I found a number of other causeways with similar access roads. Three of them—the two Courtney Campbell trails and the Clearwater Memorial Greenway—are included in this book. If you look around you'll find others, including one on the Dunedin Causeway and one on the north end of the Sunshine Skyway on the east side of the road.

ELAPP SITES

ELAPP sites are the most intriguing category of hikes in this book. ELAPP stands for "Environmental Lands Acquisition and Protection Program." Hillsborough

County has ushered these sites into public ownership to protect and preserve their natural resources. Many of them are located in highly urbanized areas, but aren't well known. In many cases, the trail that we've profiled is simply the most obvious of a number of footpaths on a site.

I encourage you to investigate more of the ELAPP areas than the eight I've included in the book. Get a copy of *Hidden Treasures of Tampa Bay* from the Hillsborough County Parks and Recreation Department and go exploring.

Hiking Recommendations

Hikes under 1 Mile
Bobcat Loop
Bonner Park Trail
John Chesnut Sr. Park Trail I
Eagle Trail
McGough Nature Park Loop
Otter Loop
Pam Callahan Nature Preserve Trail
Picnic Island Loop

Hikes from 1 to 3 Miles
Alderman's Ford Park Loop
Al Lopez Park Trail
Anderson Park Trail
Boyd Hill Nature Park Trails
Brooker Creek Preserve Loop
Caladesi Island State Park Loop
John Chesnut Sr. Park Trail II
Clearwater Mem. Causeway Greenway
Dead River Trail
Fishhawk Trail
Flatwoods Park Trail I
Fort De Soto Park Main Trail
Hammock Park Trail
Hillsborough River S.P. Nature Trails
Hillsborough River Wetlands Trail
Honeymoon Island Nature Loop
Lake Park Loop
Lake Rogers Park Loop
Lake Seminole Park Trail
Lettuce Lake Regional Park Loop
McKay Bay Wildlife Park Trail
Philippe Park Trail
Pioneer Park to Vinoy Park Greenway
Sawgrass Lake Park Trail
Taylor Park Nature Trail
Town and Country Greenway
Trout Creek Trail
Vance Vogel Park Loop
Vinoy Park to Flora Wylie Park Greenway
Violet Cury Nature Preserve Loop
Walsingham Park Trail
War Veteran's Memorial Park Trail
Weedon Island Preserve Trail

Hikes from 3 to 6 Miles
Balm-Boyette Scrub Loop
Bayshore Linear Greenway Rec. Trail
Courtney Campbell Causeway West
Friendship Trail Bridge
Hillsborough River S.P. Main Trail
Medard Park Trail
Morris Bridge Main Trail
Morris Bridge Primitive Trail
Rhodine Road Loop
Upper Tampa Bay Trail
Wortham County Park Loop

Hikes over 6 Miles
Bayshore Boulevard
Bruce B. Downs Trail
Clearwater East-West Trail
Courtney Campbell Causeway East
Flatwoods Park Trail II
Fort De Soto Nature Trail
Little Manatee River Loop
Pinellas Trail Expansion

Hikes Good for Young Children
Alderman's Ford Park Loop
Al Lopez Park Trail
Anderson Park Trail
Bayshore Boulevard (short sections)
Bayshore Linear Greenway Rec. Trail
  (short sections)
Bobcat Loop
Bonner Park Trail
Boyd Hill Nature Park Trails
John Chesnut Sr. Park Trail I
John Chesnut Sr. Park Trail II
Dead River Trail
Eagle Trail
Friendship Trail Bridge
Hammock Park Trail
Hillsborough River S.P. Nature Trails
Hillsborough River Wetlands Trail
Lake Rogers Park Loop
Lake Seminole Park Trail
Lettuce Lake Regional Park Loop
McGough Nature Park Loop

McKay Bay Wildlife Park Trail
Otter Loop
Pam Callahan Nature Preserve Trail
Philippe Park Trail
Picnic Island Loop
Pioneer Park to Vinoy Park Greenway
Sawgrass Lake Park Trail
Taylor Park Nature Trail
Town and Country Greenway
Upper Tampa Bay Trail (short sections)
Vinoy Park to Flora Wylie Park Greenway
Walsingham Park Trail

Urban Hikes

Al Lopez Park Trail
Anderson Park Trail
Bayshore Boulevard
Bayshore Linear Greenway Rec. Trail
Bobcat Loop
Bonner Park Trail
Boyd Hill Nature Park Trails
Bruce B. Downs Trail
John Chesnut Sr. Park Trail I
John Chesnut Sr. Park Trail II
Clearwater East-West Trail
Clearwater Mem. Causeway Greenway
Courtney Campbell Causeway East
Courtney Campbell Causeway West
Eagle Trail
Fort De Soto Park Main Trail
Fort De Soto Nature Trail
Friendship Trail Bridge
Hammock Park Trail
Lake Park Loop
Lake Seminole Park Trail
McGough Nature Park Loop
McKay Bay Wildlife Park Trail
Otter Loop
Pam Callahan Nature Preserve Trail
Philippe Park Trail
Picnic Island Loop
Pinellas Trail Expansion
Pioneer Park to Vinoy Park Greenway
Sawgrass Lake Park Trail
Taylor Park Nature Trail
Town and Country Greenway
Upper Tampa Bay Trail
Vinoy Park to Flora Wylie Park Greenway
Walsingham Park Trail
War Veteran's Memorial Park Trail
Weedon Island Preserve Trail

Causeway Hikes

Clearwater Mem. Causeway Greenway
Courtney Campbell Causeway East
Courtney Campbell Causeway West
Friendship Trail Bridge

Hikes with Elevation Gain/Loss

Anderson Park Trail
Boyd Hill Nature Park Trails
Caladesi Island State Park Loop
Clearwater East-West Trail
Friendship Trail Bridge
Lake Rogers Park Loop
Little Manatee River Loop
Philippe Park Trail
Walsingham Park Trail

Lake Hikes

Al Lopez Park Trail
Anderson Park Trail
Balm-Boyette Scrub Loop
Boyd Hill Nature Park Trails
John Chesnut Sr. Park Trail I
John Chesnut Sr. Park Trail II
Lake Park Loop
Lake Rogers Park Loop
Lettuce Lake Regional Park Loop
Sawgrass Lake Park Trail
Taylor Park Nature Trail
Walsingham Park Trail

Oceanside/Bayside Hikes

Bayshore Boulevard
Bayshore Linear Greenway Rec. Trail
Bonner Park Trail
Caladesi Island State Park Loop
Clearwater Mem. Causeway Greenway
Courtney Campbell Causeway East
Courtney Campbell Causeway West
Eagle Trail
Fort De Soto Park Main Trail
Fort De Soto Nature Trail
Friendship Trail Bridge
Honeymoon Island Nature Loop
McKay Bay Wildlife Park Trail
Philippe Park Trail
Picnic Island Loop
Pioneer Park to Vinoy Park Greenway
Vinoy Park to Flora Wylie Park Greenway
Weedon Island Preserve Trail

Scenic Hikes

Alderman's Ford Park Loop
Bobcat Loop
Bonner Park Trail
Brooker Creek Preserve Loop
Caladesi Island State Park Loop
John Chesnut Sr. Park Trail I
John Chesnut Sr. Park Trail II
Clearwater East-West Trail
Dead River Trail
Eagle Trail
Fishhawk Trail

Flatwoods Park Trail I
Flatwoods Park Trail II
Fort De Soto Park Main Trail
Fort De Soto Nature Trail
Hammock Park Trail
Hillsborough River S.P. Main Trail
Hillsborough River S.P. Nature Trails
Hillsborough River Wetlands Trail
Honeymoon Island Nature Loop
Lake Rogers Park Loop
Lake Seminole Park Trail
Lettuce Lake Regional Park Loop
Little Manatee River Loop
Medard Park & Reservoir Trail
Morris Bridge Primitive Trail
Otter Loop
Philippe Park Trail
Picnic Island Loop
Pioneer Park to Vinoy Park Greenway
Rhodine Road Loop
Sawgrass Lake Park Trail
Trout Creek Trail
Upper Tampa Bay Trail (some areas)
Vance Vogel Park Loop
Vinoy Park to Flora Wylie Park Greenway
Violet Cury Nature Preserve Loop
Walsingham Park Trail

Hikes on or near Historic Sites
Bayshore Boulevard
Fort De Soto I
Fort De Soto Nature Trail
Hillsborough River S.P. Main Trail
Hillsborough River S.P. Nature Trails
Hillsborough River Wetlands Trail
Philippe Park Trail
Pioneer Park to Vinoy Park Greenway
War Veteran's Memorial Park Trail
Weedon Island Preserve Trail

Hikes for Wildlife Viewing
Alderman's Ford Park Loop
Balm-Boyette Scrub Loop
Bobcat Loop
Boyd Hill Nature Park Trails
Brooker Creek Preserve Loop
Caladesi Island State Park Loop
John Chesnut Sr. Park Trail I
John Chesnut Sr. Park Trail II
Dead River Trail
Eagle Trail
Fishhawk Trail
Flatwoods Park Trail II
Fort De Soto Park Main Trail
Hammock Park Trail
Hillsborough River S.P. Main Trail
Hillsborough River S.P. Nature Trails

Hillsborough River Wetlands Trail
Honeymoon Island Nature Loop
Lake Park Loop
Lake Rogers Park Loop
Little Manatee River Loop
McKay Bay Wildlife Park Trail
Morris Bridge Primitive Trail
Otter Loop
Pam Callahan Nature Preserve Trail
Picnic Island Loop
Rhodine Road Loop
Sawgrass Lake Park Trail
Vance Vogel Park Loop
Violet Cury Nature Preserve Loop
Wortham County Park Loop
Trout Creek Trail

Hikes for Bird-watching
Alderman's Ford Park Loop
Balm-Boyette Scrub Loop
Bayshore Boulevard
Bayshore Linear Greenway Rec. Trail
Bobcat Loop
Bonner Park Trail
Boyd Hill Nature Park Trails
Brooker Creek Preserve Loop
Caladesi Island State Park Loop
John Chesnut Sr. Park Trail I
John Chesnut Sr. Park Trail II
Clearwater Mem. Causeway Greenway
Courtney Campbell Causeway East
Courtney Campbell Causeway West
Dead River Trail
Eagle Trail
Fishhawk Trail
Flatwoods Park Trail II
Fort De Soto Park Main Trail
Fort De Soto Nature Trail
Hammock Park Trail
Hillsborough River S.P. Main Trail
Hillsborough River S.P Nature Trails
Hillsborough River S.P Wetlands Trail
Honeymoon Island S.R.A Trails
Lake Park Loop
Lake Seminole Park Trail
Lake Rogers Park Loop
Lettuce Lake Regional Park Loop
Little Manatee River Loop
McGough Nature Park Loop
McKay Bay Wildlife Park Trail
Morris Bridge Main Trail
Morris Bridge Primitive Trail
Otter Loop
Pam Callahan Nature Preserve Trail
Philippe Park Trail
Picnic Island Loop

Pioneer Park to Vinoy Park Greenway
Rhodine Road Loop
Sawgrass Lake Park Trail
Taylor Park Nature Trail
Trout Creek Trail
Vinoy Park to Flora Wylie Park Greenway
Violet Cury Nature Preserve Loop
Walsingham Park Trail
Weedon Island Preserve Trail
Wortham County Park Loop

Hikes for Wildflowers
Alderman's Ford Park Loop
Boyd Hill Nature Park Trails
Fort De Soto Park Main Trail
McKay Bay Wildlife Park Trail
Pam Callahan Nature Preserve Trail
Town and Country Greenway
Upper Tampa Bay Trail (some areas)
Walsingham Park Trail

Trails for Runners
Al Lopez Park Trail
Bayshore Boulevard
Bayshore Linear Greenway Rec. Trail
Boyd Hill Nature Park Trails
Bruce B. Downs Trail
Clearwater East-West Trail
Clearwater Mem. Causeway Greenway
Courtney Campbell Causeway East
Courtney Campbell Causeway West
Flatwoods Park Trail II
Fort De Soto Nature Trail
Friendship Trail Bridge
Lake Park Loop
Lake Seminole Park Trail
Lettuce Lake Regional Park Loop
Philippe Park Trail
Pinellas Trail Expansion
Pioneer Park to Vinoy Park Greenway
Town and Country Greenway
Upper Tampa Bay Trail
Vinoy Park to Flora Wylie Park Greenway
Walsingham Park Trail

Trails for Cyclists
Al Lopez Park Trail
Bayshore Boulevard
Bayshore Linear Greenway Rec. Trail
Boyd Hill Nature Park Trails
Bruce B. Downs Trail
Clearwater East-West Trail
Clearwater Mem. Causeway Greenway
Courtney Campbell Causeway East
Courtney Campbell Causeway West
Flatwoods Park Trail I

Flatwoods Park Trail II
Fort De Soto Nature Trail
Friendship Trail Bridge
Lake Park Loop
Lake Seminole Park Trail
Lettuce Lake Regional Park Loop
Morris Bridge Main Trail
Philippe Park Trail
Pinellas Trail Expansion
Pioneer Park to Vinoy Park Greenway
Town and Country Greenway
Upper Tampa Bay Trail
Vinoy Park to Flora Wylie Park Greenway
Walsingham Park Trail
War Veteran's Memorial Park Trail
Wortham County Park Loop

Less Busy Hikes
Alderman's Ford Park Loop
Balm-Boyette Scrub Loop
Bobcat Loop
Bonner Park Trail
Brooker Creek Preserve Loop
Caladesi Island State Park Loop
Dead River Trail
Eagle Trail
Fishhawk Trail
Lake Rogers Park Loop
Little Manatee River Loop
Morris Bridge Primitive Trail
Pam Callahan Nature Preserve Trail
Rhodine Road Loop
Vance Vogel Park Loop
Violet Cury Nature Preserve Loop

Heavily Traveled Hikes
Al Lopez Park Trail
Anderson Park Trail
Bayshore Boulevard
Bayshore Linear Greenway Rec. Trail
Bruce B. Downs Trail
Friendship Trail Bridge
Hillsborough River S.P Main Trail
Hillsborough River S.P Nature Trails
Lettuce Lake Regional Park Loop
McGough Nature Park Loop
Medard Park & Reservoir Trail
Morris Bridge Main Trail
Philippe Park Trail
Pioneer Park to Vinoy Park Greenway
Sawgrass Lake Park Trail
Upper Tampa Bay Trail
Vinoy Park to Flora Wylie Park Greenway
War Veteran's Memorial Park Trail

Introduction

Welcome to *60 Hikes within 60 Miles: Tampa!* If you're new to hiking or even if you're a seasoned trail-smith, take a few minutes to read the following introduction. We explain how this book is organized and how to use it.

HIKE DESCRIPTIONS

Each hike contains six key items: a locator map, an In Brief description of the trail, an At-a-Glance Information box, directions to the trail, a trail map, and a hike narrative. Combined, the maps and information provide a clear method to assess each trail from the comfort of your favorite chair.

Locator Map

After narrowing down the general area of the hike on the overview map (see pp. viii–ix), use the locator map, along with driving directions given in the profile, to find the trailhead. At the trailhead, park only in designated areas.

In Brief

This synopsis of the trail offers a snapshot of what to expect along the trail, including mention of any historical sights, beautiful vistas, or other interesting sights you may encounter.

At-a-Glance Information

The At-a-Glance Information boxes give you a quick idea of the specifics of each hike. There are 13 basic elements covered.

Length The length of the trail from start to finish. There may be options to

shorten or extend the hikes, but the mileage corresponds to the described hike. Consult the hike description to help decide how to customize the hike for your ability or time constraints.

Configuration A description of what the trail might look like from overhead. Trails can be loops, out-and-backs (that is, along the same route), figure eights, or balloons. Sometimes the descriptions might surprise you.

Difficulty The degree of effort an "average" hiker should expect on a given hike. For simplicity, difficulty is described as "easy," "moderate," or "hard."

Scenery Rates the overall environs of the hike and what to expect in terms of plant life, wildlife, streams, or historic buildings.

Exposure A quick check of how much sun you can expect on your shoulders during the hike. Descriptors used are self-explanatory and include terms such as shady, exposed, and sunny.

Traffic Indicates how busy the trail might be on an average day. Trail traffic, of course, will vary from day to day and season to season.

Trail surface Indicates whether the trail is paved, rocky, smooth dirt, or a mixture of elements.

Hiking time How long it took the author to hike the trail.

Season Times of year when this trail is accessible. In most cases, the limiting factor

1

is the weather. Fortunately Tampa's trails are generally accessible year round.

Access   Notes fees or permits needed to access the trail.

Maps   Which map is the best, in the author's opinion, for this hike. See Appendix B for places to buy maps.

Facilities   Notes any facilities such as rest rooms, phones, and water available at the trailhead or on the trail.

Special comments   Provides you with those little extra details that don't fit into any of the above categories. Here you'll find information on trail hiking options and facts such as whether or not to expect a lifeguard at a nearby swimming beach.

Directions

Check here for directions to the trailhead. Used with the locator map, the directions will help you locate each trailhead.

Description

The trail description is the heart of each hike. Here, the author has provided a summary of the trail's essence as well as highlighted any special traits the hike offers. Ultimately the hike description will help you choose which hikes are best for you.

Nearby Activities

Not every hike will have this listing. For those that do, look here for information on nearby dining opportunities or other activities to fill out your day.

WEATHER

The best time to go hiking in the Tampa Bay area is any time you can. This area has been blessed with mild winters, and with few exceptions, you can get out and hike almost any day of the year.

During the winter, the morning temperature falls below 40 degrees on occasion, and we may even have frost a few mornings in January and February. If that's too cold, wait until the middle of the day and you'll

almost certainly have temperatures warm enough to go hiking.

On the hottest days of summer, from late July to early September, go hiking first thing in the morning; even if you wait until late in the day, the temperature and humidity won't have dropped enough to be really comfortable. The most pleasant times, though, are mid-September to early December, and late February to mid-May.

Although Tampa Bay doesn't have much in the way of fall foliage, we do have sunny Indian summer days when the light pours down like melted butter and covers everything in a kind of golden glow just before sunset.

Average Daily (High/Low) Temperatures by Month, Tampa, Florida

Month	High	Low
January	50	70
February	52	72
March	56	76
April	61	82
May	67	88
June	73	90
July	74	90
August	74	90
September	73	89
October	66	84
November	57	77
December	52	72

Into the winter, the weather sometimes turns nasty, as cold fronts sweeping down from the north may bring a day or two of cold rain. But once the front is past, you'll have several days of bluebird skies that are just the best for getting out on a trail. As the weather turns toward spring and the jacarandas and other semi-tropical trees and plants start to bloom, you'll find bright flowers everywhere. Starting during this time, and extending through the summer, be aware of the possibility of thunderstorms; this is the worst weather hazard we face (short of hurricanes), and you need to be careful not to get caught by one when you're out on a trail.

MAPS

The maps in this book have been produced with great care and, when used with the hiking directions, will help you get to the trailhead and stay on course. But as any experienced hiker knows, things can get tricky off the beaten path.

For even more information on a particular trail look to the United States Geological Survey's 7.5 minute series topographic maps (topos). Recognizing how indispensable these are to hikers and bikers alike, many outdoor shops and bike shops now carry topos of the local area.

If you're new to hiking, you might be wondering, "What's a topographic map?" In short, these differ from standard "flat" maps; topos indicate not only linear distance but elevation as well. One glance at a topo will show you the difference: contour lines spread across the map like dozens of intricate spider webs. Each contour line represents a particular elevation, and at the base of each topo a particular contour interval designation is given.

Let's assume that the 7.5 minute series topo reads "Contour Interval 40 feet," that the short trail we'll be hiking is 2 inches in length on the map, and that it crosses 5 contour lines from its beginning to end. What do we know? Well, because the linear scale of this series is 2,000 feet to the inch (roughly 2.75 inches representing one mile), we know our trail is approximately 0.8 miles long (2 inches are 2,000 feet). But we also know we'll be climbing or descending 200 vertical feet (5 contour lines are 40 feet each) over that distance. And the elevation designations written on occasional contour lines will tell us if we're heading up or down.

In addition to outdoor shops and bike shops, you'll find topos at major

universities and some public libraries, where you might try photocopying the ones you need to avoid the cost of buying them. But if you want your own and can't find them locally, contact:

USGS Map Sales
Box 25286
Denver, CO 80225
(888) ASK-USGS(275-8747)
www.mapping.usgs.gov/esic/

Visa and MasterCard are accepted. Ask for an index while you're at it, plus a price list and a copy of the booklet *Topographic Maps*. In minutes you'll be reading topos like a pro.

A second excellent series of maps available to hikers is distributed by the United States Forest Service. If your trail runs through an area designated as a National Forest, look in the phone book under the United States Government listings, find the Department of Agriculture heading, and run your finger down that section until you find the Forest Service. Give them a call, and they'll provide the address of the regional Forest Service office, from which you can obtain the appropriate map.

TRAIL ETIQUETTE

Whether you're on a city walk or on a long hike, remember that great care and resources (from nature as well as from tax dollars) have gone into creating these trails. Taking care of the trails begins with you, the hiker. Treat the trail, wildlife, and your fellow hikers with respect. Here are a few general ideas to keep in mind while hiking:

1. Hike on open trails only. Respect trail and road closures (ask if you're not sure), avoid trespassing on private land, and obtain any required permits or authorization. Leave gates as you found them or as marked.

2. Leave no trace of your visit other than footprints. Be sensitive to the land beneath your feet. This also means staying on the trail and not creating any new ones. Be sure to pack out what you pack in. No one likes to see trash someone else has left behind.

3. Never spook animals. Give animals extra room and time to adjust to you.

4. Plan ahead. Know your equipment, your ability, and the area in which you are hiking—and prepare accordingly. Be self-sufficient at all times; carry necessary supplies for changes in weather or other conditions. A well-executed trip is a satisfaction to you and not a burden or offense to others.

5. Be courteous to other hikers, or bikers, you meet on the trails.

WATER

"How much is enough? One bottle? Two? Three?! But think of all that extra weight!" Well, one simple physiological fact should convince you to err on the side of excess when it comes to deciding how much water to pack: While working hard in 90-degree heat, we each need approximately 10 quarts of fluid every day. That's 2.5 gallons—12 large water bottles or 16 small ones. And, with water weighing in at approximately 8 pounds per gallon, a 1-day supply comes to a whopping 20 pounds.

In other words, pack along one or two bottles even for short hikes. Most of these hikes have water at the trailhead or along the way. But if you must use water that's not from a tap, make sure you purify it. If you drink it untreated, you run the risk of disease.

Many hikers pack along the inexpensive and only slightly distasteful tetraglycine hydroperiodide tablets (sold under the names Potable Aqua, Globaline, and Coughlan's, among others). Time for these tablets to work their magic is usually about 30 minutes—the colder the water, the longer it takes. Some invest in portable, lightweight purifiers that filter out the crud. Unfortunately, even the best filters only remove up to 98 to 99 percent of all those nasty bacteria, viruses, and other organisms you can't see.

Tablets or iodine drops by themselves will knock off the well-known Giardia. One to four weeks after ingestion, Giardia will have you bloated, vomiting, shivering with chills, and living in the bathroom.

But there are other parasites to worry about, including cryptosporidium. "Crypto" brings on symptoms very similar to Giardia, but unlike that fellow protozoan it's equipped with a shell sufficiently strong to protect it against the chemical killers that stop Giardia cold. This means either boiling the water or using a water filter to screen out both Giardia and crypto, plus the iodine to knock off viruses.

Some water filters come equipped with an iodine chamber to guarantee nearly full protection. Or you can simply add a pill or drops to the water you've just filtered (if you aren't allergic to iodine, of course). The pleasures of hiking—and the displeasure of getting sick—make this relatively minor effort worth every one of the few minutes involved.

FIRST-AID KIT

A typical kit may contain more items than you might think necessary. These are just the basics.

Sunscreen
Aspirin or acetaminophen
Butterfly-closure bandages
Band-Aids
Snakebite kit
Gauze (one roll)
Gauze compress pads (a half-dozen
  4 in. x 4 in.)
Ace bandages or Spenco joint wraps

Benadryl or the generic equivalent—
  diphenhydramine (an antihistamine,
  in case of allergic reactions)
A prefilled syringe of epinephrine (for
  those known to have severe allergic
  reactions to such things as bee stings)
Water purification tablets or water filter
  (on longer hikes)
Moleskin/Spenco "Second Skin"
Hydrogen peroxide or iodine
Antibiotic ointment (Neosporin or the
  generic equivalent)
Matches or pocket lighter
Whistle (more effective in signaling res-
  cuers than your voice)

Pack the items in a waterproof bag such as
a Ziploc bag or a similar product.

HIKING WITH CHILDREN

No one is too young for a nice hike in
the woods or through a city park. Parents
with infants can strap the little ones on
with devices such as the Baby-Björn Baby
Carrier® or Kelty's Kangaroo®. Be careful, though. Flat, short trails are probably
best with an infant. Toddlers who have not
quite mastered walking can still tag along,
riding on an adult's back in a child carrier.

Children who are walking can, of
course, follow along with an adult. Use
common sense to judge a child's capacity
to hike a particular trail. Always rely on the
possibility that the child will tire quickly
and have to be carried.

When packing for the hike, remember
the child's needs as well as your own. Make
sure children are adequately clothed for the
weather, have proper shoes, and are properly
protected from the sun with sunscreen and
clothing. Kids dehydrate quickly, so make
sure you have plenty of clean water and
other drinks for everyone.

Depending on age, ability, and the hike
length/difficulty, most children should
enjoy the shorter hikes described in this
book. To assist an adult with determining
which trails are suitable for children, a list
of hike recommendations for children is
provided on pages xix–xx.

THE BUSINESS HIKER

Whether you're in the Tampa area on business as a resident or visitor, these hikes are
the perfect opportunity to make a quick
getaway from the demands of commerce.
Many of the hikes are classified as urban
and are easily accessible from downtown
areas.

Instead of a burger down the street, pack
a lunch and head out to one of the area's
many urban trails for a relaxing break from
the office or that tiresome convention. Or
plan ahead and take a small group of your
business comrades on a nearby hike in one
of the area parks. A well-planned half-day
getaway is the perfect complement to a
business stay in Tampa.

60 Hikes Within 60 Miles:

TAMPA

Al Lopez Park Trail

W. Hillsborough Ave.
580
92
West Shore Blvd.
N. Lois
Dale Mabry Hwy.
1
N. Himes Ave.
N. Habana Ave.
Armenia Ave.
Dr. MLK Jr. Blvd.
92

IN BRIEF

This is an outstanding urban park, with a trail that goes through a variety of habitats, full facilities, and quick and easy access from anywhere in Tampa.

DIRECTIONS

From Dale Mabry Highway at Raymond James Stadium, proceed north to the first traffic light (Dr. Martin Luther King Jr. Boulevard) and turn right (east). Go one block and turn left at the traffic light on North Himes Avenue. Go north on Himes 0.5 miles and look for the park entrance on the left. After you enter the park go past the picnic pavilions on the left and turn left into the main parking lot.

DESCRIPTION

The trail is divided into two parts: a southern loop for bicycles, and a northern loop for foot traffic only. However, you will see an occasional bicycle on the northern portion. Hikers, bicyclists, in-line skaters, joggers, and casual walkers of all ages use the trail heavily.

Signs direct hikers to the trail, indicating which is for bicycles and which is for hikers only. On the boardwalk, a few very small interpretive signs give information on the hardwood hammock there. Near the stormwater retention area in the middle of the south loop, several kiosks offer educational information about the role of wetlands in water conservation.

AT-A-GLANCE INFORMATION

Length:
2.5 miles

Configuration:
Two connected loops

Difficulty:
Easy

Scenery:
Variety of woodland habitats with a lake view

Exposure:
Variable, from well shaded to exposed

Traffic:
Busy, even on weekdays

Trail surface:
Paved, except for boardwalk/nature trail

Hiking time:
1 to 1.25 hours

Season:
All year

Access:
No permits or fees

Maps:
No map published

Facilities:
Rest rooms and water fountains are available along the south loop of the trail.

9

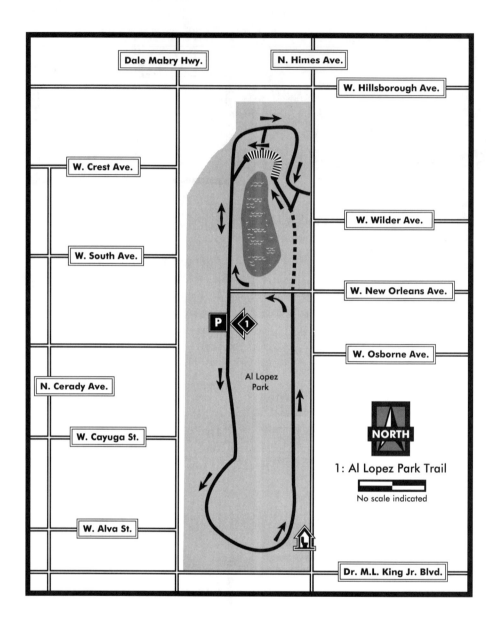

Map labels:

Dale Mabry Hwy.

N. Himes Ave.

W. Hillsborough Ave.

W. Crest Ave.

W. South Ave.

W. Wilder Ave.

W. New Orleans Ave.

P 1

W. Osborne Ave.

N. Cerady Ave.

Al Lopez Park

NORTH

W. Cayuga St.

1: Al Lopez Park Trail

No scale indicated

W. Alva St.

Dr. M.L. King Jr. Blvd.

Turn right as you leave the parking lot and you'll be on the paved road that comprises the south loop of the trail. This road is closed to traffic, so you'll have to pass the gate, which opens only to allow maintenance vehicles onto the road.

Immediately after you enter the trail, you'll see the dog park on your right.

Because of the proximity of the dog park, you'll encounter people walking dogs on this trail, but they're required to keep their dogs on leashes at all times.

Just inside the main trail and following its route is a Vita-Course which also is designated a Thera-Trail, meaning that it's designed for wheelchair users as well as able-bodied athletes. This course follows the entire southern loop of the trail.

Opposite the dog park, inside the loop, look for a large wooden castle that serves as a jungle gym and play area for children and adults. Surrounding the castle are swing sets and other conventional playground equipment. Beyond the playground, the center of the loop is an open field big enough for casual organized sports.

Past the dog park, the right side of the trail is wooded, with a nice stand of hardwoods. Further south both sides of the trail are wooded, although the trees are not large enough to create a canopy over the trail. This area is a little on the wet side, with a number of small cypress trees scattered among the oaks.

As the trail starts to curve to the left to make the bottom of the loop, there's a wonderful oak tree on the right whose branches curve over and touch the ground. Under the tree is a bench where you can sit and enjoy the sensation of being in a great green cavern.

Just past the oak, both sides of the trail open up to become grassy fields with scattered trees. In this area, several sand trails go off to the right through the woods and field in the south end of the park.

As you continue around the bottom of the loop, look for the cypress stand on the right side of the trail. This is part of a little wooded wetland that spans both sides of the trail.

Beyond the cypress stand, just as the trail swings back to the north, a sidewalk on the right takes you to rest rooms and a water fountain. This section of the trail is more open, with a nice stand of pines on the left.

As you round the loop and start back north, a spur to the left leads to a small wooden footbridge that spans a man-made wetland. This wetland is part of

The north loop of the trail is narrower and is primarily for hikers.

South Pond, a stormwater retention area. Several interpretive signs describe what a stormwater retention area is and how it works. A little farther up the trail, and set more toward the center of the loop, another spur and bridge take you deeper in the wetland.

As you near the end of the wetland area, the trail forks to the left away from the road you're on. Follow the trail past the recycling center on the right and into the edge of the picnic area again, where it winds through a small stand of pines and then turns to the left. Proceed past the four connected picnic pavilions on the left and cross the footbridge that spans a small stream. Follow the trail as it turns to the left again, until you reach the cluster of cypress trees. Here, you can take a dirt path to the right from the trail to the edge of the parking lot.

Instead of turning left to return to your vehicle, turn right and proceed north along the edge of the parking lot until you reach the road. Cross the road and you'll be on the second loop of the trail. This loop is designated for hikers only, but you'll still see an occasional bicycle on it.

On this loop the trees are smaller, but closer to the trail, than on the southern loop. Look through the trees to the right and you'll catch several views of the stocked Fish Management Area where anglers can fish. Just as you reach the head of the pond, you can see a fish feeder that's 30 feet or so out into the water.

As you pass the head of the pond you're into some bigger trees that are part of a hardwood hammock at the north end of Al Lopez Park. Look to the right and you'll see a boardwalk that traverses the hammock; don't take it now, because you'll be coming back on it in just a few minutes.

Follow the paved trail around to the right through the oak and cypress trees; there's a little bit of a hill here, which is the only part of the trail with any elevation gain. As the trail swings around the hammock and back to the south it becomes a little more open. Continue on it as it makes a left-hand turn around the maintenance yard and reaches the back gate of the park.

At the back gate, turn around and start back past the maintenance yard. As you pass the yard, take the first sand trail on the left into the woods. A short distance in, you'll come to a metal bridge on your left. Turn right, away from the bridge, and you'll be on the trail that leads to the elevated boardwalk along the edge of the pond.

A short distance down the boardwalk you'll see a spur to the left; this leads to one of two fishing docks on the pond. Don't swim in this pond; there are alligators here.

After you pass the fishing dock the boardwalk turns to the left and traverses the hardwood hammock. As it enters the hammock there's another spur to the right where you can leave the boardwalk and walk through the woods to return to the paved trail.

Continue on the boardwalk for a walk through the cypresses and ferns of the hammock. Look on several posts for small signs explaining the hammock, although they're hard to see. At the end of the boardwalk you'll re-enter the paved portion of the trail; turn left and return to the parking lot for the entire 2.5-mile hike.

NEARBY ATTRACTIONS

Al Lopez Park is in the shadow of Raymond James Stadium, where the 2001 Super Bowl was held. The winter home of the New York Yankees is across from the stadium on Dale Mabry Highway, where you can see a Yankees game or visit the baseball gift shop.

Within the park, there are many places where families can have a picnic or spend the day. Inside the north loop of the trail, a stocked lake provides fishing opportunities from two piers.

Alderman's Ford Park Loop

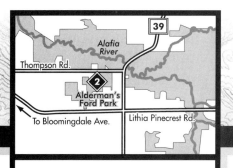

IN BRIEF

Alderman's Ford Park is one of Hillsborough County's ELAPP sites. One portion is already developed as a park, but much of the area is still in its original condition.

DIRECTIONS

From downtown Tampa, take Interstate 75 south to US 301. Go south on 301 to Bloomingdale Avenue and turn left (east). Turn right (south) at Lithia Pinecrest Road. When the road curves east, look for County Road 39 and head north on it less than a mile to Alderman's Ford Park, on the left.

DESCRIPTION

Alderman's Ford Park is part of a much larger site for which future development is planned. Plans include a hiking trail network that could link the park with Lithia Springs Park. Alderman's Ford Park Loop is a good example of a number of combination sites being developed by Hillsborough County, on which existing parks are supplement by recreational use on adjoining wild lands that still have large blocks of native flora and fauna. This is a great trail for families armed with a couple of guidebooks about Florida's wildlife and plants.

There is a recreation area near the trailhead with full facilities, including a picnic area, playground, rest rooms, fishing, and a canoe launch into the Alafia

AT-A-GLANCE INFORMATION

Length:
1.9 miles

Configuration:
Loop

Difficulty:
Flat, easy walking

Scenery:
Oak canopy

Exposure:
Scattered shade throughout

Traffic:
Underutilized, even on weekends.

Trail surface:
Hard-packed dirt and sand

Hiking time:
1 to 1.5 hours

Season:
All year

Access:
No fees or permits

Maps:
Site can be located on *Hidden Treasures of Tampa Bay*, map published by the Hillsborough County Department of Park and Recreation.

Facilities:
Rest rooms located near the trailhead in main portion of park

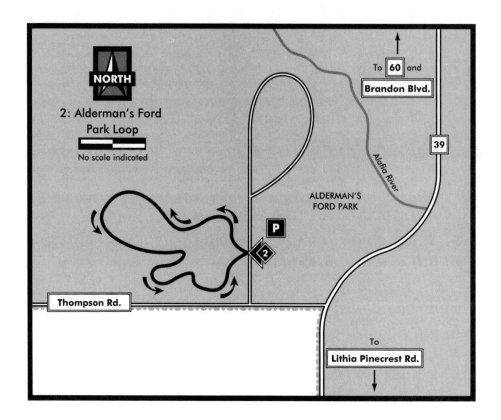

2: Alderman's Ford
Park Loop

No scale indicated

To 60 and
Brandon Blvd.

39

Alafia River

ALDERMAN'S
FORD PARK

P

2

Thompson Rd.

To
Lithia Pinecrest Rd.

River. The trail is designed as a nature trail but is long enough for hikers as well.

At the very beginning of the trail, look up into the oak canopy to see an excellent example of Spanish moss draped over the branches. Spanish moss is not actually a moss, nor is it a parasite on the trees, but is a flowering plant in the Bromeliad family. Historically, the upholstery industry used Spanish moss as a vegetable "hair," and as a packing material. However, because of the introduction of synthetic fibers, the industry no longer uses Spanish moss, and the commercial harvesting of this plant has stopped. Birds use the strands in their nests; lizards and other animals make their homes or nests in thick bunches of this plant. In many areas, Spanish moss is

dying off, perhaps because of poor air quality, or because of a fungus, no one is quite sure.

As you proceed along the trail, watch on both sides for large stands of saw palmetto and wax myrtle, ready fuel for a very fire-prone habitat. Also along the way, look for the lovely large patches of ferns mixed into the understory.

Underfoot, watch for animal tracks. Because the trail is hard-packed sand, tracks are easy to see. On the day we hiked it, we saw deer and possibly hog tracks (it's almost impossible to tell the difference), and many other tracks crossing the trail.

As you proceed, you'll soon come to the first of several open meadows covered with native flowers and grasses. Watch here for box turtles, as well as doves, which spend a lot of time feeding on seeds in these open areas.

At the top of the loop, although the oak canopy is denser, the moss drape becomes less abundant. Watch here for pileated woodpeckers hammering on the oaks. Although this bird has been removed from the Endangered Species List, there's still cause for concern. Big old pine trees, which the woodpeckers need for nesting, are becoming scarce..

In the same section of oaks and ferns we saw owls high in the great oaks. They were awake and watching us, despite the fact that we were there in the middle of the day.

Perhaps the nicest surprise we had on this hike took place in the last quarter of the trail. High in the tops of several towering royal palms, we heard the distinctive, and at times annoying, screeching of green parrots. The nest there is huge, and on that day the parrots seemed intent on spending all their time making it even larger. It's worth stopping for a little while to watch their antics as they screech at each other while adding on to the already giant nest.

The Alafia River meanders near the trail.

Anderson Park Trail

IN BRIEF

This is a short nature trail with a board-walk loop, lots of butterflies, and views of Lake Tarpon.

DIRECTIONS

From Tampa, take the Courtney Campbell Causeway across Old Tampa Bay all the way to US Highway 19. Take US 19 north approximately 12 miles. The park entrance is on the right. After you enter the park, drive straight through to the back parking area. The trail begins on the right side of the parking lot.

DESCRIPTION

A. L. Anderson Park is a well-developed Pinellas County park of 128 acres. Water and rest rooms are available. This hike is unusual in that is has a bit more relief than most other hikes in the area. Because of its short length and its placement between picnic and play areas, this trail is heavily used by families with young children. Just as you enter the trailhead, stop for a minute and look for the small butterfly garden on the left, where there's a small planting of butterfly plants. This is a good place to watch for butterflies during most of the year.

The trail begins in an interesting grove of pines and live oaks that despite their small size appear to be very old. Follow the trail as it winds downhill through the trees and curves to the left,

AT-A-GLANCE INFORMATION

Length:
1.5 miles

Configuration:
Out and back with a boardwalk loop in the middle

Difficulty:
A couple of gentle slopes, easy

Scenery:
Nice views of Lake Tarpon

Exposure:
Mostly shaded

Traffic:
Busy on weekends

Trail surface:
Shell and boardwalk

Hiking time:
20 to 30 minutes

Season:
All year

Access:
No permits or fees

Maps:
Park map available at the park office

Facilities:
Rest rooms and water fountains are available throughout the park.

16

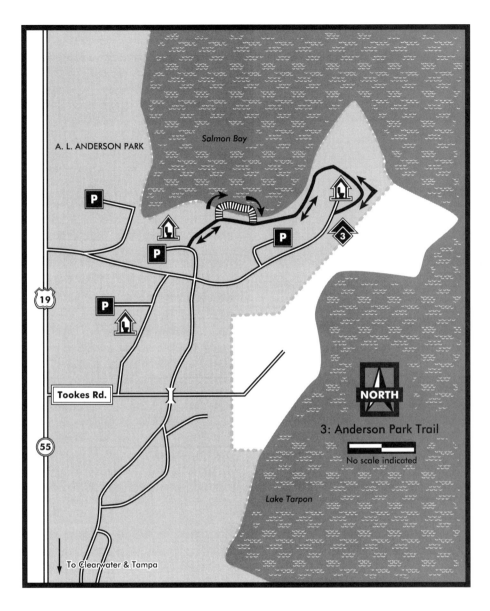

A. L. ANDERSON PARK

Salmon Bay

P

P

P

P

19

Tookes Rd.

55

To Clearwater & Tampa

3

NORTH

3: Anderson Park Trail

No scale indicated

Lake Tarpon

where you'll come to the first set of rest rooms. At this point you enter an area of much larger pines and oaks; despite the popularity of this area, the trail maintains a woodland feel. During the winter, watch for the large planting of azaleas on the left side of the trail, which flowers in January and February.

As you walk among the oaks, pines, and sabal palms, you'll see Lake Tarpon to your right through the trees; this is a good place to fish, although there is no swimming in Lake Tarpon. This area is typically very busy on the weekends with families enjoying the picnic and recreation areas.

As you leave this picnic area, the trail turns left again and follows the shore of Salmon Bay. Proceed through the sabal palms and large oaks along the trail, and enter the wooded area along the lake. As you continue, you'll come to several areas where there are picnic tables and benches, and where you can stop and sit down and look out over the lake.

As you proceed along the trail, eight spurs to the right lead to small individual picnic areas, complete with picnic tables and grills, right on Salmon Bay. At the third spur a water fountain is on the left-hand side of the trail, which at this point is heavily wooded. Many of the plants in this area are philodendrons and other exotic species that have been planted to enhance the beauty of the mixture of the native species here.

After you pass the last spur, you'll see the entrance to the boardwalk loop on the right. Don't take this yet, as you'll come back on the boardwalk in a few minutes. Proceed on the main trail through the woods past the other end of the boardwalk, until the trail ends at another picnic pavilion and a playground.

Return the way you came until you reach the boardwalk, which is now on your left, and turn onto it for a lovely view of Salmon Bay and Lake Tarpon beyond it. The boardwalk passes through a cypress swamp, complete with cypress knees and large ferns, and takes you out into the edge of Salmon Bay. Although you can fish elsewhere in the park, there's no fishing from the boardwalk. When the boardwalk rejoins the main trail, take it back to the parking lot where you began this hike for the full 1.5 miles.

NEARBY ATTRACTIONS

Near the west end of the trail, a boat launch area provides access to Lake Tarpon. Outside the park, you'll find restaurants and other amenities typical of urban areas.

Balm-Boyette Scrub Loop

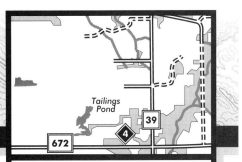

IN BRIEF

Balm-Boyette Scrub Park is an undeveloped ELAPP site. That makes this hike a real adventure.

DIRECTIONS

From downtown Tampa, take Interstate 75 south to US 301. Take 301 south to Balm Riverview Road, which forks off to the left. Follow Balm Riverview Road until it makes a sharp left turn and becomes Balm Road (County Road 672). Look for the main gate on the left just before you reach CR 39.

DESCRIPTION

Although the 5,000-acre Balm-Boyette ELAPP site is currently undeveloped. . Access points are located at existing gates on both sides of Balm Riverview Road and at the main gate on the east side of Balm-Boyette Road. If you like to fish, you might want to bring a pole to angle in the phosphate pits about 2.5 miles from the main gate. This area is open during daylight hours, but no facilities are available.

As you begin the hike on the right side of the loop, you'll be able to tell that this trail is seldom used, which is part of what makes this hike so interesting. The trail is overgrown in many areas by tall native grasses. Because the wildlife isn't accustomed to the presence of human beings, animals are not particularly wary, so you may see quite a number of them.

AT-A-GLANCE INFORMATION

Length:
5 miles

Configuration:
Loop

Difficulty:
Flat, but trails are not maintained so walking can be difficult

Scenery:
View of large pond

Exposure:
Shady with a few exposed areas

Traffic:
Very little use

Trail surface:
Sand

Hiking Time:
1.5 hours

Season:
All year

Access:
No fees or permits.

Maps:
Hidden Treasures of Tampa Bay, published by the Hillsborough County Department of Parks and Recreation.

Facilities:
None

19

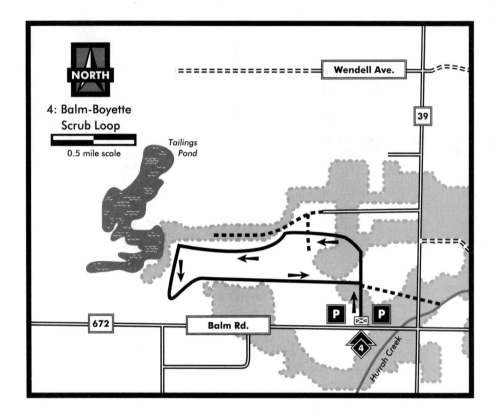

Tailings
Pond

Wendell Ave.

39

672

Balm Rd.

P P

4

Hurrah Creek

Also, watch the trail itself for animal tracks and other sign. We spotted wild hog and deer tracks within the first 100 yards.

The trail is bordered on each side by a mixture of scrub and oaks, sabal palms and saw palmetto. At almost any point on the trail you should stop at the saw palmetto clusters you encounter. Look at the base of the plant; there you can see the berries used in a nutritional supplements of the same name. The berries also are great wildlife food for a number of species, including wild (feral) hogs.

Beginning at the one-mile point, look up into the great oaks. Both there and in the oaks around the pond at the 2.5-mile point, you'll see huge air plants in the overhanging limbs. As you get closer to

the pond, you'll start to see small pockets of cypress trees. Watch closely—you may see fox squirrels as well as several species of herons in this area. Fox squirrels are protected by Florida law, and are absolutely fearless of hikers.

The biggest attraction on this hike is the large pond about 2.5 miles into the hike. The pond is greatly under-fished; on the day we were there we could see both bass and bream near the bottom of the pond, and the bass were flashing on the surface in pursuit of bait fish. Only one person was cane-pole fishing that day, and he had more than 40 bluegills on a stringer!

Many species of birds live around the pond, including wood ducks and anhingas, as well as several species of egrets

Watch ahead on the Balm-Boyette Trail. You may be able to see deer or other wildlife at any time.

and herons. As you follow the loop around to the starting point, be sure to watch for songbirds as well, including towhees, cardinals, warblers, and wood-peckers of various species.

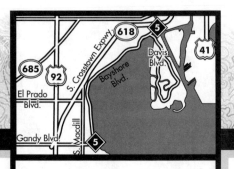

Bayshore Boulevard

IN BRIEF

This urban hike is popular for many reasons, including its dramatic view of Tampa and Hillsborough Bay area. It's close to downtown, and provides quick and easy access to a hiking area from anywhere in south Tampa.

DIRECTIONS

From anywhere in south Tampa between Gandy Boulevard on the south and Kennedy Boulevard on the north, go east until you reach Hillsborough Bay. Bayshore Boulevard follows the seawall along Hillsborough Bay between these two streets. Be careful where you park, because there are a number of tow-away zones in the area.

To get onto Bayshore at the southernmost point, take Gandy Boulevard east until it ends at Bayshore, turn left, and take the first left onto Hawthorne Road. You can park along the street here, and walk back to the southern end of the trail.

DESCRIPTION

Bayshore Boulevard is a main north-south thoroughfare that borders Hillsborough Bay. Between the street and the bay is a wide strip of grass and sidewalk, with a balustrade on the seawall. This is a very popular area for walkers, hikers, joggers, bicyclists, and parents with young children. It is very urban and close to downtown, but easily and

AT-A-GLANCE INFORMATION

Length:
8.6 miles

Configuration:
Out and back

Difficulty:
Very easy

Scenery:
Outstanding view of Hillsborough Bay and downtown Tampa

Exposure:
No shade

Traffic:
Very busy

Trail surface:
A wide sidewalk

Hiking time:
3.5 to 4 hours

Season:
All year

Access:
No fees or permits

Maps:
No published map

Facilities:
A few water fountains. Portable toilets in the median of Bayshore Boulevard, depending on festivals or other activities in the Bayshore area. Publix supermarket across Bayshore at the upper end of the trail.

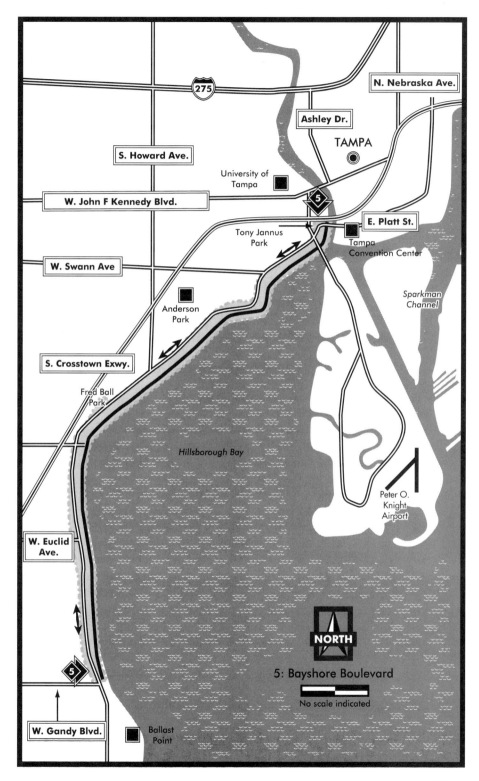

275

N. Nebraska Ave.

Ashley Dr.

TAMPA

S. Howard Ave.

University of
Tampa

W. John F Kennedy Blvd.

5

E. Platt St.

Tony Jannus
Park

Tampa
Convention Center

W. Swann Ave

Sparkman
Channel

Anderson
Park

S. Crosstown Exwy.

Fred Ball
Park

Hillsborough Bay

Peter O.
Knight
Airport

W. Euclid
Ave.

NORTH

5: Bayshore Boulevard

No scale indicated

5

W. Gandy Blvd.

Ballast
Point

quickly accessible from anywhere in South Tampa, which accounts for its high rate of use.

Bayshore Boulevard is a good place to watch evening or nighttime launches from Cape Canaveral. Even though the Cape is all the way across the state, the view of the shuttle lifting off just after sunset is nothing short of spectacular, and a lot of residents gather on the sidewalk to watch.

As you start north, you'll have a wonderful view of downtown Tampa to the east across Hillsborough Bay. As you hike, look down the side streets to the left to see some of the big trees, mostly live oaks, in this part of the city. Look here for some of the most expensive homes in Tampa.

Just after you start walking north, you'll pass a small island that abuts the trail; look for shorebirds, as well as some of the smaller egrets and herons. Throughout your hike, watch for all the birds that inhabit saltwater areas: gulls, terns, pelicans, ducks, and even an occasional loon during the winter. A short distance into the hike, you'll reach a historical plaque with a lengthy inscription.

Built into the balustrade are little alcoves where you can stop, sit on benches looking out over the water, and watch the birds go by. At intervals, you'll also find steps that go from the sidewalk level down to the water, where a small boat can dock and pick up or let off passengers.

As you walk farther up the trail, look back and to your right to see the park that's previously been hidden by the point of land at the south end of Bayshore. Extending east into Hillsborough Bay, this is Ballast Point Park, made famous by Jules Verne in his book *From the Earth To the Moon.*

Continue north to see the full sweep of the balustrade along Hillsborough Bay to the Davis Island Bridge and to Tampa General Hospital, and you'll realize just how long the "world's longest sidewalk" really is. Before long, across the street you'll see The Colonnade Restaurant. This well-known seafood restaurant has overlooked the bay in this same location since 1935, making it almost as old as Bayshore Boulevard's balustrade and walkway. Just behind The Colonnade is a small area of streetside parking for access to Bayshore.

Just north of The Colonnade is the Academy of the Holy Names, Tampa's oldest school. In July, 1881, two nuns traveled from Key West to Tampa with nothing more than their meager personal possessions to start a Catholic school. With help from the soldiers at Fort Brooke, they started the Academy of the Holy Names in a former gunsmith's shop. By 1891, the school had moved to its own building at Twiggs and Marion streets. In 1928, the school moved to its present location on Bayshore Boulevard.

Several blocks north of the Academy, at the intersection of Bayshore Boulevard with Bay to Bay, look on the southwest corner for Bayshore Park. This new park opened in early 2001, and provides a small parking and picnic area for hikers on Bayshore.

Another block north, on the corner of Barcelona, don't miss the house with all the arches. This building was converted from a filling station to a dwelling, and you can see its former use still reflected in its architecture.

In the median at the corner of Bayshore and Rubideaux, check out the sculpture. This city-commissioned art, titled *Wave,* is by Mary Ann Unger. *Wave* looks like a giant slinky quivering on its two ends.

Straight across the street from *Wave* is Fred Ball Park, a very small Tampa park with a picnic area. At the other end of the park you'll find another small

Early morning sunlight laces Bayshore Boulevard with the shadow of the balustrade.

another area where you can park and access the Bayshore.

As you continue north, just south of the intersection of Bayshore with Howard, another plaque on the balustrade gives additional historical information about both the city of Tampa and the Bayshore balustrade. According to the information here, the city of Tampa restored the balustrade in 1991, resulting in its present-day appearance.

North of the intersection with Howard, Bayshore continues to parallel a high-end residential neighborhood. Watch in the median for the horse sculpture, *Equinimity*, by Bud Oleson.

Just past the sculpture, the trail takes a little bit of a jog to the right, and at the same time the greenway on the left becomes much wider so that you're farther from the street. This is where the fitness trail, VitaCourse 2000, which parallels the sidewalk for the next mile or so, begins. Also at this point is the largest of the boat landings.

As you continue north, about halfway between the fourth and fifth VitaCourse stations, and at the intersection with south Boulevard, you'll find two water fountains. Proceed until you reach the foot of the Davis Island Bridge, where you must cross the right-hand on-ramp for the bridge.

Just after you cross the ramp, the sidewalk takes a turn to the right and rejoins the balustrade before it continues under the left-hand on-ramp and the return lanes of the Davis Island Bridge. If you bear to the right here, you can take a pedestrian walkway across to Davis Island and the shopping and dining there. However, bear to the left past the stairs that go up to the elevated pedestrian walkway over Bayshore, and cross the exit ramp for the bridge.

When you once again rejoin the balustrade, you're in the City Marina. Be sure you stay on the street side of the balustrade, as there's no trespassing in the marina.

As you walk through the marina, watch for the Gasparilla pirate ship, which is anchored here a good part of the year. Here, too, is a water fountain where you can stop for a drink. Cross the parking area, which is paved with old brick like all of Tampa's streets once were.

From here, you have an excellent view of the Convention Center, as well as the entire Channelside district across the river. On your left, a sign gives some history of the area.

Also on your left, don't miss the little plaza and fountain. Unseen by most of the traffic that passes, a statue of Christopher Columbus presides over a tiny park.

Just ahead of you is the Platt Street Bridge. From Bayshore Boulevard, this looks like the end of the Bayshore hike. But on foot, you can see that it's not. Follow the balustrade to the right and under the Platt Street Bridge.

Be careful here—don't take this portion of the hike at night. The area under the bridge is a favored hiding spot of vagrants, and is not recommended near or after dark.

On the other side of the bridge, the balustrade turns left and brings you up to Tony Jannus Park. There's another statue on this side, of one blade of an airplane's propeller.

Follow the concrete railing north through the edge of Jannus Park to the Brorein Street Bridge. At this point you're at the edge of downtown Tampa, having walked from the bottom of Bayshore Boulevard almost to the center of the city.

If you need to take a break before you return the length of Bayshore, there's a Publix across the street where you can get refreshments and find a rest room. Alternatively, if you want to hike only the top end of Bayshore, you can park in the Publix lot and access this hike from there.

NEARBY ATTRACTIONS

Because this is an urban trail, hikers are close to many amenities. You can stop for lunch at The Colonnade Restaurant, located across the street from the trail at the intersection of Bayshore Boulevard and El Prado. Several small parks along the route offer places for the hiker to sit and cool off and enjoy the sea breeze coming in from the bay. Art commissioned by the City of Tampa provides several points of interest in the median of Bayshore Boulevard.

At the Davis Island Bridge, a walkway across the river will take you to the shopping areas of Davis Island. Another walkway over the bridge at Platt Street provides access to the Convention Center and to the Channelside District beyond it, where you'll find high-end dining and shopping.

Bayshore Linear Greenway Recreation Trail

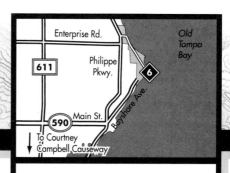

IN BRIEF

This parklike multi-use trail connects Philippe Park with Cooper's Bayou Park and with the Clearwater East–West Trail.

DIRECTIONS

From Tampa, take the Courtney Camp-bell Causeway across Old Tampa Bay and turn right at the first stoplight after the causeway ends, which is Bayshore Boulevard. Follow Bayshore north, as it becomes Philippe Parkway, for about four miles. Look for the entrance to Philippe Park on the right, just after the intersection of Philippe Parkway with Enterprise Road. After you enter the park, turn right on the main road and follow it to the parking area at the end near the footbridge. You can extend this hike by going north on the Philippe Park road, or south and west on the Clearwater East–West Trail.

DESCRIPTION

This trail was developed in 1998 to provide a measured multi-use trail connecting Philippe Park with Cooper's Bay Park and the Clearwater East–West Trail.

Cross the footbridge at the end of the Philippe Park road. This takes you right onto the Bayshore Linear Greenway trail. On the right you'll see a small oak hammock where there is a convenient bench to rest.

The first section of this trail parallels a quiet neighborhood on the right; on the

AT-A-GLANCE INFORMATION

Length:
4.8 miles

Configuration:
Out and back

Difficulty:
Flat, easy

Scenery:
A mixture of saltwater habitats and upscale homes, with one short section through an expensive resort

Exposure:
Mostly open

Traffic:
Moderately busy

Trail surface:
Paved

Hiking time:
About 2 hours

Season:
All year

Access:
No fees or permits needed

Maps:
A trail map is available at the Philippe Park office

Facilities:
Water fountains are available in the middle of the trail and at Cooper's Bayou Park. No rest rooms are available.

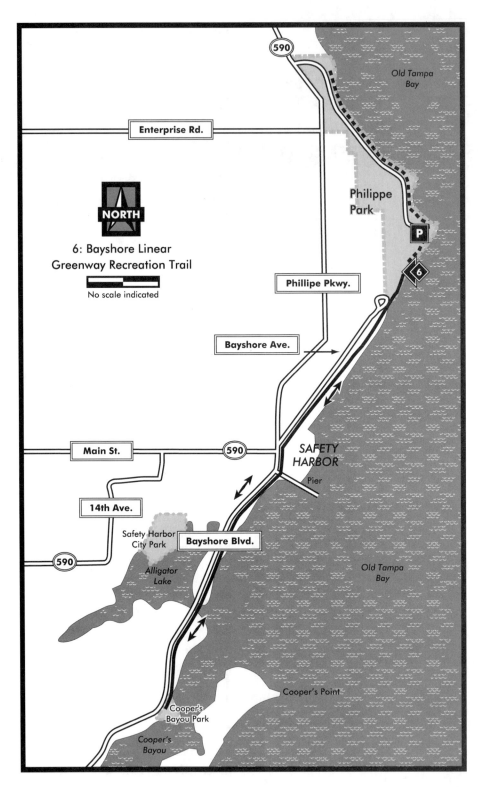

6: Bayshore Linear Greenway Recreation Trail

No scale indicated

590

Old Tampa Bay

Enterprise Rd.

NORTH

Philippe Park

P

6

Phillipe Pkwy.

Bayshore Ave.

Main St.

590

SAFETY HARBOR

Pier

14th Ave.

Safety Harbor City Park

Bayshore Blvd.

590

Alligator Lake

Old Tampa Bay

Cooper's Point

Cooper's Bayou Park

Cooper's Bayou

left you'll see a typical central Florida coastal habitat with many small mangrove trees and a stand of elderberry plants.

Just past the mangrove area, the marsh opens up, providing a wide view of Old Tampa Bay. Look south and east and you can see the Courtney Campbell Causeway.

This section of the trail has a very parklike feel, with a lot of open greenspace on the left side of the trail, backed by areas of mangroves and salt marsh plants. Keep an eye out for purple martins; a number of residents in the houses on the west side of the street have put up martin houses in the more open areas on the east side of the trail. Also look in the shallows during low tide; although they're a short distance off the trail, you often can see groups of small wading birds flying or feeding. White ibises and, during the warmer months, cattle egrets, are common on the grass of the greenway, and you can see and hear songbirds along the length of the trail.

You'll soon move into an area where there are tall pines and a few big oaks on the left side of the trail, remnants of a small flatwoods that once grew here. Just past these trees, you'll cross a small bridge where you can get a good look at a mangrove habitat on both sides of the canal that the bridge crosses.

Just on the other side of the bridge, you enter Safety Harbor. This part of the trail isn't particularly appealing, as you must cope with traffic and sometimes a lot of people. As you enter Safety Harbor, continue straight and cross the brick street to pick up the sidewalk on the other side. Follow the sidewalk one block through a grove of several large oaks, to the resort entrance. At the

entrance turn right (away from the building) and cross the street to the short section of sidewalk on Main Street. At the end of the sidewalk turn left, cross Main Street, and get back on the sidewalk that parallels Philippe Parkway. In one block, this sidewalk will return you to the Bayshore Linear Greenway.

After you pass a construction area, the parklike greenway continues past a small parking area on the left that provides access to the trail. Just beyond is a park with benches where you can rest, and a big stand of larger mangroves between the trail and the water's edge. Look in this park for a water fountain tucked back against the trees; here, a dog lover has chained a dog bowl to a tree branch, so if you have your dog with you, you can give water to it also.

After you leave the park, you'll cross the driveway of a house hidden in the trees on the left. Walk through another parklike area, cross another small bridge, and you'll enter a residential area. Look on the right of the trail for a wonderful oak tree that's smaller than some of the others you've already passed, and must have grown just to be a climbing tree.

As you leave this residential area, watch on the left for a group of trees with an unmowed understory beneath them. This is the Cooper's Bayou Park Habitat Restoration Project, which has been undertaken by the city of Clearwater and the Florida Department of Transportation. Follow the last section of the greenway south to Cooper's Bayou Park. A fitness trail runs through Cooper's Bayou, and the greenway connects to the Clearwater East-West Trail just north of Cooper's Bayou. A water fountain is available in Cooper's Bayou Park. Return the way you came to reach your car.

Bobcat Loop

IN BRIEF

This short nature trail traverses an interesting mix of coastal habitats. It's suitable for families with young children who are just learning to hike, as well as for hikers interested in unique habitats and landscapes.

DIRECTIONS

Take either Dale Mabry or Memorial Highway to Hillsborough Avenue. Turn west on Hillsborough Avenue and follow it to Double Branch Road. Turn left on Double Branch Road and follow it almost to the end, where you will see the entrance to Upper Tampa Bay Regional Park on the right. Turn right and follow the road into the park. When you reach the nature center, park across from it; the trail starts just to the right of the boardwalk at the front of the nature center.

DESCRIPTION

This portion of Upper Tampa Bay Regional Park is a 596-acre peninsula bordered on the east by Double Branch Creek and on the west and south by Old Tampa Bay. Archaeological evidence indicates that the area was inhabited long before the arrival of European explorers in the sixteenth century.

The park environment contains a wide diversity of natural habitats that result from subtle interactions between moisture and salinity. The area is quite

AT-A-GLANCE INFORMATION

Length:
0.4 miles

Configuration:
Loop

Difficulty:
Easy

Scenery:
Unique coastal habitats

Exposure:
Mixture of exposed and shaded

Traffic:
Some traffic on weekends

Trail surface:
Boardwalk and sand

Hiking time:
30 minutes

Season:
All year

Access:
$1 fee to enter the park

Maps:
A park map with the trail shown on it is available at the nature center.

Facilities:
Rest rooms and a water fountain are located at the nature center.

Special comments:
You can combine this trail with the Otter Loop to create a hike that's a total of 1.25 miles. A sign near the nature center gets you on the trail.

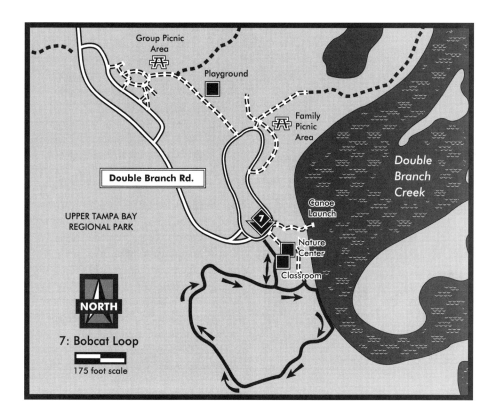

Group Picnic Area

Playground

Family Picnic Area

Double Branch Rd.

Double Branch Creek

UPPER TAMPA BAY REGIONAL PARK

Canoe Launch

7

Nature Center

Classroom

NORTH

7: Bobcat Loop

175 foot scale

flat, with a maximum elevation of only six feet. As a result, much of the park floods several times a year during periods of high tides. The rest of the park is dominated by pine flatwoods, although there are hardwood hammocks growing around a number of small ponds.

Because of the environmentally sensitive nature of the park, there's little development here, with only a nature center, a few picnic shelters, and a centrally located playground. Other than that, this park is pretty much the way Native Americans left it five centuries ago.

From the trailhead, walk along the side of the nature center and beyond it until you come to a **T** in the trail. Here you'll find a sign indicating that the trail runs left and right from this point, forming a loop.

Take the left side of the trail and follow it to the boardwalk. Don't make the mistake of making the left turn onto the boardwalk spur, which will take you right back to the nature center. Instead, go straight, which will take you out to the main boardwalk along part of Double Branch Creek. Here, you can see a mangrove forest all around you.

Keep following this boardwalk around to the right and back through the mangroves until it emerges from the trees. Here, the boardwalk ends and the trail's surface becomes sand and shell. As you traverse this area you'll see a number of salt marsh grasses in an open prairie area. During periods of high water you'll definitely get your feet wet here!

As you continue around the loop, you'll enter a drier area with a lot of small oaks and a number of sabal palms.

Look for lots of saw palmetto on this trail.

In this area, watch to the right for some very low growing mangroves that are a part of this prairie. This is a really unique habitat that you won't see many on other trails in this book.

As you proceed, you'll see that the habitats on the two sides of this trail are quite different. On the right, inside the loop, is a saltwater marsh or prairie, but on the left, outside the loop, you'll see an oak–palm hammock that's fairly typical of many areas in this part of Florida. The difference between the two sides of the trail is very striking.

This trail is a good place to watch for ospreys and possibly even eagles. Also watch for wildlife on the ground. You may see armadillos digging here even in the middle of the day. These comical little creatures see and hear poorly, so if you're quiet, you can get quite close to them before they know you're there. Once they discover your presence they freeze for just a moment and then jump straight up and scurry off as if to say, "Oh my, I'm late for tea!"

Follow the trail back around to the right as it continues to run along the edge of the wet prairie. When you reach the point where you entered the trail, turn left to return to the nature center and the parking area.

NEARBY ATTRACTIONS

The nature center offers interpretive and environmental information about the park area. Several shelters provide a place for families or groups to have lunch in the shade, and a playground and an open field near them offer a site for recreation.

Bonner Park Trail

143rd St.

Gulf Blvd.

Oakhurst Rd.

Walsingham Rd.

IN BRIEF

This very short trail won't appeal to distance hikers, but families with young children will love it as a "starter" hike for the kids.

DIRECTIONS

Take Interstate 275 (the Howard Frankland Bridge) across the bay, and get off at the Ulmerton Road exit. Proceed west on Ulmerton Road until you reach the intersection where Highway 688 goes to the left and Highway 686 goes to the right. Take the left-hand fork and stay on Ulmerton Road (now also Highway 688) as it goes toward Indian Rocks Beach. Stay on Ulmerton Road as it swings to the left (south) at 119th Street and becomes Walsingham Road. Follow Walsingham Road to 143rd street. Make a right turn onto 143rd street and follow it to the end, where you will see John Bonner Nature Park. Turn left into the parking area.

DESCRIPTION

This trail provides an excellent hike for families with very young children who have no experience on trails. The first segment takes hikers through some lovely and shady woods, while the second segment passes through a mangrove habitat and out over the water. When young children become bored with hiking, they can take advantage of the small playground in the park.

AT-A-GLANCE INFORMATION

Length:
0.4 miles

Configuration:
One short loop and one short out and back

Difficulty:
Very easy

Scenery:
Nice woods and salt marsh

Exposure:
About half shaded and half exposed

Traffic:
Quiet even on weekends

Trail surface:
Paved and boardwalk

Hiking time:
About 30 minutes

Season:
All year

Access:
No fees or permits needed

Maps:
No maps are published.

Facilities:
Rest rooms and a water fountain are located at the trailhead.

Special comments:
This park has been nominated for inclusion on the Florida Audubon Society's West Coast Birding Trail.

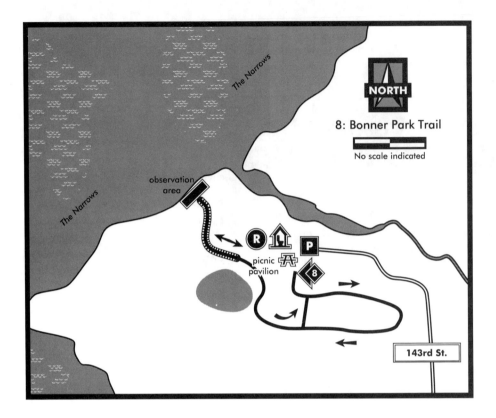

143rd St.

To reach the trailhead, walk south to the edge of the parking area, just past the picnic pavilion. Take the paved trail to the left through an open area between the picnic tables and a number of ornamental trees that are planted here. When you reach the first intersection in the trail, turn left and enter the woods.

In just a moment the trail forks again; take the left-hand fork. At this point you're in an oak hammock area, although the understory does contain many exotic plant species.

After a very short distance, you'll pass a side trail to the left that will take you out onto the road. However, continue straight ahead and you will go deeper into the woods. Watch here for songbirds, cardinals, blue jays, and other woodland bird species—this is the area where some of the unusual and rare species have been seen.

As the trail bends back to the right, it passes close by a residential area for a short distance and then turns back into the woods. Despite the fact that this is an urban trail, it is very quiet and is little used, even on the weekends. There's a good bit of poison ivy along this trail, so stay on the trail and don't stray off into the woods.

Follow this trail as it winds through the oak hammock and passes a bench where you can sit to enjoy the woods. The trail once again passes close to the residential area, then re-enters the back side of the open space where the trail begins. Here, the trail swings to the right and follows the edge of the open area where it borders a small pond; this is a good area to watch for wading birds. However, there are alligators in the pond, so use caution and don't allow children to approach the water. Follow the trail past the pond and a bench where you can sit to look out over the water, and beyond to where it rejoins the main trail.

Turn left and pass the picnic pavilion, and you'll see the entrance to the boardwalk. Turn left on to the boardwalk and follow it into the salt marsh. Stop here and listen; this is a good place to look for marshland birds, including red-winged blackbirds. Follow the boardwalk to the right and into a mangrove swamp. As you continue deeper into the wetland you'll be able to see the water. Proceed to the end of the boardwalk, where you'll find a large observation area over the water. There are benches here and a cool sea breeze that makes this a nice place even on a hot day. Retrace your steps back to the beginning of the boardwalk and turn left to return to the parking area.

Hikers can follow the boardwalk out to the pavilion over the water.

NEARBY ATTRACTIONS

Just around the corner, the George C. McGough Nature Park offers a similar hiking experience, as well as a nature center where visitors can learn more about the habitats and the area. See pages 123–25.

Boyd Hill Nature Park Trails

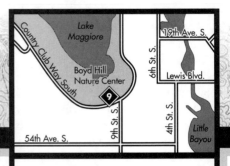

IN BRIEF

This network of six miles of trails through a lovely nature park can be combined in a multitude of ways to make hikes of many lengths.

DIRECTIONS

From Tampa, take Gandy Bridge west to Interstate 275 on the St. Petersburg side of Old Tampa Bay. Follow I-275 south to the 54th Avenue South Exit. Turn left (east) on 54th Avenue South and go 1.8 miles to Dr. M. L. King Street (also 9th Street South). Turn left (north) and go four blocks. Turn left at the traffic light, which is Country Club Way South. Boyd Hill Nature Center is on the right.

DESCRIPTION

This is an ideal hike for families with varying degrees of experience and endurance. The networked nature of the trails makes the park adaptable for everyone. Like many other trails in the area, this one has a lot of poison ivy along it, so be careful where you step.

At the trailhead, take the Main Trail to the right. After a short woodland walk, a spur to the right leads to the Swamp Woodlands Trail. The Main Trail continues to the left, however, and takes you through a very nice example of a live oak hammock. There also are a lot of ferns here, indicating that this section of the trail can be rather damp. Throughout the trail, look for interpretive signs that

AT-A-GLANCE INFORMATION

Length:
1.25 miles

Configuration:
Overlapping loops with spurs

Difficulty:
Easy; flat with one small hill

Scenery:
Varied and pleasant

Exposure:
More shaded than exposed

Traffic:
Quiet even on weekends

Trail surface:
Mostly paved; some spurs have sections of boardwalk or sand

Hiking time:
30 minutes

Season:
All year

Access:
Adults, $1; children ages 3–17, 50 cents

Maps:
Available at nature center and trail entrance.

Facilities:
Water and rest rooms are available at the nature center, water stations at several points on the trails.

Special comments:
All the named trails are well signed.

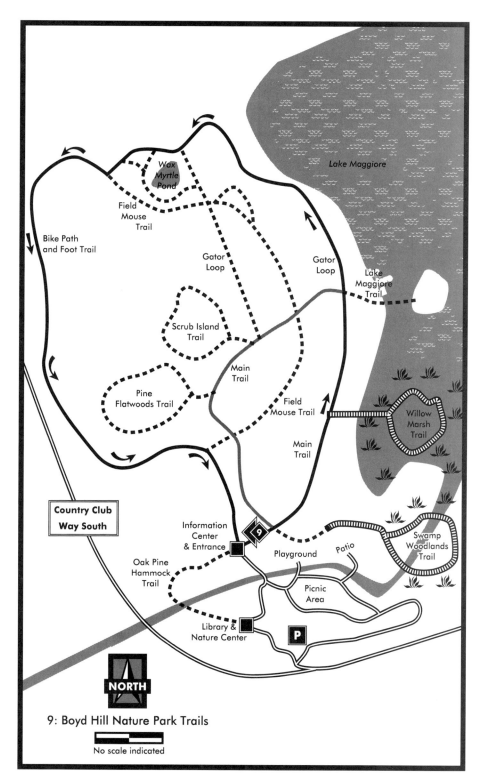

Lake Maggiore

Wax Myrtle Pond

Field Mouse Trail

Bike Path and Foot Trail

Gator Loop

Gator Loop

Lake Maggiore Trail

Scrub Island Trail

Main Trail

Pine Flatwoods Trail

Field Mouse Trail

Willow Marsh Trail

Main Trail

Country Club Way South

Information Center & Entrance

Oak Pine Hammock Trail

Playground

Patio

Swamp Woodlands Trail

Picnic Area

Library & Nature Center

P

NORTH

9: Boyd Hill Nature Park Trails

No scale indicated

tell you about the plants and animals of the area.

A little further, another spur to the right leads to the Willow Marsh Trail, a boardwalk loop through a wetland area. Continue on the Main Trail, however, and you'll pass a very nice laurel oak on the left, with a bench where you can sit if you wish. The trail traverses a mixed habitat here, with palmettos in the understory, and some wetland and upland species growing together, as well as some exotics. This entire area is good for butterfly watching—look for gulf fritillaries, zebra longwings, gold-fringed swallowtails and sulphurs, as well as some of the woodland butterflies.

Soon you'll come to an intersection of three trails. A short spur to the right, the Lake Maggiore Trail, leads out to a small island in the lake. If you turn left, you can return to the entrance using the Main Trail. However, go straight ahead and follow the Gator Loop, a section of trail that takes you deeper into the woods.

At this intersection, you'll also find a shelter, as well as a water station. After you've stopped for a drink, proceed across the intersection and take the Gator Loop.

According to the park's map, just past the intersection on the right, you'll find a blind for bird-watching. However, at the time we were there, we weren't able to find it—it's either well hidden or not there to find. This area of the trail passes through a stand of Brazilian pepper trees, also known as Florida holly. This tropical exotic is one of the scourges of land managers in Florida, who often go to great lengths to try to eradicate it from an area. A large stand of wax myrtle, a native wetland species, also inhabits this area.

As you proceed along the trail, you'll pass a path to the right. This side trail makes a loop and brings you back to the Gator Loop farther on. However, stay on the Gator Loop and you'll find some semi-wild citrus trees growing beside the trail. As you continue on around, you'll come to a place where you can make a left turn to go back to the Main Trail. Don't take the shortcut, but do stop and look down it. You'll see the first of two metal armadillo sculptures over-looking Wax Myrtle Pond.

Continue straight ahead, and in just a moment you'll see the pond—this is a good place to look for some of the larger wading birds, such as the big herons. As you pass Wax Myrtle Pond, the trail goes up a hill, the only one along the trail. At the top of the hill is the second armadillo sculpture. Look closely and you'll see that it's made of automobile parts, manhole covers, and other odd and sundry metal parts. A sign asks hikers not to climb on the armadillo.

Just beyond the armadillo, the trail goes back down the hill past a small oak hammock. Stay to the right so you don't go around the pond, but proceed to the intersection of the Field Mouse Trail with the Bike Path and Foot Trail. The left-hand fork follows the Field Mouse Trail, which winds through the center of the park. However, you want the right-hand fork, the Bike Path and Foot Trail, which will take you around the outside of the park.

This section of the trail is more open. The habitat is fairly dry, with a lot of sandhill vegetation and a number of loblolly pines. Watch here for gopher tortoises, which are typical of this kind of habitat. This area looks like its been subjected to a very hot burn, as there's quite a bit of pine regeneration going on, with lots of young trees and several dead ones.

Shortly after this trail makes a left turn, you'll pass a bench and another

Wax Myrtle Pond, along Gator Loop, is a good place to watch for wading birds.

water station where you can stop for a rest and a drink. In this area also are a couple of little unpaved trails that go off into the woods on the right. This portion of the trail is quite open and sunny, with some pretty good stands of wiregrass in the understory. Given the habitat, this is a homey place for rattlesnakes, so watch your feet and legs.

As you continue around the trail, the habitat shifts suddenly back to flatwoods, which also shows evidence of a hot burn. Then the habitat changes again, and becomes an oak hammock. As the trail turns to the left, though, you'll re-enter the flatwoods and then cross a maintenance road. Just past the crossing you'll come to a fork in the trail; the left-hand side will take you up the Field Mouse Trail, but take the right-hand side to continue toward the end of the trail.

As you head back, the trail becomes open once again. Just before you go back into the trees, look on both sides of the trail for a good stand of maypops, or native passion flowers. During the winter these plants die back and disappear, but if you're on the trail at any other time of the year, you may see either gulf fritillary or zebra longwing caterpillars on these vines. Hike through a short stretch of pines, oaks, and sabal palms, and you'll be back at the trailhead.

NEARBY ATTRACTIONS
Near the trailhead, Pinellas County operates a nature center, the Oak Hall Environmental Studies Area. At the entrance to the trail, look for the birds of prey exhibit; these birds are permanently disabled and can't be released into the wild.

Brooker Creek Preserve Loop

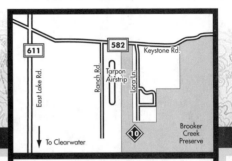

IN BRIEF

This lovely and secluded trail has no facilities and very little foot traffic at any time.

DIRECTIONS

From Tampa, take the Courtney Campbell Causeway west to Clearwater. Turn right on McMullen Booth Road, which is the first major intersection on the west side of the bay. Follow McMullen Booth Road for about 13.75 miles north as it becomes East Lake Road, to the intersection of Keystone Road. Turn right on Keystone and go 1.75 miles to Lora Lane. Turn right on Lora Lane and follow it to the end. The trail begins on the right.

DESCRIPTION

Brooker Creek Preserve is an 8,000-acre, 41-square-mile preserve that comprises part of the Lake Tarpon watershed. Despite its proximity to urban areas, this is quite an isolated trail, so hikers should do the same kind of planning they do to hike in remote areas. This is good habitat for rattlesnakes, so watch where you put your feet.

This trail is a delight as it winds through a variety of typical Florida habitats. It begins as a straight path into the woods that at one time was a two-track road. On the left, a ditch that was created when the road was built now contains a

AT-A-GLANCE INFORMATION

Length:
1.75 miles

Configuration:
Loop

Difficulty:
Flat, easy

Scenery:
Mixture of typical Florida woodland habitats

Exposure:
Shaded

Traffic:
Little-used trail

Trail surface:
Sand, grass, and pine needles

Hiking time:
45 minutes

Season:
All year

Access:
No permits or fees

Maps:
Available at the trailhead

Facilities:
None

Special comments:
A wooden sign at the trailhead lists trail rules and shows a map of the trail. Red-topped wooden posts mark the trail itself.

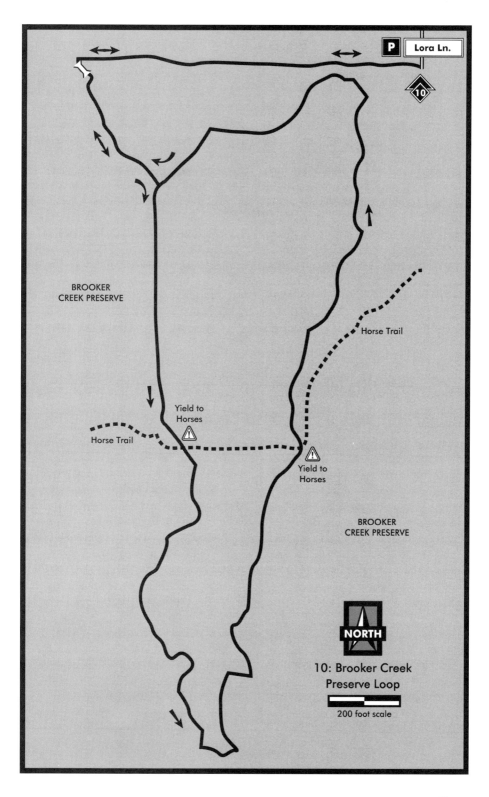

P Lora Ln.

10

BROOKER
CREEK PRESERVE

Horse Trail

Yield to
Horses

Horse Trail

Yield to
Horses

BROOKER
CREEK PRESERVE

NORTH

10: Brooker Creek
Preserve Loop

200 foot scale

number of wetland species; a nice pine flatwoods is on the right. Listen for the birdsong here and throughout the length of this trail; there's a lot to hear. There's also a lot of poison ivy in this section of the trail, so be careful.

A short distance in, there's a short spur to the right that leads to an observation platform overlooking a mitigation area. This is a good place to sit and watch for wildlife, although you also can see into the back of a small residential area from here.

A little farther in, the trail makes a sharp turn to the left and crosses a little footbridge over the ditch. The residential area is now to your right, but this is the last you'll see of it. This area is very quiet except for birdsong and cicadas; this is as remote as it gets in an urban area.

Before long you come to a fork in the trail, which is the beginning of the loop. Take the right-hand side, which takes you through pines that are a little younger and smaller than the flatwoods at the beginning of the trail. This section of the trail is more open as well, and is a good place to look for woodland butterflies.

As you proceed, you leave the younger pines and enter a more mixed habitat, with oaks and other species. Before long you'll see the horse trail on the right, where this trail takes a bit of a left turn. In just a few more yards the trail crosses the horse trail, where a sign reads, "Yield to Horses."

The trail passes through some oaks and back into pines of varying ages with a grassy understory. As you near the top of the loop you're getting closer to Channel A of Brooker Creek, and the area becomes slightly wetter; look for ferns and gallberries here, typical of central Florida pine woodlands. The trail

jogs to the left and then back to the right, and traverses some palmettos, also typical of central Florida. After passing through some larger and older pines, and some palmettos that have grown so big that they've actually stood up and become small trees, you'll enter a section of the trail with more oaks and other hardwoods.

At the bottom of the loop, the trail turns to the left and parallels Channel A of Brooker Creek. This channel of the creek is seasonal; during dry times it doesn't have any water in it. However, look around you and you'll see a lot of wetland hardwoods in the area. Also look on the ground—feral pigs like these wet areas, and you'll likely see a lot of disturbance where they've rooted up the soil.

When you come to the "Keep Out" sign where a closed trail continues to parallel the channel, follow the main trail as it makes a sharp left turn. Look for lots of ferns as the trail continues through a fairly wet flatwoods habitat. As you get farther from the creek, the trail moves into drier flatwoods and crosses the horse trail again. The pines here are smaller, some of them quite young; the older pines in this area appear either to have been logged, or to have been damaged and subsequently cut down, to make room for the younger trees. Consequently, this area is very open.

After shifting to a narrow, winding path through the young pines, the trail turns to the left and becomes more distinct again, and more open. This is a good area to watch for sulphur butterflies. Continue on until you reach the end of the loop, where a sign directs you back to the right. Cross the footbridge and return to the parking area.

Bruce B. Downs Trail

IN BRIEF

This multi-use trail connects the Flatwoods–Morris Bridge–Trout Creek series of parks with suburban areas in north Tampa.

DIRECTIONS

From downtown Tampa, take Interstate 275 north to the Fletcher Avenue exit. Take Fletcher Avenue east approximately 1.7 miles to Bruce B. Downs Boulevard. Turn left on Bruce B. Downs and follow it north and then northeast approximately six miles. The parking area for the Bruce B. Downs Trail and Flatwoods Wilderness Park is on the right, just after the I-75 overpass.

DESCRIPTION

Exit the parking lot on the street side of the parking area, and turn right to follow the trail as it passes a wooded area and crosses a bridge through a small wetland. Continue past the woods and into another little wetland. In this area, look into the wetland for red marsh mallow, a native wildflower that looks somewhat like a wild hibiscus.

After a short hike you'll reach the north end of the trail at Hunter's Green Drive. Return the way you came until you reach the parking area again, and then continue past it to stay on the trail. Within a few hundred yards you'll enter a congested area where you'll pass several restaurants, fast food places, and a

AT-A-GLANCE INFORMATION

Length:
Approximately 8.5 miles

Configuration:
Out and back

Difficulty:
Easy, but intersections add difficulty

Scenery:
Woodland, greenway, and urban

Exposure:
Mostly exposed with a little shade at the south end of the trail

Traffic:
Moderately busy

Trail surface:
Paved

Hiking time:
3 to 4 hours

Season:
All year

Access:
No fees or permits required

Maps:
No trail map is published.

Facilities:
Rest rooms and drinks available at convenience stores along the road that the trail parallels.

Special comments:
Heavy traffic at several intersections, particularly along the northern portion of the trail, can make the hike difficult at peak traffic times.

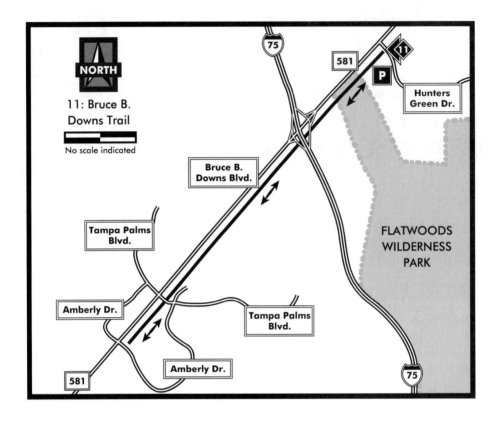

NORTH

11: Bruce B.
Downs Trail

No scale indicated

Bruce B.
Downs Blvd.

Tampa Palms
Blvd.

Amberly Dr.

Tampa Palms
Blvd.

Amberly Dr.

581

Hunters
Green Dr.

FLATWOODS
WILDERNESS
PARK

convenience store where you can stop if you need to.

Cross Highwoods Preserve Parkway at the light and proceed past another convenience store, a couple more fast food restaurants, and a pharmacy. After another crossing at Dona Michelle and a few more businesses, you'll enter a more rural area.

Hike past a wooded area, cross the Interstate 75 entrance ramp, and pass under the highway. Use caution here; although there's a crossing light at each of the two ramps, this is a high-use intersection with a lot of traffic, making it a potentially dangerous crossing.

Once you've passed I-75, you'll be in a much more rural setting. Even though

you're next to a major highway, watch for wildlife; "deer crossing" signs posted for the next couple of miles indicate that wildlife hasn't been chased away by the development in this area.

The trail now traverses a lengthy wooded area. Here, you'll pass the development of Tampa Palms, which hasn't yet affected the woodland along the highway and trail.

At the end of the woods you'll come to a brick fence that forms the perimeter of Compton Place at Tampa Palms. This upscale development has done a nice landscaping job along the fence, providing some pleasant scenery until you pass by a power substation and return to the woods. All of the woods along this trail

Even though Bruce B. Downs Trail is very urban, you may see wildlife crossing the trail.

are a sort of mixed hardwood wetland, with cypress, oak, and a few pines.

As you near the end of the trail you come to the developed portion of Tampa Palms. This area is landscaped, with a lot of big trees next to the trail, so that it's shaded in this section. In this area you'll cross Tampa Palms Boulevard. Although there's a walk light here, it's a very large crossing, so use caution. Just beyond the crossing you'll see a lovely manmade lake beside the trail.

The last section of trail passes through a very nice greenway that the development has created along the outside of their brick perimeter.

When you reach the next crossing at Amberly Road, you're at the end of the trail. Turn and retrace your steps for the entire 8.5-mile hike.

Caladesi Island
State Park Loop

IN BRIEF

This trail is one of the best adventures in
this book. Not only is the trail secluded
and wild, getting there is an adventure.

DIRECTIONS

From Tampa, take the Courtney Campbell Causeway to Clearwater. Turn right
on US Highway 19. Go two miles north
and turn left on Sunset Point Road. Follow Sunset Point Road until it dead
ends at Edgewater Boulevard. Turn right
(north) on Edgewater. Continue north
on Edgewater as it becomes Broadway
Bayshore Boulevard, and follow it to
State Road 586, which is also Curlew
Road. Turn left on Curlew Road, which
becomes Dunedin Causeway. Follow the
causeway until it reaches the entrance to
Honeymoon Island State Park. Inside the
park entrance, turn left at the sign to go
to the ferry.

After you reach Caladesi Island, follow
the boardwalk and porch to the back of
the building that contains the office and
snack bar, then take the boardwalk to the
beach. The boardwalk crosses a small dirt
road, then passes a foundation on your
left. Beyond the foundation take the ce-
ment trail to the left and follow it to the
sand trail. If you look down the trail you
can see a sign that reads "Nature Trail."

DESCRIPTION

This trail is exposed for much of its
length and has no water stations on the

AT-A-GLANCE INFORMATION

Length:
3 miles
Configuration:
Loop
Difficulty:
Moderate
Scenery:
Pine flatwoods and coastal commu-
nities
Exposure:
Mostly exposed, some shade
Traffic:
A little traffic on weekends
Trail surface:
Sand
Hiking Time:
1.5 to 2 hours
Season:
All year
Access:
$4 per vehicle with up to 8 occu-
pants. Ferry from Honeymoon
Island to Caladesi Island, $7 for
adults, $3.50 for kids.
Maps:
Trail map available in a box at the
trailhead
Facilities:
Rest rooms and snack bar at trailhead

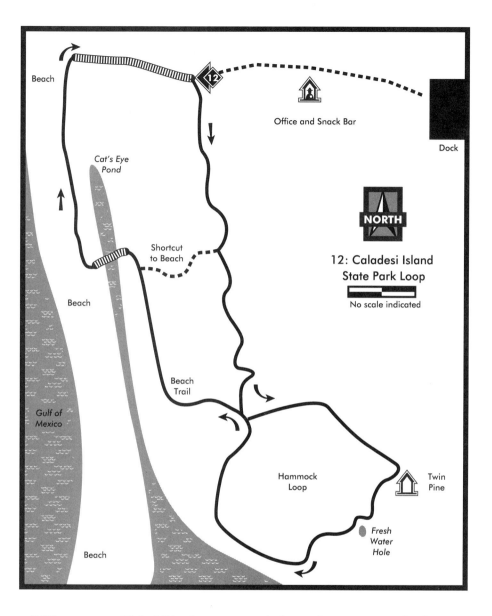

Beach

Cat's Eye
Pond

Shortcut
to Beach

Beach

Office and Snack Bar

Dock

NORTH

12: Caladesi Island
State Park Loop

No scale indicated

Beach
Trail

Gulf of
Mexico

Hammock
Loop

Twin
Pine

Fresh
Water
Hole

Beach

trail. We recommend light hiking boots or other shoes with ankle support due to soft sand on parts of the trail. Also, the population of rattlesnakes on Caladesi Island is quite large—watch where you walk!

Hike past the bathhouse on the right, where rest rooms are available, and into a wonderful palm hammock. This is a very dry environment, with lots of wiregrass

and plenty of native cacti. Before long you'll cross a maintenance road. Just past the road is a box that contains trail guides with information that corresponds to the interpretive posts. There's a good bit of poison ivy on this portion of the trail, so make sure you stay on the path.

One plant species you'll see quite a bit of in this area is salt myrtle. Salt myrtle is common on land that's been cleared or otherwise disturbed. The tree's name comes from its ability to use saltwater. Also watch for gopher tortoises, which are common in dry upland areas in Florida.

Before long you'll come to a bench where you can rest next to a wonderful bent sable palm. The tree was of great importance to early Floridians—the trunk was used by both Native Americans and pioneers for log houses and canoes. The leaves are still used today for the roofs of Seminole chickees, and the heart—called swamp cabbage—can be eaten raw or cooked, although this kills the tree.

As you continue, you'll come to a fork in the trail. Go straight ahead to complete the nature trail. You'll enter an area that's more shaded, with some pines and oaks, and a bench.

Before long the trail lightly ascends into habitat similar to that on Honeymoon Island, which sustains lots of pines. Here the surface of the trail changes from soft sand to a firmer substrate with pine needles on it.

This trail continues to pass through a lot of poison ivy, so stay on the trail and watch your feet. There's also wax myrtle in this area. This plant gets its name from the wax on the leaves and berries; the wax coating is used in Bayberry candles.

After you cross a footbridge over a seasonal stream, you'll enter an area with a lot of pines and shade. A very slight grade takes you into a habitat with lots of good-sized sabal palms and pines. Here, you'll continue to see benches where you can sit and listen to the quiet. You can hear a few cicadas but not a whole lot of birdsong; it's just a very peaceful place to spend the day.

When you spot the next intersection, you'll have to make a decision. A right turn will take you across the loop and

shorten your hike to slightly less than 2 miles. However, go left and you'll take the bottom of the loop. In this section of trail, watch for the twin pine, as well as for the freshwater hole to the trail's left.

As you swing back around to the north and the trail starts to parallel the beach, it becomes wider and more solidly packed. Here, you'll traverse a mangrove habitat on the left, while the upland habitat continues to the right of the trail. Look through the mangroves to the left to see a channel that comes into the interior of the island.

Before too much longer you'll come to a side trail to the right that will take you back to the marina. Here, you'll see an exotic plant control project, where park personnel are trying to eradicate Brazilian Pepper, which has become established on the island.

As you pass the exotic plant control project turn left and walk down to the beach. You'll find yourself on a boardwalk that passes over the channel you've been paralleling. As you leave the boardwalk you'll see a little side trail to the right that takes you to an overlook of the channel. Follow the main trail around to the left, where it traverses a palm hammock and another boardwalk over a branch of the channel. The trail continues through a mixed habitat of sable palms, saltmarsh grasses and other native grasses before it crosses the sand dunes. Here you'll find another box where you can pick up or return trail guides. These dunes are protected, so don't walk off the trail, pick any plants, or dig. Here, you'll also find a bench where you can sit and overlook what must be one of the most deserted beaches that you'll find in Florida.

Turn to the right and follow the beach back north until you come to the boardwalk that leads back to the marina and the ferry to Honeymoon Island.

John Chesnut Sr. Park
Trail I

IN BRIEF

This hike is a combination of a nature trail/boardwalk and a footpath around a park lake.

DIRECTIONS

From Tampa, take the Courtney Campbell Causeway across Old Tampa Bay to McMullen Booth Road. Take McMullen Booth Road north about 9.25 miles, where it changes to East Lake Road. Shortly after this, you'll see John Chesnut Sr. Park on the left. When you enter the park, drive straight through until you come to the parking area for Shelter 10 on the left. Park there and walk toward Shelter 10. The trailhead is between the shelter and the rest rooms at the end of the parking area.

DESCRIPTION

Part of the Pinellas County park system, the 250-acre John Chesnut Sr. Park is a well-developed park that's home to a variety of wildlife, including alligators, deer, and many wading birds.

As you pass the rest rooms near Shelter 10, step off the sidewalk and onto the gravel trail. The trail passes through a wetland pine area before you reach the boardwalk. Once you step up onto the boardwalk, though, you're in a wetter area, with cypress trees and ferns on each side of the trail, and cypress knees poking up through the ferns. Close your

AT-A-GLANCE INFORMATION

Length:
Approximately 1 mile
Configuration:
Loop
Difficulty:
Flat, easy
Scenery:
A variety of wetland habitats
Exposure:
Shaded on the nature trail and boardwalk, open around the lake
Traffic:
Moderately busy on weekends
Trail surface:
Shell, boardwalk, and grass
Hiking time:
20 to 30 minutes
Season:
All year
Access:
No fees or permits needed
Maps:
Available at the park office and at various points in the park.
Facilities:
Water fountains and rest rooms at several places in John Chesnut Sr. Park

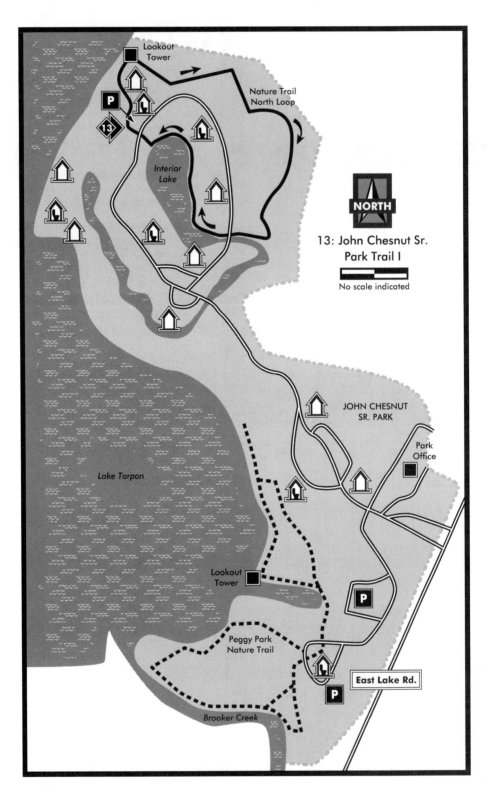

Lookout
Tower

P

13

Nature Trail
North Loop

Interior
Lake

NORTH

13: John Chesnut Sr.
Park Trail I

No scale indicated

JOHN CHESNUT
SR. PARK

Park
Office

Lake Tarpon

Lookout
Tower

P

Peggy Park
Nature Trail

P

East Lake Rd.

Brooker Creek

eyes and take a deep breath, and you can smell the wetland.

There are lots of good-sized cypresses in here, as well as lots of poison ivy, so stay up on the boardwalk. Before long you're in a full-fledged cypress wetland that continues until you leave the boardwalk and continue on another short stretch of sand trail. This section passes close by Lake Tarpon. Here there are palms to your left, and if you look through the trees to the left you can see out into the lake where there is an abundance of cattails.

A little farther on, a short spur to the left will take you to an observation platform with benches where you can sit and look out over the lake. Just beyond the spur, the main trail makes a right turn and once again becomes boardwalk as it passes through a hammock with lots of cypress trees and mixed hardwoods. As you proceed through this section of the trail, a bench provides a place to sit and look over the hammock. Despite the fact that you're in the middle of a developed park, this whole area affords a good example of what Florida look liked before industrial society changed it.

At the end of the boardwalk, step onto the gravel trail and continue on until you reach the cross trail. Don't take this trail—it's actually an emergency vehicle road. Instead, proceed straight ahead until the trail becomes a boardwalk again and takes you through another cypress wetland. In just a minute the trail crosses a little slough, where there is another bench where you can sit and enjoy the swamp. Follow the boardwalk through this fern and cypress wetland, and watch for several nice big pines and oaks close to the boardwalk.

When the boardwalk ends and the trail becomes gravel again, proceed

through the pines and large oaks until you come to the path that goes to the left. This also is a maintenance road, so do not take it. Instead, stay on the main trail until you come to another slough. Follow the trail as it curves to the right around the slough and then back to the left; it then becomes boardwalk once again. This section of the trail passes through a mixed-species wetland with more pines and hardwoods than cypress, and a lot of sabal palms. If you stand still and close your eyes and listen, it's easy to be out of civilization here.

Continue along the boardwalk until you reach the end. You'll pass a small lake on your left with an island in the middle. A little footbridge leads across to the island, where you can sit at a picnic table and watch the water. However, if you take the gravel trail to the right, you can cross the road and enter the end of the parking lot. Instead of turning right into the main part of the parking lot, though, go straight ahead through the pines. There's a bit of trail there that makes a jog to the left through the pines and then curves back to the right, past the picnic tables until you reach the lakeshore a short distance beyond.

This picturesque lake has pickerel weed along its edge—and if you look out in the middle you may see a big alligator swimming along, so don't swim. But watch for wading birds and ducks, as well as for ospreys fishing in the lake. Follow the lakeshore as it curves around to the left, go past the windmill, and angle slightly to the right so that you come out on the paved road right by the end of the fence. Cross the road, walk through the narrow strip of oaks and pines, and you'll be back in the parking lot for Shelter 10.

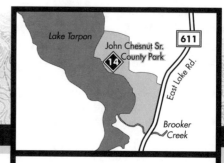

John Chesnut Sr. Park Trail II

IN BRIEF

This hike is a combination of two nature trail/boardwalks along the edge of Lake Tarpon.

DIRECTIONS

From Tampa, take the Courtney Campbell Causeway across Old Tampa Bay to McMullen Booth Road. Take McMullen Booth Road north about 9.25 miles, where it changes to East Lake Road. Shortly after this, you'll see John Chesnut Sr. Park on the left. When you enter the park, drive straight through until you come to the parking area for Shelter 10 on the left. Park there and walk toward Shelter 10. The trailhead is between the shelter and the rest rooms at the end of the parking area.

DESCRIPTION

Just north of the boat ramp, take the paved trail past several benches and the Lookout Tower sign. Follow the pavement, then proceed straight on the boardwalk. which is right on the water and exposed. Along this section, four spurs to the right take you to picnic tables (grills are not permitted). The area is a wetland with wax myrtle and lots of cypress, so when you go into these little picnic areas, they're quite private. There also are some benches along the boardwalk where you can sit and look over Lake Tarpon. At the end of this section of the boardwalk, you can go up in the

AT-A-GLANCE INFORMATION

Length:
Approximately 1.5 miles

Configuration:
Two loops with short spurs

Difficulty:
Flat, easy

Scenery:
A variety of wetland habitats

Exposure:
Mostly shaded

Traffic:
Moderately busy on weekends

Trail surface:
Shell, boardwalk, and grass

Hiking time:
40 minutes

Season:
All year

Access:
No fees or permits needed

Maps:
Available at the park office and at various points in the park

Facilities:
Rest rooms and water fountains are available throughout John Chesnut Sr. Park.

Special comments:
The south loop of this trail is named for Peggy Park, Florida's only woman wildlife officer killed in the line of duty.

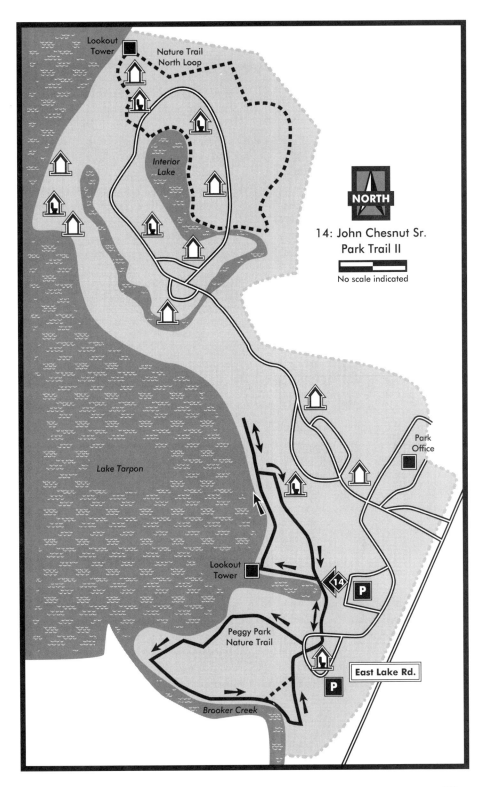

Lookout
Tower
Nature Trail
North Loop

Interior
Lake

NORTH

14: John Chesnut Sr.
Park Trail II

No scale indicated

Lake Tarpon

Park
Office

Lookout
Tower

14

P

Peggy Park
Nature Trail

East Lake Rd.

P

Brooker Creek

Lookout Tower for a good view, or follow the trail to the right into the woods. As you enter the woods, watch for many maples, wax myrtle, and cypress. As you proceed, three short spurs to the left lead to picnic areas that go out over the water.

The trail passes through more cypress trees and makes a right turn. A little further, the trail forks; the left side leads to a picnic area and the parking lot. Take the right fork through some big pines and follow it through a flatwoods area. You'll cross several little boardwalk bridges that take you through a slough and a section of ferns and large cypress trees and pines.

The trail becomes a boardwalk once again and rejoins the pavement just before it returns to the trailhead. Turn left and onto the pavement where you began. When you reach the parking lot, turn right and cross the boat ramp. Once you cross, take the left-hand sidewalk through an oak hammock and past the rest rooms and the water fountain. Then make a bit of a right turn and take the right-hand sand trail through the trees to the parking lot. When you get to the parking lot, turn right, and go around the parking circle a short distance until you reach the Peggy Park Nature Trail.

As you enter the trail, look for the box containing interpretive booklets about the trail. Return it to the box at the end of the trail.

Shortly after you pass the sign, the trail turns from gravel to boardwalk and passes through a cypress swamp with lots of ferns and cypress. As the trail makes its first sharp left-hand turn, don't miss the huge cypress tree just to the right of the corner. There's a bench here where you can sit and contemplate the swamp if you wish.

Continue on along the boardwalk as it gets closer to Lake Tarpon. Where the trail turns left again, you'll have a really nice view of this arm of the lake.

Proceed on the boardwalk as it follows the lakeshore and passes another bench, then curves to the left through a stand of ferns and large hardwoods. When the boardwalk ends and you're back on gravel, you've reached Brooker Creek. The trail continues to follow Brooker Creek back to the east, through habitat that's a little drier than where you've just been, and consists of hardwoods and sabal palms with a palmetto understory.

At the creek, you'll pass several benches overlooking the water. As you proceed, you'll pass through a hammock of young oaks. Then you'll come to a fork in the trail; the left-hand fork is a shortcut back to the parking area, but if you stay on the main trail you'll continue to parallel the creek. Look on the right for an old cypress tree that's been broken and burned; despite all the hardship, it's still going strong. Next to the cypress is a huge pine—both must be close to a century old.

As the trail swings to the left and away from the creek, you're as close to East Lake Road as you'll get in the park, and you can hear the traffic from the highway. However, as you continue along the trail, you'll soon leave that behind. Pass through the hardwood hammock as the trail turns back to the left. This portion of the trail is much drier, so you'll see a lot more upland oaks and pines than you've seen on previous sections of this trail.

When the trail crosses the end of the shortcut, turn to the right and follow the trail back to the parking area. Return the interpretive booklet to the box, turn left, and follow the parking circle back past the trailhead. A short distance past the trailhead, you'll see the path that connects the parking area to the boat ramp and the big parking lot beyond it.

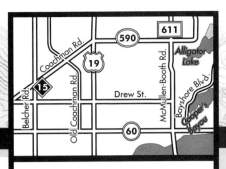

Clearwater East-West Trail

IN BRIEF

This don't-miss urban multi-use trail traverses several area parks and greenways to provide a lovely hike through some surprisingly hidden settings.

DIRECTIONS

From Tampa, take the Courtney Campbell Causeway to Clearwater. Turn right on McMullen Booth Road and take the first left on Drew Street. Go west 2.25 miles to Belcher Road, and turn right on Belcher. Go 0.8 miles and turn into the Long Center on the right. Park behind the Long Center, where you'll find the trailhead.

DESCRIPTION

This trail begins at the back of the Long Center. Look for the "Clearwater East-West Trail" sign. Start east on the sidewalk there, and go down a hill between the stream on your left and pond on your right. Although the pond is quite small, even small pockets of water will attract many of the egrets and herons.

Follow the trail as it crosses the bridge over the stream, then winds its way through an oak hammock, emerging along the edge of Coachman Ridge Park. There's public parking and a water fountain there.

The trail leads through pines and sycamores and connects to a sidewalk at Old Coachman Road. Turn right on the sidewalk, follow it up and back down a

AT-A-GLANCE INFORMATION

Length:
8.5 miles

Configuration:
Out and back

Difficulty:
Somewhere between easy and moderate, with some grades in the middle

Scenery:
A couple of urban stretches, but mostly woods and parks

Exposure:
About half shaded and half exposed

Traffic:
Light traffic on weekends

Trail surface:
Paved

Hiking time:
3.5 to 4 hours

Season:
All year

Access:
No permits or fees necessary

Maps:
Trail maps posted on signs along the trail.

Facilities:
Rest rooms and water fountains are available in several parks along the trail.

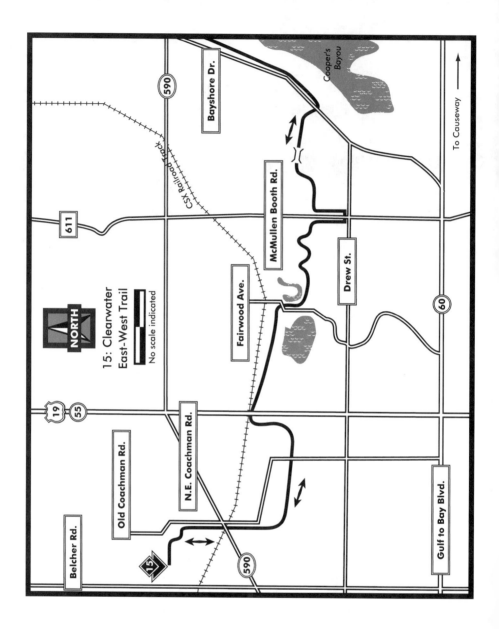

slight hill and over the railroad crossing to Northeast Coachman Road, and cross at the light.

The trail then enters Northeast Coachman Park. Traverse the hammock of large oaks as the trail turns to the right and crosses two bridges.

After you come off the second bridge, a short spur to the right takes you to a small interpretive area. The large pond is a good place to look for wading birds such as wood storks and egrets.

Follow the trail around the pond until you reach the crossing with Old

Coachman Road. There's no traffic light here, so cross with care. The trail continues up a slight rise behind a youth baseball field. Continue around the back of the complex between the playing fields and follow the trail to the left as it crosses the bridge over the stream. Take care here, as a bicyclist may not be able to see you coming.

Here, the trail follows the greenway around to the right and under US 19, then turns back to the right just a bit and enters another oak hammock before it crosses a small bridge. It winds through a shady area and enters Cliff Stephens Park. Don't miss the tree on the left that's fallen down and grown again from where it's lying on the ground.

Here, too, is another large pond where you can bird-watch. Don't swim in this pond, though—alligators. Follow the trail as it turns to the right and crosses a bridge. At the foot of the bridge there's a water fountain.

Take the trail through the rest of the park to Fairwood Avenue. Take care at this crossing, as there is no light, and turn right on the sidewalk across the street. On your left you'll see another pond with a "No Swimming" sign. Follow the trail to the left around the pond as it parallels Brigadoon Drive.

In a moment the trail swings to the right and crosses Brigadoon Drive, then makes a sharp turn to the left. Climb the hill, and you'll be on a linear greenway between two apartment complexes.

At the end of the greenway, the trail turns to the right and winds through a remarkable hidden hardwood hammock. Here the grade is as much as 10 percent, both up and down, making this the hardest portion of the trail.

As the trail emerges from the woods, it flattens and turns left to skirt the edge of the hammock as it traverses the back of another youth sports field. Then the trail plunges back into the woods for a short distance before it emerges between another youth sports complex on the right and a small residential area on the left.

As you leave the sports fields, the trail reaches McMullen Booth Road. Take McMullen Booth road one block south until you reach Drew Street, cross Drew Street at the light, and turn left to follow McMullen Booth Road back to the north. Cross three streets and turn right into Del Oro Park.

Del Oro Park has rest rooms and a water fountain on the right side of the trail. Behind the rest rooms, the trail passes a small playground and picnic area before turning left and entering the woods again. After a short distance the trail turns back to the right and enters a wide greenway between a residential area on the left and an apartment complex on the right.

Follow the greenway until you reach Bayshore Drive. Cross Bayshore Drive carefully, as there is no light here, and turn left to follow the sidewalk. After a short hike you'll reach Cooper's Bayou, where you'll find parking, a fitness trail, and a water fountain.

From this point you can either turn around and traverse the trail in the opposite direction for the 8.5 miles, or continue straight to the Clearwater East-West Trail. which connects with the Bayshore Linear Greenway.

NEARBY ACTIVITIES

Here, you can take advantage of the Cooper's Bayou Fitness Trail or proceed on foot for the last short stretch of the Clearwater East-West Trail until it connects with the Bayshore Linear Greenway, and, beyond that, Philippe Park.

Clearwater Memorial Causeway Greenway

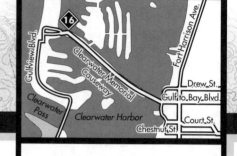

IN BRIEF
This park-like multi-use greenway trail parallels the Clearwater Memorial Causeway.

DIRECTIONS
From Tampa, take the Courtney Campbell Causeway west to Clearwater, and stay on the causeway road west as it becomes Gulf-to-Bay Boulevard and then Court Street. When it dead-ends at Pierce Boulevard, turn right, and take the first left onto the Clearwater Memorial Causeway. Cross the causeway and go around the roundabout until you're headed back east. As soon as you cross the short span onto the causeway, turn right into the parking area. The trail is accessible from the back side of the parking area.

DESCRIPTION
This paved trail was designed with an eye toward aesthetics. Its gentle turns wind between mangroves and other estuarine species, and landscape-type plantings. Despite the fact that it parallels a major highway, it offers a restful view of the Clearwater Pass.

Be aware that Clearwater Beach is a major destination for students during spring break. Despite the fact that this is a wonderful short hike, it's not recommended during that time of year because of the amount of time you'll sit in traffic getting there.

AT-A-GLANCE INFORMATION
Length:
2.3 miles
Configuration:
Out and back
Difficulty:
Flat, easy
Scenery:
Parklike, pleasant
Exposure:
Exposed
Traffic:
Moderately busy
Trail surface:
Paved
Hiking time:
About an hour
Season:
All year
Access:
No fees or permits needed
Maps:
No map is published.
Facilities:
None

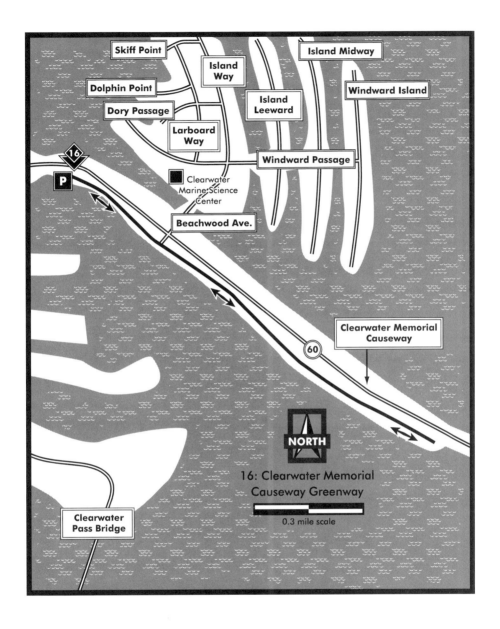

16: Clearwater Memorial
Causeway Greenway

0.3 mile scale

If you're interested in a longer hike, there are several ways to extend this one. One way is to go west from the parking area across the bridge. Once you cross the bridge you enter the Clearwater Municipal Marina, where you can continue on the sidewalk around the circle and return east on the north side of the causeway. You can stay on the sidewalk on the west side of the causeway, which also traverses a pleasant area, all the way to the bridge where the described route ends and hikers turn around to return to the trailhead.

If you don't want to extend the hike quite that far, you can cross the causeway at a light at Island Way and take the sidewalk from that point to the east.

As you leave the back of the parking lot and head east, the trail has a very park-like feel, due to the wide, grassy greenway through which it winds. On the right is the Clearwater Pass, and on the left you'll see palms of several species along the shoulder of the causeway.

As you continue east, you'll pass a number of fairly large mangroves along the shoreline and tall sable palms on the causeway side of the trail. In this area there are a couple of benches where you can sit and look out over the water.

Three-tenths of a mile east of the trailhead, there's a crosswalk light where you can cross the causeway at Island Way. From here you can either hike the other side of the causeway, or visit the Clearwater Marine Aquarium.

As the trail continues east, mangroves continue to line the shore, and there are several benches where you can sit and watch the water. The wide grassy shoulders in this area are places to look for cattle egrets and ibises. There are a few sea grapes here as well; early settlers used the fruit of this small tree to make jellies, although few people eat them today.

About two-thirds along the length of the trail, the pavement swings away from the causeway and toward the water, and passes behind a small, secluded parking area accessible from the causeway. There are a lot of oleanders planted around the parking area, so be aware of your security if you're in this area after dark.

Also in this area, the shoreward side of the greenway becomes a small grassy beach, where a few families and sunbathers picnic on weekends. Given the urban nature of the area, this is a surprisingly secluded little beach.

After you pass the parking area the trail swings back a little closer to the causeway, but is still closer to the shoreline than it is for the rest of its length. From here to the end of the trail the scenery is more open, with fewer mangroves and more palms, as well as several benches to sit on.

As you approach the drawbridge back to the mainland, the trail terminates in a little turnaround at the end of the greenway. Return the way you came for the full 2.3 miles of the hike.

NEARBY ATTRACTIONS

West of the trail is the Clearwater Municipal Marina, where anglers can either hire a fishing guide or get on a party boat for a day of fishing. Across the causeway, a small shopping center provides beach-related shopping as well as personal watercraft rentals.

West of the marina, Crabby Bill's Seafood offers a place to eat. Continue and you'll reach Clearwater Beach, one of the premier beaches in the area.

To learn more about the aquatic life of the region, you can visit the Clearwater Marine Aquarium across the causeway from the trail. The aquarium is located on Island Way, and is accessible by crossing the causeway at the crosswalk light near the trailhead.

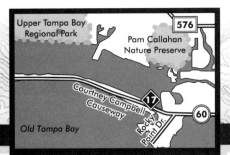

Courtney Campbell Causeway East

IN BRIEF
This long hike is within a short distance of downtown Tampa. The trail follows the water along the Courtney Campbell Causeway as it crosses Old Tampa Bay.

DIRECTIONS
From Tampa, take the Courtney Campbell Causeway west toward Clearwater/St. Petersburg. Take the first access point from the westbound lane onto the frontage road. You can park on the right-of-way under one of the two groups of sabal palms.

DESCRIPTION
For hikers who want a long hike that is literally within sight of downtown Tampa, this is a good place to go. This is a paved frontage road along the Courtney Campbell Causeway that is open to anglers, hikers, and bicyclists, but because it doesn't go anywhere, traffic is very light. It passes through a number of conservation easement areas with protected nesting sites, so hikers can expect to see nesting shorebirds from January through August. The county has made an attempt to landscape some sections of the right-of-way. If you're planning to bird-watch while you hike, this trail is best done during the week, as boaters and Jet Skiers use this area of the bay on weekends.

Start this trail by going east to the gate that keeps this portion of the road closed

AT-A-GLANCE INFORMATION

Length:
10.4 miles

Configuration:
Out and back

Difficulty:
Flat, easy

Scenery:
Water and conservation easements

Exposure:
Exposed

Traffic:
Moderately busy

Trail surface:
Paved

Hiking time:
4 to 5 hours

Season:
All year

Access:
No permits or fees

Maps:
No map is published.

Facilities:
None

Special comments:
A few signs indicate habitat areas near the trail that are closed to visitors.

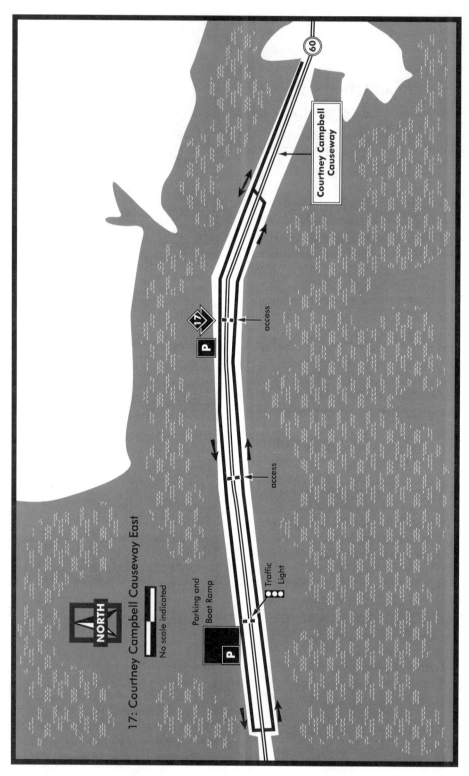

17: Courtney Campbell Causeway East

NORTH

No scale indicated

Parking and
Boat Ramp

Courtney Campbell
Causeway

access

access

Traffic
Light

60

P

P

P

to motorized vehicles. Walk around the end of the fence and hike east along the road. In this area, a number of mangrove trees have taken root in the riprap, so you'll pass a number of mangrove clumps of various sizes.

This entire area is a good place to look for herons and egrets, both on the rocks and on the tidal flats. During the winter, you may see large rafts of diving ducks of various species. Watch them for their amusement value; they'll all decide to feed at about the same time and disappear from view, only to bob up like so many bathtub ducks a minute later. Also watch for pelicans, cormorants, and other species, fishing or perching on the channel markers. And if you're into fish watching, you can see schools of mullet in the water as you walk.

When the trail ends at the Embassy Suites hotel, return the way you came to complete the first leg of this hike.

When you reach the parking area where you began, continue west. After you've walked by a short stretch of the same kind of mixed-size mangroves as on the first leg of the trail, you'll enter an area of larger mangroves where there are more tidal flats. This gives way to a real shoreline on the bay side of the trail, where the habitat is classified as a conservation easement site and is posted against trespassing. You won't have a problem as long as you stay on the trail, since the road you're walking on is open for public access. Between January and August, watch this locale for nesting birds.

Throughout this area, the left side of the trail consists of the grassy shoulder between the trail and the Courtney Campbell Causeway. The shoulder has been planted with clumps of sabal palms and oleander. Keep in mind that the oleander is extremely toxic; as pretty as the flowers are, don't pick them or handle them. In areas where the oleander is planted, you may encounter flying insects that look like glossy blue-black wasps. Don't be concerned about them, as these are actually harmless oleander moths, whose larvae feed on oleander bushes.

The conservation easement site continues past the next access point from Courtney Campbell to the frontage road, on to the third access point, where a parking lot and boat launch area are located. This area is busy on weekends, so watch carefully as you cross the parking lot.

Just past the parking area, the landscape changes. On the left side is a long row of sabal palms, providing a small amount of shade during the winter months when the sun is to the south. On the bay side, once again there's riprap where small mangroves have taken hold. In this area you'll encounter a lot of anglers on the rocks, particularly during weekends.

At the end of this section the trail turns, passes under the bridge, and swings back to the east. After you make the turn the shoreline is still riprap, but the water comes in with more energy than on the other side, so there are no mangroves there. This area also has a wider shoulder than the north side, and is frequently used by sunbathers. There's plenty of parking here between the trail and the causeway.

Just past the turn, don't miss the cluster of coontie, a cycad native to Florida. On this wider shoulder are more plantings of sabal palms and oleander as well. The entire southern side of the trail lacks the woodsy feel of the north side, but provides more of an open waterside walk; be sure you bring your sunscreen if you're going to hike the entire length.

The bird life on this side is different also. Because it's more open and exposed than the north side, herons and egrets are not common here. However, you often can see American oystercatchers and other similar species, especially during the winter.

At the next access point to the causeway, you can cross at a light and re-enter the parking lot where the boat ramp is located. At the following access point, however, you cannot safely cross the causeway, due to a high concrete median, blocking the way. The last section of the trail is totally exposed, with just riprap and open grass. At the stop sign you can choose to either return the way you came for the total 10.4 miles, or cross the causeway at the light and return to the parking area, for a hike of about 6 miles.

NEARBY ATTRACTIONS

This entire area is open for fishing except in the protected conservation easement sites.

Courtney Campbell Causeway West

IN BRIEF

This seaside trail offers a long hike within a short distance of downtown Tampa.

DIRECTIONS

From Tampa, take the Courtney Campbell Causeway west toward Clearwater/ St. Petersburg. Cross the main span of the causeway and watch for an access point once you're off the main span. Turn right onto the access road, and pull off to the left to park on the right-of-way between the road and the causeway.

DESCRIPTION

Like its sibling to the east, this site offers a long hike within sight of downtown Tampa. This is a paved frontage road along the Courtney Campbell Causeway that's open to anglers, hikers and bicyclists, but because it doesn't go anywhere, traffic is very light.

There are two access points from the westbound lane and two from the eastbound lane. One word of warning: if you drive a high-profile vehicle, be sure you get off at the first access point westbound, not the second one, so you can get back onto the Courtney Campbell Causeway westbound. At the western end of the loop, the road goes under a short span of bridge that's barely high enough for a Jeep to pass under, so you won't be able to drive around the loop to get back onto the causeway.

AT-A-GLANCE INFORMATION

Length:
6 miles

Configuration:
Loop

Difficulty:
Flat, easy

Scenery:
Lots of water and some planted areas

Exposure:
Exposed

Traffic:
Moderately busy any time

Trail surface:
Paved

Hiking time:
2.5 to 3 hours

Season:
All year

Access:
No permits or fees

Maps:
None

Facilities:
None

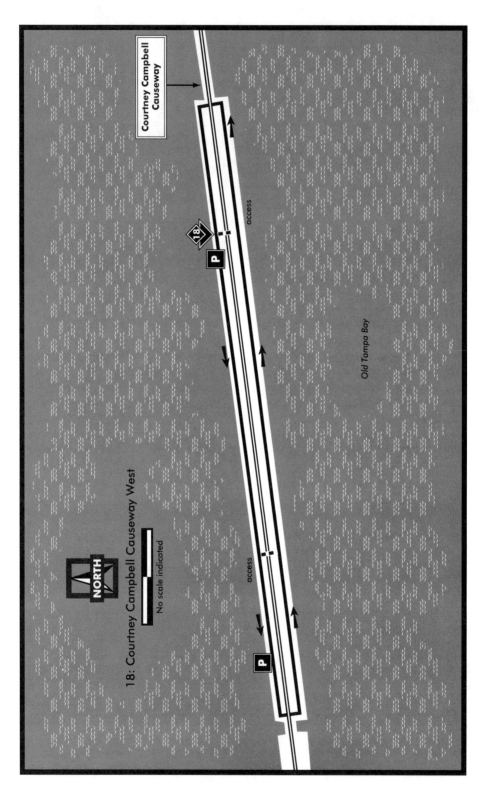

18: Courtney Campbell Causeway West

NORTH

No scale indicated

Courtney Campbell Causeway

access

Old Tampa Bay

access

66

As you begin this hike to the west, you'll be in habitat that's similar to much of the Courtney Campbell Causeway East trail—riprap with some small mangroves. Look across Old Tampa Bay to your right and you can see a power plant with high-voltage lines marching west.

Before long, you'll pass Australian pines planted on the right side of the trail. These are large trees and provide some shade for this section of the trail during the summer when the sun is to the north. They're planted intermittently along this section of the trail; since this entire area is open to fishing, expect to encounter anglers in the shady areas these trees create.

Past the first stand of pines, on the left, you'll see a stand of sabal palms and oleander. As you walk through the oleander, both here and on other trails, watch for blue-black insects about the size of a large wasp flying across the trail. Don't be afraid of them; they're oleander moths, which resemble wasps.

Continue on past more Australian pines, and you'll see a stand of sea grapes on the left. Old-time Floridians used sea grapes to make jelly, although they're not used for anything today.

For the next mile or so, the landscape is fairly uniform, with riprap, and intermittent Australian pines (with anglers) on the right and sabal palms, oleander, and sea grapes on the left. Then the shoreline widens just a bit, and small mangroves mix with the Australian pines growing on the riprap and the narrow shoreline on the right, although the mixture of sabal palms, oleander, and sea grapes on the left continues. When you reach the next access point for the Courtney Campbell Causeway, continue straight ahead on the trail.

As you near the terminus of the trail, the plantings end and the sides of the trail are open, offering good visibility across the north side of Old Tampa Bay. In this area expect to see more anglers than on the rest of this side of the trail. As you pass beneath the bridge, watch your head; this is a low, narrow passage, and if you're up on the apron under the bridge at all, you run the risk of connecting with the underside of the span.

As you turn the corner to head east, there's a fairly decent stand of mangroves on the corner to your right; although this side of the trail is a bit more high-energy than the north side, you'll see quite a few small mangroves along the length of this section of trail. You can cross over the causeway at this access point, but there is no walk light.

On windy days, expect to get wet; this trail is close enough to the water that breakers wash up onto the road when the surf is rough.

On this section of trail, look to the east. This is perhaps the best view of the Tampa skyline that you'll see from any of the hikes in this book. After dark it can be quite beautiful.

When you reach the sign indicating that you're leaving Pinellas County and entering Hillsborough County, the trail takes a little jog to the right. Throughout this section of trail the landscape is open, with a very narrow shoulder.

Continue until you reach the second access point to the causeway. You can cross the causeway here, which allows you to shorten the hike if you wish.

Hike straight ahead and you'll soon reach the second turn in the trail, where it swings to the left to go under the bridge again. Pass under the bridge and turn back to the west. Continue west between the riprap on the right and the sabal palms and oleander on the left until you reach the first access point to the Courtney Campbell Causeway, where you parked your car and began this hike.

Dead River Trail

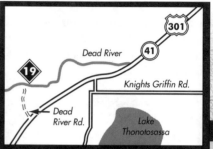

IN BRIEF

The Dead River trail parallels Dead River, which is a tributary of the Hillsborough River.

DIRECTIONS

From downtown Tampa, take Interstate 4 to the US 301/Zephyrhills Exit. Drive north on US 301 and go approximately nine miles. Look for Dead River Road on the left.

DESCRIPTION

This trail is one of the best-kept secrets in Hillsborough County. Dead River is a tributary of the Hillsborough River and is surrounded by diverse and beautiful wild land that's relatively undisturbed because of the trail's lack of significant mid-week foot traffic.

As soon as you make the turn into the park from US 301, you know you're in for a treat. The lane that leads to the trailhead is made of compressed shell and is canopied by the branches of heritage oaks. The tunnel of trees is so thick and rich that the sun just barely breaks through; when you get out of your car, you'll find that the temperature is cooler.

The trailhead is located at the edge of a small parking area between a bridge to the camping area in Dead River County Park and the trail. Approximately 30 feet from the entrance, the trail branches. If you take the left fork you'll cross the bridge into the camping area. But take

AT-A-GLANCE INFORMATION

Length:
2.5 miles

Configuration:
Out and back

Difficulty:
Easy, flat except for one slight rise in elevation

Scenery:
Outstanding example of hammock-type flora and fauna with a pleasant view of the river

Exposure:
Shady throughout

Traffic:
Very little use

Trail surface:
Sandy soil with occasional roots

Hiking time:
1 to 1.5 hours

Season:
All year

Access:
General public access, no fee

Maps:
No trail map is published.

Facilities:
None

Special comments:
Access road is open to vehicular traffic on weekends to facilitate access to the camping areas. Bike and foot traffic only, Mon.–Thurs.

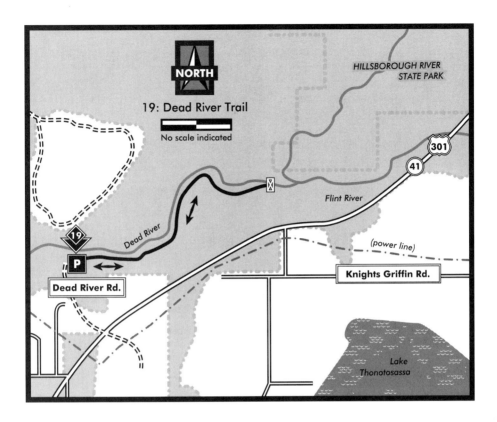

the right fork and you'll enter the trail. This is a multi-use trail, with biking allowed, but the trees have some serious root systems that could make biking a real challenge.

As you begin your hike you'll see Dead River to your left. Watch for the alligator slides on both sides of the river; if you look closely you'll see alligator tracks on the banks. Be sharp! During the warm months you WILL see alligators, and while they're fun to watch, they can be dangerous—an alligator can come up out of the water after prey faster than a horse can run.

Alternating cypress heads and oak hammocks flank the right side of the trail. The cypress hammocks are full of cypress knees, and air plants abound in the trees. Deer and hog tracks cross the trail, showing where the animals have moved from the woods to the river and back. The trail is shaded by mostly heritage oaks, and their acorns create a plentiful food source for a wide variety of animals, so watch for wildlife. On the day we took this hike we saw deer, hogs, armadillos, raccoons, alligators, otters, squirrels, and countless bird varieties. If you take this trail during the winter months you'll see a lot of migratory birds and possibly otters, although the alligators are dormant.

About midway on the trail, a massive, magnificent grandfather oak curves over the trail, creating a picturesque arch. The trail widens at this point from 8 feet across to about 20 feet, making this a great place to stop and explore the riverbank, which at this point is wider than

Hikers along the Dead River Trail will see some lovely views of the river.

the rest of the trail, or to rest near this magical oak.

At the end of the trail is a deserted farmhouse. Although it's not accessible to the public, it provides a nostalgic and picturesque end to the trail before you begin the trip back.

As you retrace your steps, the trail takes on a new look. Now the river is on your right and flows toward you. This change in the way you see the river's current also changes the things you see. Hiking back, look for the otters' den on the far side of the river, especially in early morning or evening.

On the river side of the trail, look for magnolias, Spanish moss–draped oaks and sabal palms. The oaks and the palms on the river side occasionally sport air plants and wild orchids.

As you approach the trailhead, continue past the parking area until you come to the bridge that separates the nature trail from the camping area, and look over the side at the river. This is a good place to see baby alligators, largemouth bass, and catfish. It's a nice end to what is truly one of the most beautiful trails in Hillsborough County.

NEARBY ATTRACTIONS
Hillsborough River State Park is adjacent to Dead River and is accessible from the same parking lot.

Eagle Trail

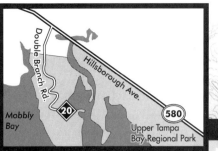

IN BRIEF

This short nature trail passes through several unique central Florida coastal habitats. It's suitable for families with young children who are just learning to hike and hikers who enjoy seeing different habitats.

DIRECTIONS

Take either Dale Mabry or Memorial Highway north to Hillsborough Avenue. Turn west on Hillsborough Avenue and follow it west to Double Branch Road. Turn left on Double Branch Road and follow it almost to the end where you will see the entrance to Upper Tampa Bay Regional Park on the right. Turn right and follow the main road through the park, watching for a small parking area for the Eagle Trail on the right.

DESCRIPTION

Upper Tampa Bay Regional Park is a 596-acre peninsula bordered on the east by Double Branch Creek and on the west and south by Old Tampa Bay. Archaeological evidence indicates that the area was inhabited long before the arrival of European explorers in the six-teenth century.

The park environment contains a wide diversity of natural habitats that result from subtle interactions between moisture and salinity. The area is quite flat, with a maximum elevation of six feet above sea level. As a result, much of

AT-A-GLANCE INFORMATION

Length:
0.3 miles each way; 0.6 miles total

Configuration:
Out and back

Difficulty:
Easy

Scenery:
Flatwoods and salt marsh

Exposure:
Mixture of shaded and exposed

Traffic:
Some on weekends

Trail surface:
Sand and boardwalk

Hiking time:
40 minutes

Season:
All year

Access:
No permits required, but a $1 fee is necessary to enter the park.

Maps:
A park map available at the nature center; a trail guide provides infor-mation about the habitats.

Facilities:
Rest rooms and a water fountain are located at the nature center.

Special comments:
A sign near the trailhead provides interpretive information about the area.

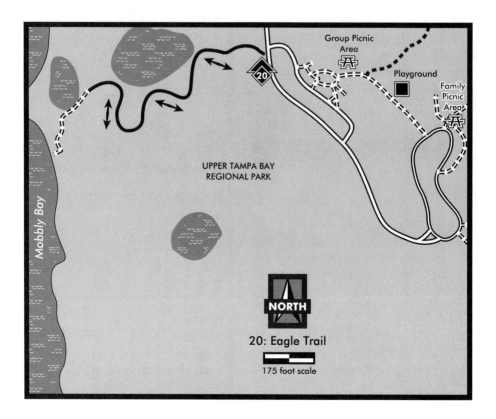

Group Picnic Area

Playground

Family Picnic Area

UPPER TAMPA BAY REGIONAL PARK

Mobbly Bay

NORTH

20: Eagle Trail

175 foot scale

the park floods several times a year during periods of high tides. The rest of the park is dominated by pine flatwoods, although there are hardwood hammocks growing around a number of small ponds.

Because of the environmentally sensitive nature of the park, there's little development here, with only a nature center, a few picnic shelters, and a centrally located playground. Other than that, this park is pretty much the way Native Americans left it five centuries ago.

The boardwalk portion of this trail was renovated during early 2001. The Eagle Trail has much more shade on it that either the Otter Loop or the Bobcat Loop, both of which are also in Upper Tampa Bay Regional Park.

As with the other two trails, the main factors influencing the habitat are moisture and salinity.

The trail begins in a pine flatwoods with some good-sized trees and a lot of palmettos in the understory, fairly typical of central Florida flatwoods. This is some of the highest ground in the park.

Within a short distance you'll pass into a hardwood hammock area, as the trail goes around a freshwater marsh on the right side. The most common plant in the freshwater marsh is needle rush, which you'll see quite a bit of here.

This area is a really good place to watch for both songbirds and for small wildlife, including quail, armadillos, raccoons, rabbits, and other critters. It's also excellent rattlesnake habitat, so watch your feet!

The Eagle Trail is the prettiest of the three trails in Upper Tampa Bay Regional Park.

In this area, look for some large live oaks; this is really a lovely hammock to see. And watch overhead, the large live oaks support a thriving community of air plants called epiphytes. However, don't wander off of the trail—besides rattlesnakes, you'll also encounter quite a bit of poison ivy here.

Before long you'll pass into a more open savanna or prairie area. This wet prairie contains a saltwater pond, another really unique habitat that's found in this park. The most common plants here are salt-tolerant species such as keygrass, saltwort, and glasswort.

Continue on the boardwalk as it leaves the open savanna and traverses another really unique habitat, a salt barrens. A salt barrens forms because saltwater floods the area at high tide, and poor drainage keeps it there during low tide. The hot sun evaporates the water, leaving the salt behind. The sand is so salty that even salt-tolerant plants can't grow.

Before long you'll enter a stand of mangroves. The mangroves are an important nesting area for wading birds such as herons, egrets, and spoonbills, so you might see any of them here.

In a moment you'll reach Mobbly Bay. Watch here for lots of wading birds such as herons and egrets, and don't forget to look overhead; this is a good place to see ospreys and even eagles. Also watch the shoreline; this is a low-energy beach, and you may see crabs, horseshoe crabs, and other tidal creatures along the edge of the water. Return the way you came for the full 0.6-mile round trip.

NEARBY ATTRACTIONS
The nature center offers interpretive and environmental information about the park area. Several shelters provide a place for families or groups to have lunch in the shade, and a playground and an open field near them offer a site for recreation.

73

Fishhawk Trail

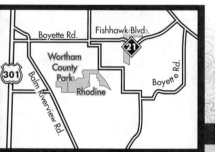

IN BRIEF
This hike traverses a 285-acre nature preserve that only recently has become accessible to the public.

DIRECTIONS
From Tampa, take the Crosstown Expressway to US Highway 301 (*Alternate directions:* take Interstate 4 east to I-75, and take I-75 south to US 301 at the Riverview exit.). Follow 301 south until you reach Boyette Road, then turn east on Boyette Road. When Boyette Road reaches Bell Shoals Road, continue straight ahead onto Fishhawk Boulevard. The entrance to the preserve is marked with a six-foot county sign and is about three miles east of the intersection of Boyette and Bell Shoals Road.

DESCRIPTION
Hillsborough County purchased this 285-acre nature preserve from the Fishhawk ranch in 1991. The area was left untouched for the next eight years, until bird watchers and hikers discovered it and began to open trails. In 2000, the site became accessible to the public when the planned community of the same name opened.

The trails that exist on this site are very primitive—this is really a "find your own trail" situation. We picked a trail that was fairly clear to profile, but you may find your feet taking you in other directions from where we went. We

AT-A-GLANCE INFORMATION
Length:
2 miles
Configuration:
Out and back
Difficulty:
Moderate
Scenery:
Hardwood hammocks and Florida pine flatwoods
Exposure:
Mostly open
Traffic:
Becoming more popular
Trail surface:
Should be paved by press time
Hiking Time:
About 1.5 hours
Season:
Year round
Access:
No permits or fees required
Maps:
None
Facilities:
None
Special comments:
Experienced hikers looking for a bit of a challenge will enjoy this trail. However, it's definitely not suitable for families with small children.

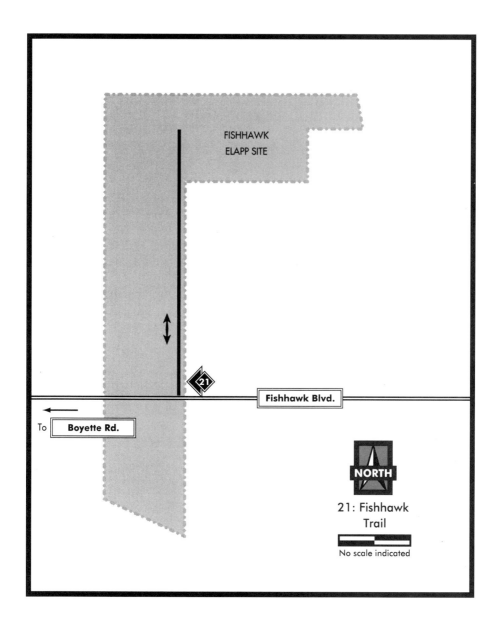

FISHHAWK
ELAPP SITE

21

Fishhawk Blvd.

To Boyette Rd.

NORTH

21: Fishhawk
Trail

No scale indicated

suggest you carry plenty of water and a compass if you take this trail, and encourage you to wear light hiking boots with good ankle support.

This trail will become more accessible and better maintained as the planned community of Fishhawk becomes better established.

The trails on this site begin as soon as you enter. The first 100 yards are quite open, and the trail (and the surrounding area) consists mostly of deep sand, adding challenge to the footing.

Follow the trail north as it hugs the eastern fence line, until you enter an area with a lot of scrub oaks and saw palmettos. We encountered a pair of Red-tailed Hawks within the first quarter mile. They were not intimidated by our presence, and one watched us from the top of a tree before it rose to soar above us. One of the birds seemed to follow us for most of the hike, circling above us as we walked.

The trail becomes wider and more clearly defined as it passes between very large oak trees that are home to boundless numbers of squirrels. Watch in this area for many species of songbirds, including blue jays and mockingbirds. The undergrowth is very thick, and it's clear to even a casual observer that little or no maintenance has been done in this area for many years. A thick carpet of dead leaves and grass covers the ground, and clumps of Spanish moss have fallen from the trees. Early in Florida's history, furniture makers used Spanish moss to stuff the upholstery of couches, and, later, car seats. My experience with Spanish moss is that it often contains vast numbers of redbugs, tiny mites, that burrow into the skin of anyone unfortunate enough to encounter them. The red welts they leave behind itch fiercely for up to a week.

As the trail continues straight, you'll come upon a quarter-mile section that the neighboring cattle herd has discovered. The moss has been evenly trimmed at the animals' eye level, leaving a distinct browse line.

As your proceed also watch for deer. If you keep an eye on open, you may see their heart-shaped tracks. Keep an eye out for the animals themselves, particularly if you hike during the early morning or late afternoon. Most wildlife is more active during these hours, and deer are no exception. Often you'll just catch a glimpse of one crossing the trail in front of you, just a brown wraith slipping silently through the trees. If you see one, stand perfectly still and watch the same area for at least a minute or two, as deer frequently pass through an area in single file, sometimes as much as several minutes apart.

In its last quarter mile, the trail once again traverses an area of flatwoods and saw palmetto. On the day we took this hike, some of the taller pines were the perches of choice for about half a dozen turkey vultures, not the most appealing birds to watch, but certainly an impor tant species in the overall web of life in the woods.

When you reach the end of the trail, retrace your steps and return to the entrance for the full two-mile hike.

Flatwoods Park Trail I

IN BRIEF

Flatwoods Park is connected by paved trail to Trout Creek and Morris Bridge Park. All three, plus Dead River, are part of the large Wilderness Parks complex in northern Hillsborough County.

DIRECTIONS

Take Interstate 75 north to the Fletcher Avenue exit. Turn east on Fletcher and follow it as it turns north and becomes Morris Bridge Road. Morris Bridge Road passes the entrance to the Flatwoods/Four River Basins Park. Turn left into the park and stop at the second parking area.

DESCRIPTION

The trail begins immediately at the edge of the paved parking lot, where its tightly-packed sand and shell surface makes for an easy walk.

The trail passes through a mixture of habitats, including flatwoods, cypress domes, oak and palmetto hammocks, and some low, often swampy ground. As a result, you're likely to contend with mosquitoes and other biting insects, so bring insect repellent. If you forget your repellent, try using a trick the old Florida Crackers learned from the Seminoles: pick up a dry palmetto frond and use it to keep the biting flies, gnats, and mosquitoes off your back and legs.

About a quarter of a mile into this trail, you'll cross the first of three small

AT-A-GLANCE INFORMATION:

Length:
3 miles
Configuration:
Out and back
Difficulty:
Flat and easy to hike
Scenery:
Typical central Florida mixture of live oak and flatwoods with palmettos and cypress domes
Exposure:
Mostly shaded
Traffic:
Bikers often use this trail
Trail surface:
Hard-packed sand and shell
Hiking Time:
About 2 hours
Season:
All year
Access:
No fees or permits required; a donation of $1 is requested.
Maps:
Trails in this park complex are shown on a Hillsborough County Parks and Recreation map, *Trail Guide for Hikers and Bikers on the Wilderness Park Off Road Trails.*
Facilities:
Rest room at the park office, located at the park entrance

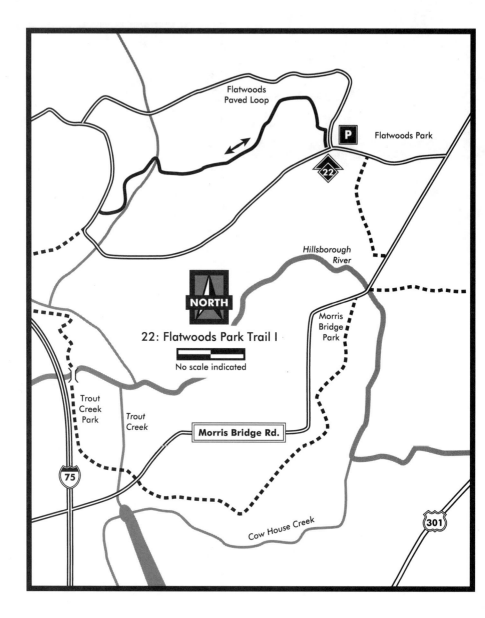

Flatwoods
Paved Loop

P   Flatwoods Park

22

Hillsborough
River

NORTH

Morris
Bridge
Park

22: Flatwoods Park Trail I

No scale indicated

Trout
Creek
Park

Trout
Creek

Morris Bridge Rd.

75

Cow House Creek

301

wooden bridges. In the rainy season, these bridges cross standing water on the low ground.

When it's not so wet, watch for armadillos under the bridges. They're very active as they dig for dinner during the cool mornings as well as in the early evening. They're a lot of fun to watch as they noodle around through the leaves.

If you sneak up on them before they know you're there, they hold very still, then jump straight up and head for the underbrush at a high rate of speed.

The trail is about six feet wide and well cleared. Because this is a multi-use trail, expect to encounter mountain bikers, particularly on weekends. Although a few riders are children, most of them are

This trail is about six feet wide and well maintained.

older kids and adults, and often ride quite fast. So be prepared to get out of the way.

After you cross the first small bridge, watch on your left where you'll see the first of several cypress domes. Cypress domes are a characteristic Florida habitat, and usually are found in a pine flatwoods or other similar habitat. Despite what its name implies, a cypress dome doesn't rise, but falls, creating a depression that catches and holds water. The water in these ponds slowly drains into the water table.

Cypress swamps once were widely distributed across Florida and North America, but today most of the prehistoric forests are gone. Geologists believe cypress trees have grown in this area in southwest Florida for more than 5,000 years. Cypress swamps, ponds, and domes provide habitat for many wildlife species, including a number that are endangered.

After you pass the cypress dome, look to your left for possible bird nesting activity. On our hike we saw a White Ibis nest at the edge of the wetland.

Follow the trail as it curves slightly to the right, and watch for the half-acre of saw palmetto. Be careful if you stop to pick any berries; the fronds of the palmetto are covered with small sharp spines. Also, look out for snakes!

The second small bridge also passes over a low wet area. About a hundred yards beyond the bridge, the habitat changes to an open field of knee-high grasses that provides a real contrast to the first part of the trail. Although you'll be tempted to strike out across the field, park rangers don't encourage hikers to leave the trail. If you're hiking in the early morning or late afternoon, watch the field for deer.

Continue past the field, into the woods. On a third small bridge, cross a wet area. Stay on the trail to the turnaround point, then start back toward the trailhead.

Flatwoods Park
Trail II

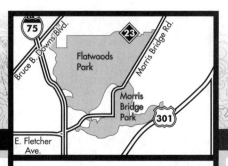

IN BRIEF

Flatwoods Park is connected by paved trail to Trout Creek and Morris Bridge Park. All three, plus Dead River, are part of the large Wilderness Parks complex in northern Hillsborough County.

DIRECTIONS

Take Interstate 75 north to the Fletcher Avenue exit. Turn east on Fletcher and follow it as it turns north and becomes Morris Bridge Road. Morris Bridge Road passes the entrance to the Flatwoods/Four River Basins Park and continues through the park proper. Park at the ranger station and walk in on the road another hundred yards or so, and watch for the trail marker where the trail crosses the road.

DESCRIPTION

This section of the Flatwoods/Four River Basins Park trail is paved and canopied. The combination makes it a popular trail for families, particularly on weekends. On weekdays, only serious hikers and bicyclists use the trail.

A canopy of live oak and laurel oak trees covers the first mile of the trail. The trees are very dense in this section of the trail, so it's a pleasant and cool first mile, even on a hot and humid Florida summer day. For the first two miles of the trail, be on the lookout for small plant and tree identification placards placed

AT-A-GLANCE INFORMATION

Length:
7 miles

Configuration:
Loop

Difficulty:
Flat and easy

Scenery:
Mixture of live oak, myrtle, and flatwoods with palmettos and a few cypress domes

Exposure:
Mostly shaded

Traffic:
Quite popular on weekends with cyclists and hiking families; basically deserted on weekdays

Trail surface:
Paved

Hiking Time:
3–3.5 hours

Season:
All year

Access:
No fees or permits required; a donation of $1 is requested.

Maps:
Map available at main entrance

Facilities:
The main entrance has full rest room facilities; rest room facilities at the top of the loop.

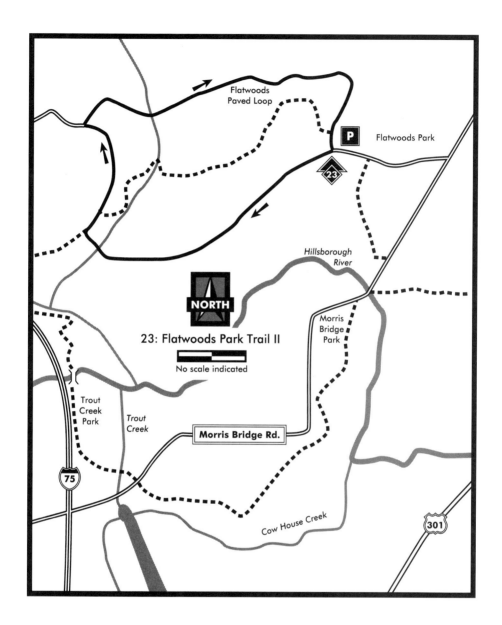

Flatwoods Paved Loop

P Flatwoods Park

23

Hillsborough River

Morris Bridge Park

NORTH

23: Flatwoods Park Trail II

No scale indicated

Trout Creek Park

Trout Creek

Morris Bridge Rd.

75

Cow House Creek

301

along the side of the trail, the work of a Hillsborough County Scout troop.

The most interesting part of the trail's first mile is the cypress dome to the right of the trail. The pond here is home to several species of wading birds, including Great Blue Herons, which we saw hunting in the shallows of the dome habitat. At the same time, we also saw

gopher tortoises coming out of their holes in the drier area around the cypress dome. It's a good example of how much the habitat can change over a short distance in Florida, depending on the condition of the soils.

Throughout the second and third miles of the trail, watch for hog sign, including tracks, rubs, and rooting. Feral hogs are

Keep watch on trails like this one; you may see wildlife at any time.

plentiful in the Four Rivers area, and this section of the Flatwoods trail abounds with acorn bearing trees. This combination creates, literally, a hog heaven. The hogs leave the ground looking like it's been freshly plowed. Some of the tracks you see may be deer tracks; they're almost impossible to tell apart from hog tracks, and deer also love acorns.

At the top of the trail you'll discover a palmetto grove. These small members of the palm family supply the berries used to produce the dietary supplement known as saw palmetto. Be careful if you want to examine the berries: the fronds have small thorns at their bases. In areas like this, watch where you put your hands and feet as well. This is prime rattlesnake habitat.

After you pass the top of the loop and start down the back side of the trail, you'll find a good example of the habitat that gives the park its name. As you pass through the pines, you'll see the palmet-

to and wiregrass understory that's typical of a southern pine flatwoods. This habitat once covered most of the Southeast; today, only about 3 percent of the original flatwoods habitat, with its giant pines, remains. Most of the flatwoods habitat you see throughout the Southeast today is second or third growth.

On this section of the trail you'll see a lot of interesting birds and other wildlife. Watch for small flocks of white ibis searching in the grass for food. Overhead, watch for the red-tailed hawks that seem to be on constant aerial patrol over the trees. Also look for gopher tortoises and box turtles. In the early evenings you'll see armadillos nosing through the leaves in search of insects and other invertebrates.

The last two miles of the trail traverse the same oak habitat the first part goes through, with a heavy oak canopy over the trail. In this area you may find a lot of trumpet-shaped flowers scattered along the trail. These flowers come from the trumpet creeper vines that run up into the limbs of the overhanging oaks. Where these are common, hummingbirds also are common. Although they're hard to spot, listen for the low drone of their wings and you may be able to see one. Ruby-throated hummingbirds are resident in central Florida from March to October.

This trail does warrant one caution: on weekends it's very popular with bicycle riders, many of whom seem to have the attitude that they have the ultimate right-of-way. Other than that, this is a pleasant and easy-to-hike trail that's a nice, longer hike for novices and families.

NEARBY ATTRACTIONS
The nearby Hillsborough River State Park offers camping, canoeing, fishing, and recreational facilities.

Fort De Soto Park Main Trail

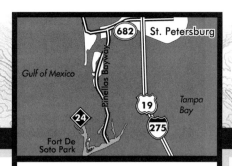

IN BRIEF

This multi-use recreation trail follows a beautiful sand beach on Mullet Key and passes by a historic Army post from the Spanish-American War.

DIRECTIONS

From Tampa, take Gandy Bridge west to Interstate 275. Take I-275 south to the Pinellas Bayway, which is Exit 4. A sign indicates that Exit 4 is the correct exit for Fort De Soto Park. Take the Pinellas Bayway—which is a toll road (50 cents)— west until it turns south (left) and becomes State Road 679. Once you turn left, you'll pay another toll (35 cents). Follow the Bayway south to the entrance to the park. Follow the Bayway until it reaches a **T**. Turn right and follow the Bayway west and then back to the north until you pass the "leash free zone" for dogs. Park in the next parking lot on the left; the trail begins here.

DESCRIPTION

This trail begins without fanfare at the south end of the parking lot; a road crossing sign is all that tells you you're on it. As soon as it crosses the Bayway, the trail parallels the road on the edge of a coastal habitat. After a short distance it crosses back over the Bayway, passes through the end of another parking lot, and follows the back side of the beach.

Before long the trail passes through a small grove of Australian pines and sabal palms, which provide shade for a section

AT-A-GLANCE INFORMATION

Length:
About 8.5 miles

Configuration:
Out and back with a spur

Difficulty:
Flat, easy

Scenery:
Oceanside, bayside, and historic

Exposure:
Mostly exposed

Traffic:
Busy on weekends

Trail surface:
Paved

Hiking time:
3 to 4 hours

Season:
All year

Access:
Except for toll roads, no permits or fees are required.

Maps:
Available at the campground office and the park office

Facilities:
Rest rooms and water fountains are available at several points along the trail. In addition, a gift shop and snack bar are located near the fort.

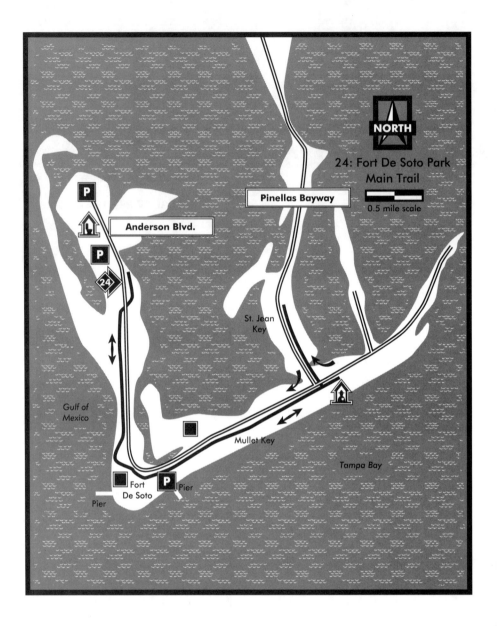

North

24: Fort De Soto Park
Main Trail

0.5 mile scale

Pinellas Bayway

Anderson Blvd.

St. Jean
Key

Gulf of
Mexico

Mullet Key

Tampa Bay

Fort
De Soto

Pier

Pier

of trail that is quite open otherwise. Past the trees, the trail continues to wind along the back side of the dunes.

Beyond the dune area the trail swings away from the road, and goes behind the gift shop and snack bar, where you can stop and get something cold to drink if you like. Here the trail passes a number of sea grape trees and more sabal palms,

fairly typical coastal species that park planners have wisely left intact.

Just past the snack bar, the trail swings back toward the road and passes through more sabal palms as it approaches the main point of historical interest in the park, Fort De Soto. This fort was built in 1898, and is open to the public.

A stop at Fort De Soto, built in 1898, is well worth the time.

Beyond the fort, the trail passes several picnic pavilions and parallels the road as it winds between a number of small oak trees. The trail crosses a small bridge over a little slough, then crosses the entrance to the fishing pier parking lot. Hike past the sabal palms, then cross the entrance to the parking lot for the second pier.

From here, the trail traverses a greenway that has a lot of sabal palms along it. After crossing another small bridge over a saltwater slough that's full of mangroves, you'll pass through a lightly wooded area of pines, cedars, and some sabal palms. In this area you'll also find benches to rest on.

At the end of the greenway you'll see a giant American flag, which flies in front of the park headquarters. Here, for an interesting side trip, turn right into the parking lot and look for the barrier-free interpretive trail. As soon as you step onto the trail, a sensor picks up your presence and starts an audiotape that tells you about the area you're entering and what you'll see on the trail.

On the main trail, however, walk straight ahead onto the short spur that takes you to the East Beach swim area. When you return down it and reach the park headquarters once again, turn right, cross the Bayway, and pick up the main trail as it parallels the road. You're about to see the prettiest part of the trail.

Watch on the right until you can see out over the mangrove bay. A sign here tells you that this is the Fort De Soto Wetland and Aquatic Management Area, and gives a bit of interpretive information about the area. Other signs indicate that there are deep holes in this area, and recommend against either swimming or shell fishing here.

The trail winds through a small oak hammock with some shade. There's a bench here where you can sit down and rest. Continue on until the trail crosses the Bayway again and enters the camping area. Return the way you came for the entire 8.5-mile trip.

Fort De Soto Park
Nature Trail

IN BRIEF

This seaside trail traverses several saltwater and beach habitats.

DIRECTIONS

From Tampa, take Gandy Bridge west to Interstate 275. Take Interstate 275 south to the Pinellas Bayway, which is Exit 4 for Fort De Soto. Take the Pinellas Bayway (toll road, 50 cents) west until it turns south (left) and becomes State Road 679. Once you turn left, you'll pay another toll (35 cents). Follow the Bayway south to the entrance to the park. Inside the park, follow the Bayway until it reaches a T. Turn right and follow the Bayway until you reach the Arrowhead Picnic Area. The entrance to the trail is across the road from the parking area.

DESCRIPTION

Enter the trail through a grove of sabal palms to an interpretive sign about prescribed (controlled) burns. Take the trail to the left, following the directional arrows.

In this area the habitat is quite dry; prickly pear cactus is common along this section of trail. Follow the trail around to the right through coastal flatwoods with sabal palms and small oaks.

Follow the trail to the right past a Station 4 through 7 sign and through a pine woodland. Before long you will reach a fork in the trail. A sign indicates that the trail leads to the left, but take the right

AT-A-GLANCE INFORMATION

Length:
About 1.75 miles

Configuration:
Out and back with loops and a spur

Difficulty:
Flat, easy

Scenery:
Varied and unusual salt marsh and mangrove habitats

Exposure:
Mostly shaded

Traffic:
Moderately busy on weekends

Trail surface:
Sand and mowed grass

Hiking time:
45 to 60 minutes

Season:
All year

Access:
Except for toll roads, no permits or fees are required.

Maps:
Available at the campground office, the park office, and box at the trailhead

Facilities:
Water fountain at trailhead

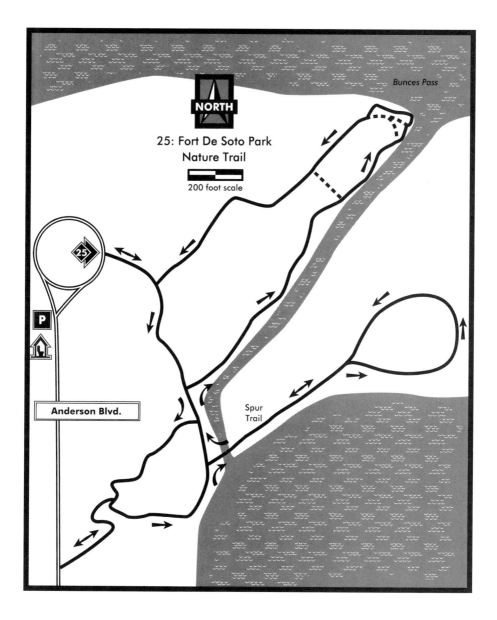

25: Fort De Soto Park
Nature Trail

200 foot scale

NORTH

Bunces Pass

Spur
Trail

Anderson Blvd.

fork instead. Just beyond that there is another fork; again take the fork to the right (and watch for a large stand of poison ivy right where the trail splits).

As you traverse this portion of the trail, you're going to pass through a wonderful coastal pineland with a grassy understory that's significantly different in appearance from most of the other piney woods you'll see on the hikes in this book. When you reach Station 5, don't follow the main trail to the left; rather, take the spur to the right, away from the main trail. This spur takes you on a short walk through a little-used portion of the park, past a communications tower and some Australian pines, and through some sabal palms before ending at the main road through the park. This whole area is good bird and

At Bunces Pass, the trail reaches the water's edge.

butterfly watching territory; while we were there, we passed a birder who was watching a painted bunting, quite an unusual species in central Florida. This area also is good for gopher tortoises.

Return down the spur, turn right, and continue around the loop of the main trail. This section of trail traverses an area that's mostly grassy, with a number of sabal palms.

Just after Station 6, another spur goes to the right. Ignore this one or take it as you choose; it's a very short walk back to the communications tower you passed on the previous spur.

Continue following the main around to the left. When you reach Station 7, bear to the right to take the Spur Trail. This takes you through a variety of habitats in quick succession. First you'll be in a sabal palm area, then you'll pass through a mangrove habitat. Shortly you're into some large oaks mixed with sabal palms in a hammock. Before long this Spur Trail forks around a large oak

tree. From here the trail makes a short loop, so taking either side will soon bring you close to the water. Don't miss the poison ivy that's growing up some of the trees in this area—it is unbelievable.

Return down the Spur Trail to the main trail, and go to the right at Station 7. At the next fork, turn right and follow the Stations 8 to 13 sign.

As you proceed along this loop you'll see a couple of cross trails, but if you stay on the main trail you'll soon arrive at the water's edge at Bunces Pass. Here, you'll be in an area of sabal palms that's quite open with a lot of salt marsh grasses, even though the trail is dry. The trail swings left, and left again, so that you're headed back down to the other side of the loop. Follow the loop around; it goes back into the sabal palms and then into the coastal flatwoods. Just past Station 13, this loop trail rejoins the main trail. Turn right here and follow the main trail back to the parking lot.

Friendship Trail Bridge

IN BRIEF

The Friendship Trail Bridge was developed from the old Gandy Bridge, and stretches from the Hillsborough County side of Old Tampa Bay to the Pinellas County side.

DIRECTIONS

To reach the Hillsborough end of the trail, go west on Gandy Boulevard until you cross West Shore Boulevard. The turnoff to the trail is one-half mile past Westshore on the right.

DESCRIPTION

This trail was opened in 1999, and upgrading continues with minor construction taking place from time to time. The Friendship Trail Bridge was retooled from the old Gandy Bridge that connected South Tampa with Pinellas County. No vehicles are allowed on the trail except for maintenance and repair vehicles. However, joggers, in-line skaters, and bicyclists use the trail. Its proximity to downtown and to all of South Tampa makes for easy and quick access, so the Trail Bridge is very popular.

As you leave the parking lot and start west on the Trail Bridge, you're beginning one of Tampa Bay's unique hikes. Although the Pinellas Trail crosses one bridge, the Trail Bridge is the only trail that is over water for its entire length.

In the first section of the trail, a suspended catwalk on either side of the

AT-A-GLANCE INFORMATION

Length:
5.2 miles

Configuration:
Out and back

Difficulty:
Easy; flat except for the center span of the old bridge

Scenery:
Spectacular view of Old Tampa Bay

Exposure:
Completely exposed; no shade at all

Traffic:
Quite busy, especially on weekends

Trail surface:
Paved

Hiking time:
1.5 to 2 hours

Season:
All year

Access:
No permits or fees

Maps:
No published map

Facilities:
None

Special comments:
Half-mile intervals are painted on the pavement.

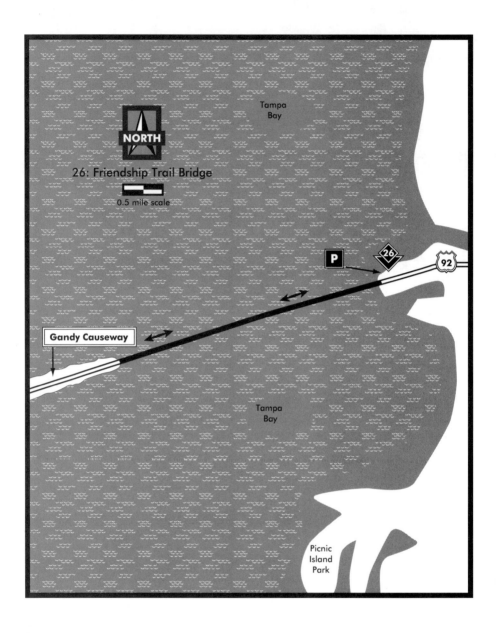

bridge is open for fishing. This is a popular spot for anglers, and a good place to fish, so you'll likely see people catching fish at any time.

As you proceed west, the fishing catwalk ends and the trail begins to climb rather steeply as you approach the channel under the Gandy Bridge into Old

Tampa Bay. From the top of the span, you can see the entire sweep of the bay, including the Howard Frankland Bridge and the Courtney Campbell Causeway to the north. If you can get in the right place on a clear day, you may even be able to look under the new Gandy Bridge and see the Sunshine Skyway

From the Trail Bridge, you have a great view of Old Tampa Bay.

Bridge far to the south, where Interstate 275 crosses the mouth of Tampa Bay and links Pinellas, Hillsborough, and Manatee counties. As you continue down the center span, you can see the entire length of the trail to its terminus in Pinellas County. In the middle of the trail, keep a sharp eye on the water. Not only will you see the usual pelicans and other aquatic birds, but this also is an excellent location to watch for dolphins and the occasional spotted eagle ray as they break the surface of the water.

As you near the Pinellas County end of the Trail Bridge, again you'll see a fishing catwalk on both sides of the trail. Continue to the end, then return for the full 5.2 miles.

NEARBY ATTRACTIONS

The Friendship Trail Bridge is close to almost everything except shopping. Between Westshore and the trailhead on Gandy Boulevard you can buy any fishing tackle you need, wash your car, or get gas. Or if you're hungry, you can find something to eat at Jimmie Mac's just south of Gandy Boulevard on the water. Just north of the east end of the trail, a small beach offers wade fishing or just a place to play in the water.

At the west end of the trail, beaches on both sides of Gandy Boulevard provide popular recreation spots during most of the year. Proceed west on Gandy for several beachside restaurants.

Hammock Park Trail

IN BRIEF

This nature park has several miles of intertwined trails that can be combined to make hikes of various lengths.

DIRECTIONS

From Tampa, take the Courtney Campbell Causeway to Clearwater. Turn right on US Highway 19. Go two miles north and turn left on Sunset Point Road. Follow Sunset Point Road until it dead-ends at Edgewater Boulevard. Turn right (north) on Edgewater. Go 3.2 miles north to Mira Vista (a sign indicates where to turn) and turn right. Cross the Pinellas Trail on Mira Vista and take the left-hand fork to San Mateo Drive. On San Mateo drive to the park entrance and turn right. The trailhead is to the right of the picnic pavilions.

DESCRIPTION

After you park, walk east until you come to the sidewalk, then follow it south (right) toward the rest rooms. Before you reach the rest rooms, turn left on the main sand trail you see there. Ahead you'll see a "Sugarberry Trail" signpost. Here, turn right onto the grass trail.

On your left watch for Cedar Creek, which parallels the Sugarberry Trail. Between the creek on your left and the woods on your right, there's just enough change in elevation to make a difference in the habitat. The area along the creek bank is a narrow wetland, while on your

AT-A-GLANCE INFORMATION

Length:
1.75 miles

Configuration:
Intertwined loops and spurs

Difficulty:
Flat, easy

Scenery:
A variety of Florida woodland habitats

Exposure:
Mostly shaded

Traffic:
Moderately busy on weekends

Trail surface:
Grass, sand, pine needles, leaves

Hiking Time:
45 to 60 minutes

Season:
All year

Access:
No fees or permits needed

Maps:
Available from the Dunedin Leisure Services Administration Office, 903 Michigan Boulevard, Dunedin, FL 34698; (727) 298-3263.

Facilities:
A rest room and water fountain are located at the trailhead.

Special comments:
Trail intersections are clearly marked.

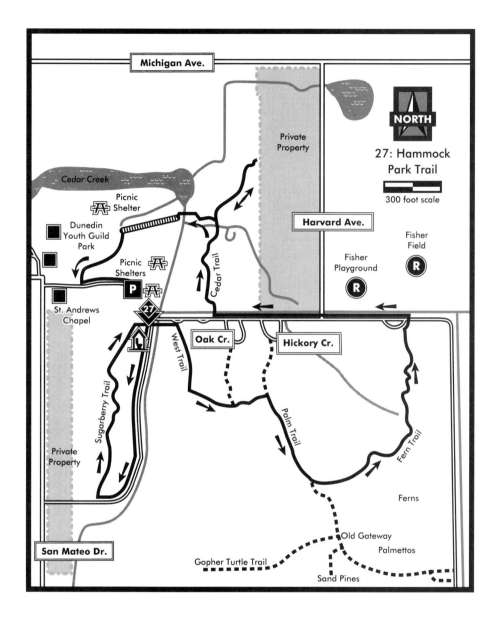

27: Hammock Park Trail

right you'll see large oaks and other hardwoods. This section of the trail is a good place to watch for butterflies, especially around the lantana bushes.

Before long, you'll see ferns on both sides of the trail. Follow the trail to the right until you see the big oak tree and the chain separating The Hammock from private property. Here you can turn

right into the woods, where you'll find a number of large oaks and other hardwoods with an understory of ferns. As you walk, you'll come to a bench where you can rest and maybe spot several species of woodland butterflies.

The Sugarberry Trail makes a loop to the playground behind the rest rooms. Pass the rest rooms and turn right, back onto the paved sidewalk where you began.

This time when you see the "Sugarberry Trail" signpost, head straight to the principal trail that goes into the main part of the park. A short distance in, turn right on the West Trail and walk through a stand of palms. Follow the trail as it winds through the citrus trees mixed with palms and native hardwoods.

The trail goes left through large hardwoods with a fern understory, then crosses a wooden footbridge over a stream. At the fork in the trail go left. deeper into the woods, where you'll cross another footbridge. Continue through the hardwoods and ferns and cross a third bridge.

When you reach the "Oak Trail" signpost, continue straight on the West Trail rather than turning onto the Oak Trail. Follow it through the trees until you reach the intersection of the West Trail and Palm Trail. Take the Palm Trail to the right.

Before long you'll see a signpost, indicating an intersection with the Fern Trail. Take the Fern Trail to the left to make a loop. As its name implies, there are ferns along this trail, but there's also a lot of poison ivy. Where the trail takes a sharp right, you'll pass a large, downed hardwood that's still alive and growing. As the trail turns to the right again it narrows; a number of exposed roots adds a little challenge to the walk.

A little further the trail turns left, and a short boardwalk takes you across another stream. Before long you'll reach a dead tree lying across the trail that you'll have to climb over. After another short walk through ferns, this trail comes out at the main east-west trail again, where there's a signpost that reads "Fern Trail" and a bench to sit on.

Turn left on the main trail and walk toward the entrance of the park. This trail parallels a canal that flows into Cedar Creek. As you continue toward the entrance, you'll pass a bridge that takes you over to a playground.

On the right, look for the Cedar Trail. There, take the bridge across the canal and onto the Cedar Trail. The habitat here is drier and more open than the area you've just hiked.

A short distance into the trail, you'll cross a bridge over another branch of Cedar Creek. Just beyond the bridge the trail turns to the left and passes an overlook and boardwalk. Don't take this yet, but proceed straight ahead for now. The trail takes you into a slightly wetter area, where you'll see more naturalized citrus trees, and ends at the edge of The Hammock's property, which is well marked.

Return on the Cedar Trail until you reach the spur that goes to the overlook and boardwalk, and turn right to follow it. When you reach the overlook, stop and look at the osprey nest that's in front of you. This is an active nest, and, during the spring, you can see the parents feeding and caring for young birds.

After a stop at the overlook, proceed on the boardwalk through the salt marsh. Where the bridge crosses Cedar Creek again, watch for wading birds, and for water birds such as ducks and mergansers. When you reach the fork in the boardwalk, take the right-hand side, which will lead you into the Dunedin Youth Guild Park. This route passes through mangroves and very close to the osprey nest.

When you exit the boardwalk, turn left onto the paved path and follow it through the oaks and palms until you reach the fork. Take the left-hand side and proceed on the path until you reach the handicapped parking area for The Hammock. From here you'll be able to see the parking lot and your vehicle.

Hillsborough River State Park Main Trail

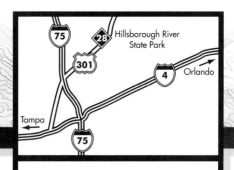

IN BRIEF
Meander beside the Hillsborough River, past live oaks, wax myrtle, and saw palmetto in one of the states oldest state parks.

DIRECTIONS
Exit off Interstate 4 north of Tampa to US Highway 301; follow 301 north approximately nine miles from the Interstate to the park entrance. Stay on the paved road through the park to the concession area. The nature trails and the main hiking trail begin there.

DESCRIPTION
A Civilian Conservation Corps (CCC) project, Hillsborough River State Park opened to the public in 1938. This 3,950-acre park now offers camping, picnicking, canoe rentals, and seasonal swimming.

From the main parking area, head through the picnic area and past the concession area. Enter the trail by crossing a small bridge over the swiftly-flowing Hillsborough River. Originating in the Green Swamp, about 30 miles northeast, the Hillsborough River is the primary freshwater source for the city of Tampa. It's a river that's teeming with wildlife, so stop and gaze into the water at every bridge.

After crossing the first bridge, you'll approach a fork in the trail. Go right to follow the loop in a counterclockwise

AT-A-GLANCE INFORMATION

Length:
3.4 miles

Configuration:
Loop

Difficulty:
Easy; flat from beginning to end

Scenery:
Very nice view of the Hillsborough River as well as typical central Florida habitats

Exposure:
Mostly open with some scattered shade throughout

Traffic:
Busy on weekends

Trail surface:
Sand and shell, boardwalk, and about a mile of paved road

Hiking time:
About 2 hours

Season:
All year

Access:
$3.50 to enter park; 8 a.m. to dusk

Maps:
A park and trail map is available at the ranger station.

Facilities:
Rest rooms, playground, picnic tables

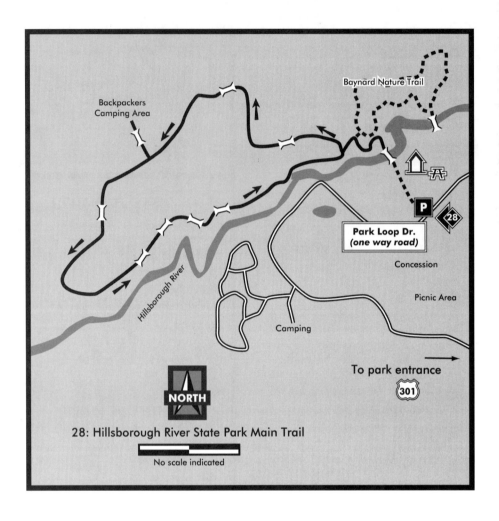

Backpackers
Camping Area

Baynard Nature Trail

Hillsborough River

Park Loop Dr.
(one way road)

Concession

Picnic Area

Camping

To park entrance

301

NORTH

28: Hillsborough River State Park Main Trail

No scale indicated

direction. Once you take the fork, the path begins to wind around portions of the Boynard Nature Trail. Look into the water here—during the spring you may see panfish on their beds. They're hungry when they're on the beds, so you may see them chasing and catching minnows.

The trail continues under a canopy of live oak and palms. Look on the oak branches above for strands of Spanish moss and other epiphytes (plants that get their sustenance from the air).

At the one-mile marker, watch for a cypress dome on the right. A cypress dome isn't a high spot, as the name

implies, but rather a slightly sunken spot made of clay or other soil that doesn't drain easily. Water collects and stands in the depression, creating a small pond even during dry times.

Around the outside of the dome, small palmettos and grasses indicate a dryer habitat. This is a good place to see gopher tortoises and box terrapins, as well as other creatures (including eastern diamondback rattlesnakes) that use holes the tortoises have dug.

On the left side of this section of the trail, you'll see cypress trees with their ever-present cypress knees. In dry

Pine flatwoods along the trail

weather, this is a great place to look for small animal tracks, as the soil is damp and holds impressions easily. On the day we took this hike we saw not only the tracks of raccoons, but also the raccoons themselves.

After the one-mile marker, you'll reach a small spur trail that crosses a bridge and goes to a campsite set aside for the use of backpackers. Continuing on the main trail, you'll come to a flatwoods area with tall pines, natural grasses, and saw palmetto. Watch your feet here; flatwoods habitats are famous for their rattlesnakes and coral snakes.

The trail continues for another mile or so with alternating habitats of live oaks and palms, and flatwoods with towering pines and native grass understory. In the flatwoods area on this trail section we saw signs of feral hog activity. The ground was uprooted and turned as though freshly plowed.

The last mile of the trail parallels the Hillsborough River. Here, you'll start to see an increase in the number and species of birds. On the day we hiked we saw great blue herons as well as a number of smaller herons and egrets wading along the banks of the Hillsborough River. Next, you'll come to four wooden bridges that cross parts of the river. Be sure to stop and spend some time peering over the side into the river. You'll see fish, small alligators, turtles and wading birds. Keep watching—you might get lucky and see a family of otters at play in the river.

Return to the trailhead and the parking area for the full 3.4-mile hike.

NEARBY ATTRACTIONS
Historic Fort Foster is located inside Hillsborough River State Park. Fort tours are available.

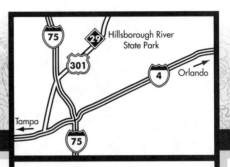

Hillsborough River State Park Nature Trails

IN BRIEF

These intertwined nature trails provide a good look at several native Florida habitats as well as a jaunt along the Hillsborough River.

DIRECTIONS

Exit off Interstate 4 north of Tampa to US Highway 301; follow 301 north approximately nine miles from the Interstate to the park entrance. Stay on the paved road through the park to the concession area. The nature trails and the main hiking trail begin there.

DESCRIPTION

A Civilian Conservation Corps (CCC) project, this 3,950-acre park offers camping, picnicking, canoe rentals, and seasonal swimming. It also has some good hiking.

At the parking area, you'll find three trailheads. The one to the far left that immediately crosses the river is the main hiking trail, profiled earlier in this book. Around to the right, you'll see the paired trailheads for the nature trails. Take the one to the left, toward the river.

On the trail, you'll find yourself in a mixed habitat of live and scrub oak with an understory of ferns. Overhead, the trees are full of squirrels that are unafraid of humans. Please don't feed them, however. It's not good for the squirrels and it's against park policy. Nonetheless, their

AT-A-GLANCE INFORMATION

Length:
2.2 miles

Configuration:
Connected loops

Difficulty:
Moderate

Scenery:
Follows the bank of the Hillsborough River

Exposure:
Mostly shaded, with a few exposed areas

Traffic:
Very busy on weekends, virtually empty during the week

Trail Surface:
Mixture of hard-packed sand and shell with boardwalks

Hiking time:
About 2 hours

Season:
Open all year

Access:
$3.50 to enter park; 8 a.m. to dusk

Maps:
A park and trail map is available at the ranger station

Facilities:
Full facilities are available at the concession and picnic area where the trails begin.

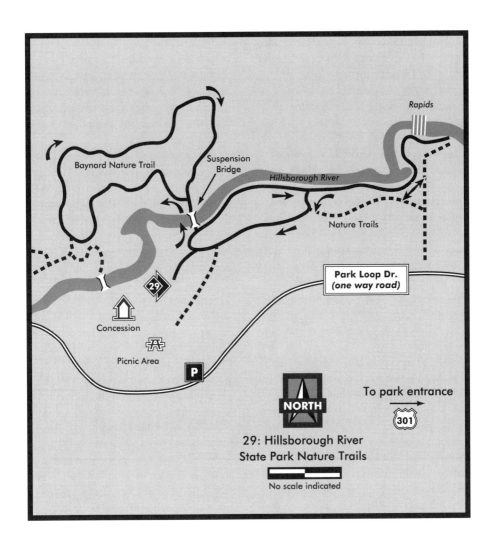

Baynard Nature Trail

Suspension Bridge

Hillsborough River

Rapids

Nature Trails

Park Loop Dr.
(one way road)

29

Concession

Picnic Area

P

NORTH

To park entrance

301

29: Hillsborough River
State Park Nature Trails

No scale indicated

boldness around people makes them great fun. If you take this hike with children, they'll get a real kick out of the little animals as they scurry up and down the tree trunks and beg for treats.

As the trail approaches the river, it begins to slope downward slightly. Here, a very nice surprise awaits—a suspension bridge spanning the Hillsborough River. It's mesmerizing as it gently sways back and forth over the river. On the weekend we hiked here, we didn't see a single hiker make it all the way across the

bridge without stopping in the middle to peer over the side. When we crossed, we found out why. Looking down, we could see some large fish swimming beneath the bridge, making us wish we'd brought our fishing rods.

On the other side of the bridge, you'll find yourself on the Baynard Nature Trail. This short nature trail is about half of a mile. Inside this small loop trail you'll find both cypress domes and oak hammocks. This is a good place to look for several species of woodpeckers, including pileated woodpeckers, which we saw busily looking for insects among the oaks. They're worth looking for since they're fairly uncommon elsewhere. Most of the time, your first glimpse of them will be as they fly from tree to tree. All you'll see is a swift black shadow; watch, and you'll likely see a second one, as the male and female usually feed together. Also listen for them, as their drumming is loud and slow, then softer at the end, quite unlike the rapid drumming of other woodpeckers.

As you walk the Baynard Nature Trail, notice where feral hogs have uprooted the ground looking for food. Park rangers say hogs are a constant problem in the park, and they appreciate having visitors tell them where they've seen any of the animals.

Along this trail, you'll see a few small signs that identify some of the plants and trees. According to park rangers, there are plans to add more interpretive signs to the park.

Once you've traversed the Baynard Nature Trail, re-cross the suspension bridge and head down river (left). Now you'll be walking under an oak canopy draped with Spanish moss. Between the river and the canopy of trees, this stretch of the trail has an almost magical feel to it. Look up in the trees for squirrel nests high in the oaks, and look for bromeliads nestled into the forks of several trees as well. When we were there, the plants had beautiful red flowers on them; park rangers said they continue to bloom throughout most of the spring and into the early summer.

When you reach the side trail to the right, continue straight ahead. Before long, you'll reach a rather sharp left turn

that follows the river. Here the trail begins to open up, and the path looks well used. A lot of people walk by here because of the rapids, which begin at this point. Although these are only Class II rapids, they're a lot of fun for both canoeists and tubers.

At the rapids, turn around and retrace your steps for about a quarter mile, until you reach the side trail again. Turn left on the side trail, then bear right through the hardwoods and Sabal palms. The undergrowth here is saw palmetto, a relative of Sabal palm, which is the Florida state tree.

As you reach the end of the trail, you have a choice of routes back to the parking area. If you take the first trail to the left you'll come out at the picnic area a short distance away from your vehicle. Stay on the main trail for a few more steps, however, and you'll find yourself at the trailhead where you began.

NEARBY ATTRACTIONS

Other activities in Hillsborough River State Park include canoeing and freshwater fishing in the Hillsborough River; swimming isn't allowed. The river has one of Florida's only class II rapids.

If you're at the park on the first weekend in December, watch for the annual Derby Day Festival. This festival includes a road race for physically challenged people of all ages and abilities.

Historic Fort Foster is located inside Hillsborough River State Park. If you're there on a day when park staff members are putting on a living history program, you can step back in time to observe fort personnel carrying out their daily duties in the year 1837. Fort tours also are available.

Hillsborough River Wetlands Restoration Trail

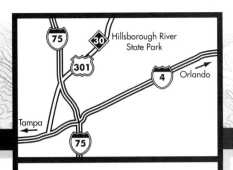

IN BRIEF

This three-mile loop hike highlights an ongoing restoration project sponsored by the State of Florida, including man-made cypress domes and a pine flatwoods restoration project.

DIRECTIONS

Exit off Interstate 4 north of Tampa to US Hwy. 301; follow 301 north approximately nine miles from the Interstate to the park entrance. After you enter the park, follow the loop drive all the way to the back of the park, to within 100 yards of the trailhead. Parking here is tricky (a parking area for the trail is on the drawing board), so either park your vehicle carefully at the trailhead, or, for safety's sake, park back at the campground and hike the quarter mile to the trailhead.

DESCRIPTION

This is an easy, open trail that highlights repair efforts of environmental damage that has taken place over the years. It's an easy and comfortable place to expose children to the wonders of a very young habitat that will grow as they do. The trail includes the newly-created cypress domes and pine flatwoods restoration projects.

The trail is hard-packed sand and shell, and is wide enough for the park's 4-wheelers to use. About 50 yards past the trailhead, on the right, you'll see the first of the manmade cypress domes.

AT-A-GLANCE INFORMATION

Length:
3 miles

Configuration:
Loop

Difficulty:
Easy to moderate

Scenery:
Florida wetlands, with pine flatwoods and palmetto

Exposure:
Open, with little canopy

Traffic:
Busy on weekends, deserted during the week

Trail Surface:
Hard-packed sand and shell

Hiking time:
1 to 2 hours

Season:
Year round

Access:
$3.50 to enter park; 8 a.m. to dusk

Maps:
Available at the ranger station

Facilities:
Full rest room facilities at the picnic and concession areas

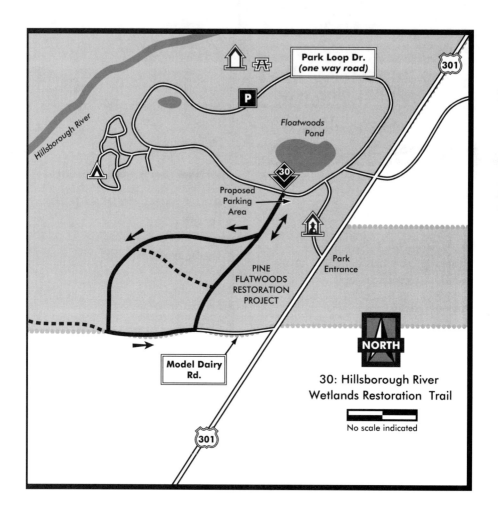

Park Loop Dr.
(one way road)

301

Hillsborough River

Floatwoods
Pond

30

Proposed
Parking
Area

Park
Entrance

PINE
FLATWOODS
RESTORATION
PROJECT

NORTH

30: Hillsborough River
Wetlands Restoration Trail

No scale indicated

Model Dairy
Rd.

301

Ditch plugs and monitoring wells are clearly visible from the trail. The ditch plugs keep water flowing toward the young cypress trees.

When you come to the fork in the trail, follow the right-hand side as it continues along the small developing cypress domes. Watch for wildlife in this area; many species are attracted to the developing habitat. Look in the dryer areas outside the cypress domes for gopher tortoises and other upland species, and look for opossums, armadil-los, and wading birds such as egrets and herons in and around the cypress domes themselves. As the cypress trees mature, more wetland species of birds and wildlife will move into the area, which will greatly enhance the hiking experience here.

When you reach Model Dairy Road, turn left and follow the road for a distance, and then turn left again. As you make your way back to the trailhead, take note of the pine flatwoods restoration project on the right side of the trail.

The tall pines and saw palmetto under-growth stand in direct contrast to the young cypress domes on the other side of the trail. Pines grow quickly, and the undergrowth of saw palmetto grows even faster. Take a moment and look at the base of the saw palmettos, where you'll see the small berries that are harvested for the popular nutritional supplement of the same name. Be careful; sharp thorns protect the berries. Also be aware that spiders and scorpions often live near the berries as well. This is excellent rattlesnake habitat—you may find either a small pygmy or ground rattler, or its larger cousin, the Eastern Diamondback, here.

NEARBY ATTRACTIONS

Other activities in the park include canoeing and freshwater fishing in the Hillsborough River; swimming isn't allowed. The river has one of Florida's only class II rapids.

If you're at the park on the first weekend in December, watch for the annual Derby Day Festival. This festival includes a road race for physically challenged people of all ages and abilities.

Historic Fort Foster is located inside Hillsborough River State Park. If you're there on a day when park staff members are putting on a living history program, you can step back in time to observe fort personnel carrying out their daily duties in the year 1837. Fort tours also are available.

Honeymoon Island Nature Loop

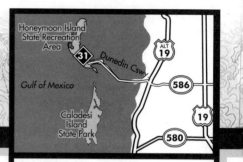

IN BRIEF

This hike follows a combination of woodland and beachside environments, introducing visitors to a virgin slash pine forest as well as a large colony of osprey.

DIRECTIONS

From Tampa, take the Courtney Campbell Causeway to Clearwater. Turn right on US Highway 19. Go two miles north and turn left on Sunset Point Road. Follow Sunset Point Road until it dead ends at Edgewater Boulevard. Turn right (north) on Edgewater. Continue north on Edgewater as it becomes Broadway Bayshore Boulevard, and follow it to State Road 586, which is also Curlew Road. Turn left on Curlew Road, which becomes Dunedin Causeway. Follow the causeway until it reaches the park entrance.

When you enter the park, proceed straight ahead almost to the end of the road, where you'll see a sign that reads "Picnic Area and Nature Trail." Park at the far end of the picnic area, where you can see the trailhead in front of you.

DESCRIPTION

Originally populated by the Tocobagans, a Native American people, Honeymoon Island has been visited by numerous groups, including Spanish explorers, pirates, traders, and fisherman. The island eventually was bought by a New York entrepreneur, who wanted to turn it into

AT-A-GLANCE INFORMATION

Length:
About 2 miles

Configuration:
Loop

Difficulty:
Easy, but deep sand adds difficulty

Scenery:
Pineland and seaside

Exposure:
Light shade in the pines, exposed on the beach

Traffic:
Moderately busy on weekends

Trail Surface:
Sand

Hiking Time:
1 to 1.5 hours

Season:
All year

Access:
Entrance to the park costs $4 per vehicle, with up to 8 occupants.

Maps:
A park and trail map is available at the gate.

Facilities:
Rest rooms at the trailhead

Special comments:
There is poison ivy throughout the pine forest. Watch where you walk!

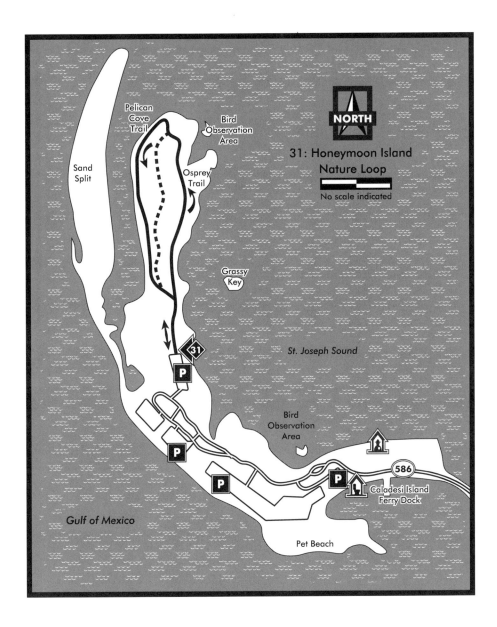

Map labels (within image):
Pelican Cove Trail
Bird Observation Area
Sand Split
Osprey Trail
NORTH
31: Honeymoon Island Nature Loop
No scale indicated
Grassy Key
St. Joseph Sound
31
P
Bird Observation Area
P
586
P
P
Caladesi Island Ferry Dock
Gulf of Mexico
Pet Beach

a newlywed resort. Unfortunately World War II broke out and the island was used to give exhausted war workers much-needed rest and relaxation. Today, the island is a part of Florida's State Park system.

From trail's start, you'll see a remarkably healthy stand of poison ivy. Though poison ivy is undesirable to hikers, dur-

ing the winter the berries are an important food source for wildlife.

Just past the trailhead, the trail swings to the right, then back to the left, and enters an area where evidence remains of a very hot controlled burn.

This entire area is open, with a scattering of pine trees and sabal palms throughout. When you reach the first bench on the side of the trail, look up and to the right. You'll see an osprey nest in a dead tree less than 40 feet from the bench.

Shortly after you pass an interpretive sign about prickly pear cactus, look straight ahead through the trees, toward the end of the island, and you'll see another osprey nest. This area is good bird watching habitat. On the day we hiked we saw doves, cardinals, yellow-shafted flickers, and other woodpeckers.

When you reach the quarter-mile post, continue straight ahead. You'll see some cedars and small hardwoods char-acteristic of beach habitats. As you pass dry areas, you'll see signs that read "Environmentally Sensitive Area—Entry Strictly Prohibited..." Take heed; we met several wildlife officers patrolling the trail.

Just past the half-mile post, continue straight ahead to a kiosk with informa-tion about fire and owls. Beyond the kiosk, look for another osprey nest just to the left of the trail—you'll literally walk right under it. From here, you're among active osprey nests that are almost as numerous as the trees they're in.

At the top of the loop, is a fork in the trail. If you take the left path, you'll stay on the Osprey Trail among this wonder-ful colony of birds. Take the right path, and you'll be on the Pelican Cove Trail that leads to the beach. This trail passes through another environmentally sensi-tive area, so don't leave the trail.

After you pass the mangroves, bear to the right and you'll come out at the beach. Turn left and follow the shoreline. As you walk, you're only a couple of feet above the high tide mark; on a windy day you'll get wet. Then the trail swings

A typical osprey nest found on Honeymoon Island.

to the left, 15 feet or more above the high tide mark.

Before long, the trail passes through an area where mangroves have become estab-lished along the shore. As you walk, the mangroves become larger and better established, with lots of small trees sprout-ing.

At last the trail turns back to the left, and you pass through a stand of Brazilian Pepper, an exotic tree that's become well established in central Florida. Watch here for a huge prickly pear cactus, as well as another great stand of poison ivy.

Bear to the right, and you'll be back on the Osprey Trail. Follow the trail until you reach a sign that points to the left for the picnic area. Turn left here and you'll come out at the trailhead.

Lake Park Loop

IN BRIEF

This multi-use trail traverses several typical Florida habitats.

DIRECTIONS

From anywhere in south or west Tampa, take the Veteran's Expressway north to where it ends at Dale Mabry Highway. Turn right, cross Van Dyke Road, and watch for the park entrance on the right. (*Alternate directions:* Take Dale Mabry Highway north to the North-lakes area, and watch for Gaither High School on the left. After you pass the high school, watch on the left for the park entrance.)

Once in the park, go to the **T**, turn right and follow the paved road until you reach a fork where the paved road goes to the left and a sand road goes straight ahead. Take the sand road and follow it until you reach the parking area for the boat ramp and hiking trail, ignoring the "trail" sign along the road. The trailhead is to the right of, and more or less behind, the fenced picnic area; just follow the fence around to the right and you'll find it.

DESCRIPTION

This hike follows the only loop currently open in the park. According to park officials we talked to, the Florida Trail Association is in the process of developing at least one additional trail on this property.

AT-A-GLANCE INFORMATION

Length:
2. 1 miles

Configuration:
Loop

Difficulty:
Easy, but deep sand on some portions of the trail adds difficulty

Scenery:
Mostly woods

Exposure:
Very exposed

Traffic:
Light on weekends

Trail surface:
About 2/3 sand and 1/3 paved

Hiking Time:
About an hour

Season:
All year

Access:
A $1 donation is requested.

Maps:
Available from the park office just inside the front gate

Facilities:
Rest rooms and a picnic area available in the park

Special comments:
This 589-acre park is a joint venture between Hillsborough County and the City of St. Petersburg.

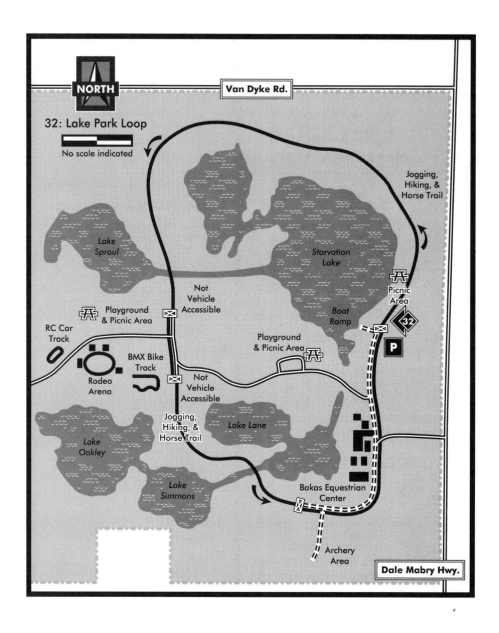

32: Lake Park Loop

No scale indicated

NORTH

Van Dyke Rd.

Jogging, Hiking, & Horse Trail

Lake Sproul

Starvation Lake

Not Vehicle Accessible

Picnic Area

Playground & Picnic Area

Boat Ramp

RC Car Track

32

Playground & Picnic Area

P

BMX Bike Track

Rodeo Arena

Not Vehicle Accessible

Jogging, Hiking, & Horse Trail

Lake Lane

Lake Oakley

Lake Simmons

Bakas Equestrian Center

Archery Area

Dale Mabry Hwy.

While exploring this park, you'll see wildlife typical of the area, but you can also spy a bird not normally found on any other trail in this book: peacocks. Park officials say the birds appeared when a housing development was built nearby. Apparently the peacocks lived on that property, and migrated to the park when their habitat was razed. Keep an eye out for them, especially near the equestrian area at the front of the park.

When ready, walk through the open gate at the trailhead and start down the wide dirt path. At this point you're walking between the picnic area on the left and woods to the right. Starvation Lake is off to your left, although the view was somewhat obscured by high weeds when we were there.

As you proceed, the trail follows the right of way of a power line for some distance. This section of the trail runs quite close to Dale Mabry Highway, so you can hear the traffic on the road. In this open area, watch for sulphur butterflies, both yellow and white, as well as a number of woodland butterflies.

Follow the trail as it turns to the left. As you move away from the highway, the footing improves because the ground is less sandy. Before long the trail swings to the left away from the power line, although it's no less open.

While on the trail, you may notice that this path is shared by horses; the large "deposits" left in their wake are hard to miss.

The trail is a good place to see snakes, both venomous and non-venomous. On the day we hiked, we surprised a large black racer sunning itself along the side of the trail.

As you hike, watch for the big snag on the right side of the trail—this is a good place to look for woodpeckers. Also in this area several side trails head into the woods. This is the general area where the FTA is developing more trails, which eventually may connect with a more complex system of trails.

Follow the trail as it continues to turn to the left. This dry area is a good place to look for gopher tortoises.

Just before you reach the gate, you'll notice a marked trail to the left. This trail will take you back to the other side of the loop just south of where you parked. However if you proceed straight ahead, you can walk around the gate and pass the playground and picnic area located next to the BMX bicycle track and the rodeo arena, which is vehicle-accessible

via a road that runs through the center of the park.

Cross the paved section of road and walk around the end of the second gate, which takes you back onto the trail. This area is very similar in habitat and appearance to the first section of trail, but if you look to the right you'll see occasional stands of cypress, indicating wet areas during times of normal rainfall.

As you proceed, a sign notes that Lake Simmons is off to the right. When there's adequate rainfall this area may be a lake, but when we took this hike it was a grassy field. In a little while you'll pass Crum Lake on the left, which also was bone dry on the day we were there.

As soon as you pass Crum Lake you'll enter the only section of this trail that's shaded; oaks spread their branches and provide a canopy for the trail. There are a lot of ferns here, and to the right you'll see the back end of the archery range. A sign cautions hikers against entering for obvious safety reasons. This area is a habitat for Zebra Longwings, the Florida State butterfly.

Walk around the end of one more gate to a gravelled section of park road. The main entrance to the archery area is on the right, and additional signs warn against entering the area.

Before long the gravel road ends and becomes pavement. This paved section passes the equestrian area and the park entrance where you entered. Follow the road straight ahead until it passes the paved fork to the left and becomes a gravel road once again; stay on it until you reach the parking area.

NEARBY ATTRACTIONS
Besides the regular rest rooms and picnic areas, this park also contains a horse stable, a rodeo arena, an archery range, and a BMX bicycle track.

Lake Rogers Park Loop

IN BRIEF

As it encircles Lake Rogers, this loop trail traverses a number of typical Florida habitats.

DIRECTIONS

Take the Veteran's Expressway north to the Erlich Road exit, and turn west on Erlich Road. (*Alternate directions from East Tampa:* Take Bearss Avenue west until it becomes Erlich Road, and follow Erlich Road until it passes under the Veteran's Expressway.)

Stay on Erlich Road until it runs into Gunn Highway, and follow Gunn Highway as it turns north. Stay on Gunn Highway as it passes South Mobley Road and Race Track Road. The next light after Race Track Road is North Mobley Road; turn left here. Go 0.4 miles on North Mobley Road and turn left into the parking lot of Lake Rogers Park. The trailhead is at the southwest corner of the parking lot.

DESCRIPTION

Opened in March 2000, Lake Rogers Park has a number of picnic areas that are entirely undeveloped; park managers have simply tucked picnic tables into openings in the trees, and in some cases installed grills next to them. Other than that, it's pack it in, pack it out.

Although this trail is basically flat, it does have a little more relief than many of the trails we've profiled in this book.

AT-A-GLANCE INFORMATION

Length:
2.5 miles

Configuration:
Loop

Difficulty:
Moderate; deep sand on some portions of the trail adds difficulty

Scenery:
Woods and lake

Exposure:
Some shade, but mostly exposed

Traffic:
Quiet on weekends

Trail surface:
Sand

Hiking Time:
2 to 2.5 hours

Season:
All year

Access:
No permits or fees

Maps:
No map is printed; a park map is on a signboard at the trailhead.

Facilities:
Portable toilets at the trailhead, and two water stations on the trail

Special comments:
We recommend that you wear light hiking boots or other shoes with some ankle support.

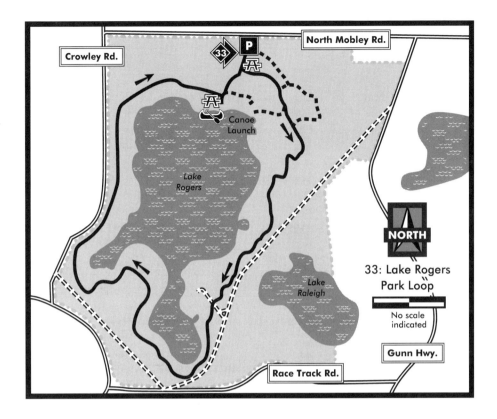

Crowley Rd.

North Mobley Rd.

33

P

Canoe
Launch

Lake
Rogers

NORTH

33: Lake Rogers
Park Loop

No scale
indicated

Lake
Raleigh

Gunn Hwy.

Race Track Rd.

A short distance past the trailhead, you'll come to a fork in the trail. A sign indicates a canoe launch area to the right, camping to the left, and fishing on either side of the fork. We chose to take the left-hand side of the trail.

The trail traverses a mixed pine and hardwood habitat with oaks throughout. These oaks aren't large enough to be called grandfather oaks, but they're old enough to have some character.

When you reach the first side-trail continue straight ahead; the left-hand trail takes you back to the parking lot. Then pass a small trail to the right as well.

At the next fork in the trail follow the sign and go right, although your intuition probably will tell you to go straight ahead.

Shortly you'll pass a primitive campsite that contains several picnic tables, a pavilion, and a fire pit. The campsite is in a nice oak grove, making this an attractive place to spend a few quiet hours or even days.

Just past the picnic site, you'll pass into an area of saw palmetto, and while we were there, a lot of banana spiders. These large orb-weavers are typical spiders of central and south Florida, and grow quite large during the long summer.

At the next fork in the trail, bear to the right, and follow the trail down through a little gully into an open area. The presence of aquatic plants to the right of the trail indicates that during wet weather, water stands in a marshy area; here you should get your first glimpse of Lake Rogers off to the right.

In the next little **S**-turn, you'll clearly see Lake Rogers; a picnic table here provides a scenic spot to stop and overlook the water. Listen here for birdsong, including blue jays and woodpeckers.

The habitat continues to be fairly uniform, with a mixture of hardwoods and a few pines. As you proceed, you'll pass a utility maintenance area to the left; don't walk into it, but bear to the right and stay on the trail. Here the trail dips down into a gully and passes what appears to be an old flood control structure or headwall. Take a look at the ferns here, which are really quite nice.

Just beyond this area the trail becomes more open and less shaded. Watch for some of the open-field butterflies flying around all the blackberry plants; we saw sulphurs, a couple of swallowtails, and a Viceroy.

As you hike around the southern shore of Lake Rogers, the trail continues to be sunny and open, then climbs back into the trees and some broken shade. When you cross a maintenance road, the trail continues straight ahead; a picnic area is located to the right at the end of the road near the edge of the lake.

The next short stretch of trail passes through a type of fern I had never before seen. This particular fern appeared to be aggressive, and showed signs of being hacked back regularly. Identify it if you can; we were at a loss as to what it was.

Continue around the west side of the lake, where you'll find a little more elevation change than you find on most of the trails in this book. A short boardwalk takes you across a small seasonal stream, then the trail emerges into a grassy area with a few small pines to the left and some native hollies—not Brazilian Pepper—to the right.

Here, watch for gopher tortoises; we saw several of them, as well as their distinctive tracks along the trail. Along this portion of the trail you'll also see several small side trails. The main trail continues to be well marked, however, and park officials don't want hikers following the side trails; they've placed piles of dirt across them, blocking them.

As you continue north, the trail continues to be quite open, and parallels Crowley Road, which is the western perimeter of the park. From here back to the trailhead, the lake is accessible for fishing in a number of places.

The trail swings to the right, away from Crowley Road, and enters an area of young pines. In this area look for the swinging bench on the right; it's a nice place to sit and read, if you're so inclined.

As you near the trailhead, the trees become thicker and the shade heavier. Before long you'll pass the canoe launch area on the right, where you'll see another picnic pavilion. A water station is on the left just past the canoe launch area.

When you come to the next fork in the trail, the right-hand side will take you down to the lake to another fishing area; the left-hand side takes you back to the trailhead and the parking lot.

Lake Seminole Park Trail

IN BRIEF

Take this pretty multi-use trail hidden in the back of a very busy county park for a restful hike that's "away from it all."

DIRECTIONS

From Tampa, take Gandy Bridge west to Pinellas County and stay on Gandy Boulevard as it becomes Park Boulevard at US Highway 19. From the intersection of Gandy/Park Boulevard, continue west 5.5 miles. The entrance to the park is on the right.

The challenge of this hike is not locating the park, but finding the trail once you're there. With no map and poor signage, you can drive through the park and never find the trail entrance. Stay on the main road past the boat ramp on the left, and then take the next right and follow the road to the second large parking area. Walk north and follow the sidewalk to the west and you'll come to the trailhead where one small sign lets you know you've arrived.

DESCRIPTION

Don't let the number of people in the park scare you off this trail. This park is located almost in the center of Pinellas County and is a very popular place for many kinds of recreation. Despite hundreds of visitors on a summer weekend day, the trail is surprisingly quiet. One thing to note is that the signs indicate that this is a one-way trail, starting from

AT-A-GLANCE INFORMATION

Length:
1 or 2 miles

Configuration:
Stacked loops

Difficulty:
Flat, easy

Scenery:
Typical Florida flatwoods, with both native and exotic plant species

Exposure:
Mostly shaded; a few sunny areas

Traffic:
Moderately busy on weekends; not as busy as hikers would expect from the congestion at the park

Trail surface:
Paved

Hiking time:
45 to 60 minutes

Season:
Open all year.

Access:
No fees or permits necessary

Maps:
Available at the park office

Facilities:
Water is available at three places on the trail. Rest rooms are located just south of the trailhead across a parking lot.

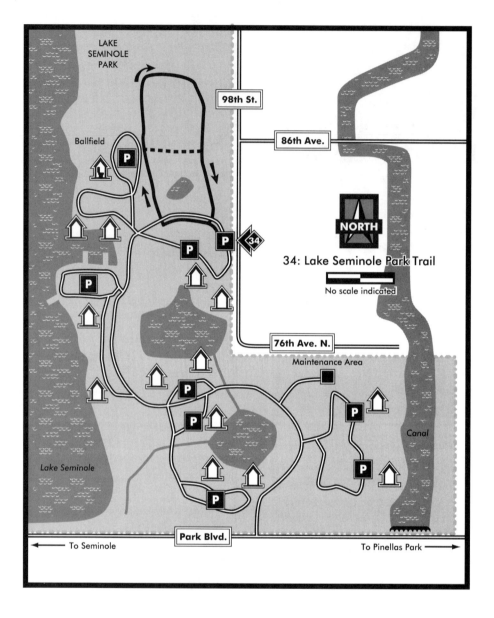

LAKE SEMINOLE PARK

98th St.

86th Ave.

Ballfield

NORTH

34: Lake Seminole Park Trail

No scale indicated

76th Ave. N.

Maintenance Area

Lake Seminole

Canal

Park Blvd.

← To Seminole

To Pinellas Park →

the western entrance and proceeding to the eastern exit. Expect to see bicyclists, joggers, skaters, and dog-walkers on this trail.

This entire trail traverses a nice stand of southern pines, typical of Florida piney woods habitat. The understory contains the palmetto and other native species you'd expect to see in the piney woods, as well as a number of exotic species.

A short distance into the trail, a large sign asks hikers not to feed the squirrels, which are numerous throughout the area. Additional signs list the trail rules and ask pedestrians to keep right and bicycles to keep left on their way around the loops.

Hikers and cyclists will find a number of places to stop and enjoy the scenery along the trail.

Before long, you'll pass a small lake on the right. This is a good place to see wading birds, especially during the winter. There's no swimming here, and a sign cautions hikers to beware of alligators; take a good look out at the lake, and you may be able to see why, as alligators often bask on the surface of the water. On the left and just past where you first see the lake, watch for the start of a huge stand of ferns that follows a seasonal stream bordering the trail.

At the north end of the lake, you'll find benches where you can sit and rest—and watch the alligators, if you like. Don't miss the big clump of native swamp lilies just before the last bench— they're spectacular when they're in bloom. And if you like, follow the little footpath that goes all around the edge of the lake.

As you continue along the trail, also watch for giant ferns on the left, part of the stand of ferns that continues to parallel the trail.

Before long, you'll have to make a choice. If you turn right at the first intersection of the trail, you'll take the shorter, one-mile loop back to the parking lot. Continue straight ahead, however, for the full two-mile loop. Just past the intersection, look to the left for the first water fountain. In this area, you'll also see the first of several unpaved side trails you can take through the woods.

As you follow the top of the loop, you'll see a sign describing controlled burns, and how they're used in the park to manage the habitat. In this area the results of a hotter-than-intended burn are clearly visible in a stand of dead pines.

Three-quarters of the way around the loop, at the second intersection with the smaller loop, you'll find another water fountain. Beyond that, you'll once again pass the little lake before returning to the parking lot at the end of the trail.

Lettuce Lake
Regional Park Loop

IN BRIEF

Part of the Wilderness Parks complex, this hike follows a boardwalk to explore native swamp and lake fed by nearby Hillsborough River and a number of habitats. An interpretive nature walk in addition to other amenities, including a ball field and picnic pavilions, make this a great hike for families.

DIRECTIONS

From downtown Tampa, take Interstate 275 north to the Fletcher Avenue exit. Take Fletcher Avenue east approximately five miles. The park entrance is on the left. Once you enter the park, drive all the way through until you reach the **T**. You may turn either left or right to enter one of two parking lots for the visitor center.

DESCRIPTION

This hike combines a number of different path to give hikers a good sampling of all this regional park has to offer. There are several opportunities to shorten the overall length of the hike, making this great for those who need to adapt to time or other constraints.

Once you've parked, walk through the trees to stop by the visitors center. Pick up a trail map then head out the back door. Follow the sidewalk to the paved bike path, turn left, and walk to the sign that reads "Boardwalk." At the sign, turn right to get on boardwalk, which is

AT-A-GLANCE INFORMATION

Length:
2.1 miles

Configuration:
Loop

Difficulty:
Easy

Scenery:
Wooded, pleasant

Exposure:
Mostly shaded

Traffic:
Busy on weekends

Trail surface:
Main trail is paved; nature trail is sand; also a boardwalk

Hiking time:
About 1 hour

Season:
All year

Access:
Donation of $1 is requested; open daily 8 a.m. to 6 p.m.

Maps:
Available at gate kiosk or at the visitors center

Facilities:
Picnic areas, and a visitor center with rest rooms, ball field and a number of pavilions with grills

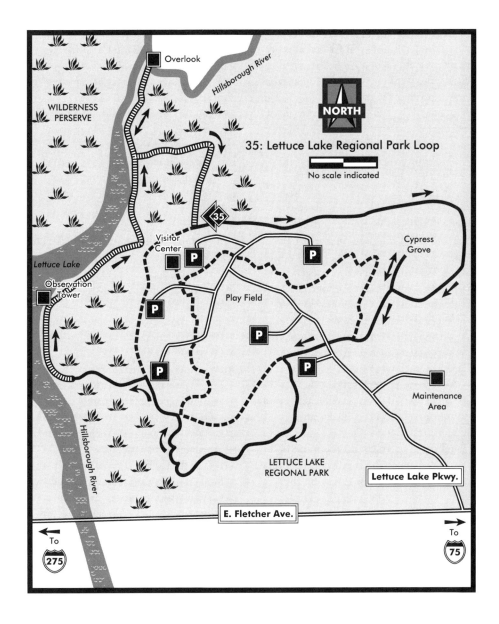

Overlook

Hillsborough River

WILDERNESS
PERSERVE

NORTH

35: Lettuce Lake Regional Park Loop

No scale indicated

35

Visitor
Center

Cypress
Grove

Lettuce Lake

Observation
Tower

P

P

Play Field

P

P

P

P

Maintenance
Area

Hillsborough River

LETTUCE LAKE
REGIONAL PARK

Lettuce Lake Pkwy.

E. Fletcher Ave.

To

275

To

75

restricted to foot traffic only. Otherwise you will encounter animals, joggers, bicycles, or roller skates here.

At the first intersection of the board-walk, do not turn left but go straight ahead. The trail takes you into a hard-wood hammock with many large oaks, as well as a lot of old growth poison ivy—fortunately you're above it so you don't have to worry about walking through it!

Follow the trail a little further, and you will see cypresses and other hard-wood species. Before long the boardwalk takes a turn to the right, so you're over-looking Lettuce Lake. Look here for a really nice big cypress. As you proceed along the lakeshore, you'll see a number of cypress trees along both sides of the trail, some with large knees. Watch overhead; you may see ospreys feeding in this area. Shortly, you'll come to a couple of benches where you can stop and overlook the swamp and lake if you like.

Continue to where the boardwalk crosses the edge of the lake, and then turns and takes you deeper into the swamp. When you reach the next intersection, proceed straight ahead instead of turning right. You'll be on a spur that takes you all the way to the Hillsborough River. Watch for some really spectacular cypress trees in this section of the trail.

Before long, you'll come to a short spur to the left that leads to an overlook. At this point you are elevated above the swamp, which during wet periods will have water standing in it.

As you continue deeper into the swamp, the shade gets heavier, and you'll continue to see a lot of really nice cypresses. At the end of this long spur, you'll come to an overlook on the Hillsborough River, which is the main source of water for Tampa. At this point the river is very narrow, and quite lovely.

From here, return down the spur to the boardwalk intersection, and make a left turn, which will take you around a boardwalk loop. This section offers less shade than earlier on the trail. As you walk, watch for bird nesting boxes. Some of the open areas along here are good places to look for songbirds. Look for water hyacinths during high water.

As you leave the woods on the boardwalk, you'll pass an intersection, where you can turn either left or right, which leads to two different picnic pavilions; proceed between them and you'll emerge onto the paved bicycle trail.

Turn left on the paved trail and proceed through open woods past a couple of picnic areas. As you pass the first picnic area on the left, don't miss the huge oaks that fell during a storm some years back; they have grown again, creating almost a double tree.

The trail continues through a mixed hardwood forest. As it swings to the right, it goes through a really lovely live oak hammock. Although the trees aren't as big as those at Philippe Park, it's still an outstanding example of an oak hammock with a nice palmetto understory.

As you continue around the trail, you will see a spur to the right, with a sign that reads "Cypress Dome." If you follow the spur through the hardwoods and ferns, you'll find a bench where you can sit in the middle of the cypress dome.

Return down the spur and rejoin the main trail, where you make a right turn. After you cross the road that comes into the park, continue straight ahead on the paved trail, past the little parking area on the right.

A short distance past the parking area, an unpaved nature trail goes off to the left. Take that left to leave the bike path behind and pass through a mixed woodland with a nice palmetto understory and into another oak hammock. You'll cross a couple of side trails, but continue walking straight. As you proceed along this section of the trail, it goes from being fairly open at the beginning to a deeper woods with more shade at the end.

When you emerge onto the paved path again, make a left turn. In this section of trail you'll pass a rest room and water fountain on the left. Just past the water fountain, the next section of the unpaved nature trail turns left and heads into the woods. This section of the nature trail is wider, a little more developed, and a good bit drier than the previous section.

After a short distance you'll arrive at a boardwalk intersection, where one boardwalk goes to a couple of picnic areas on the left. Take the right-hand boardwalk (which is also a left turn from the nature trail). This section of boardwalk very quickly takes you away from the noise of the picnic areas and into some deeper woods. Shortly you'll be back on the edge of Lettuce Lake. In this area watch for some massive cypresses at the edge of the water, as well as some old stumps that are about the same size as the trees. There are benches to sit on here, or you can proceed to a short spur to the left that takes you to an observation tower.

Beyond the tower spur the boardwalk is very open, although there are a few more cypresses and other trees. In this section of trail, watch to the right for another massive cypress tree with lots of cypress knees around it—this one is so big it must be centuries old.

After another short distance along the boardwalk, you'll end up back at the beginning of the boardwalk, where you started.

NEARBY ATTRACTIONS

Besides the nature trails and boardwalks, Lettuce Lake Regional Park contains a fitness trail that follows the paved trail and is designed for wheelchair users as well as runners. In the center of the park, a large play field provides space for many family and team activities.

The bikeway passes through a large oak hammock.

Little Manatee River Loop

IN BRIEF

This trail is adjacent to the Little Manatee River State Recreation Area. About half the trail parallels the river.

DIRECTIONS

Take Interstate 75 south to exit 46-B, the Wimauma and Little Manatee River State Recreation Area exit, which is State Road 674. On SR 674, go east 7.5 miles from Interstate 75. Turn right (south) on US Highway 301 and go five miles to the ranger station to pick up a map and get the combination to the gate. The hike area is back north on 301 about two miles; look for a utility pole with the number 205 on it on the left.

DESCRIPTION

The trailhead begins at a small shaded parking area inside a locked gate. As you proceed, you'll traverse a wet hammocky area with a lot of ferns. After about 0.1 miles, you'll come to a fork in the trail. Because we hiked this trail in the middle of summer, we took the north (right) side of the trail, so that by the middle of the day we'd be in the shade.

Shortly after you make the right turn, you'll be in a pine flatwoods area. Before long you pass the first of 19 bridges and boardwalks on the trail. Walking the trail in this direction, you're actually walking it backwards in terms of the way the bridges and boardwalks are numbered—the first one you come to is number 19.

AT-A GLANCE INFORMATION

Length:
6.3 miles

Configuration:
Loop

Difficulty:
Flat and easy, with a few sandy slopes

Scenery:
Pleasant, a lot of different Florida habitats

Exposure:
North part of trail is quite exposed with just scattered shade. The south part of the trail is mostly shaded.

Traffic:
Not particularly busy, even on weekends

Trail Surface:
Sandy woodland trail

Hiking Time:
3.5 to 4 hours

Season:
All year

Access:
Fee to enter the park, $3.25 for a vehicle and two adults

Maps:
Trail map available at the ranger station

Facilities:
None on the trail. Rest rooms are located at Little Manatee River State Recreation Area.

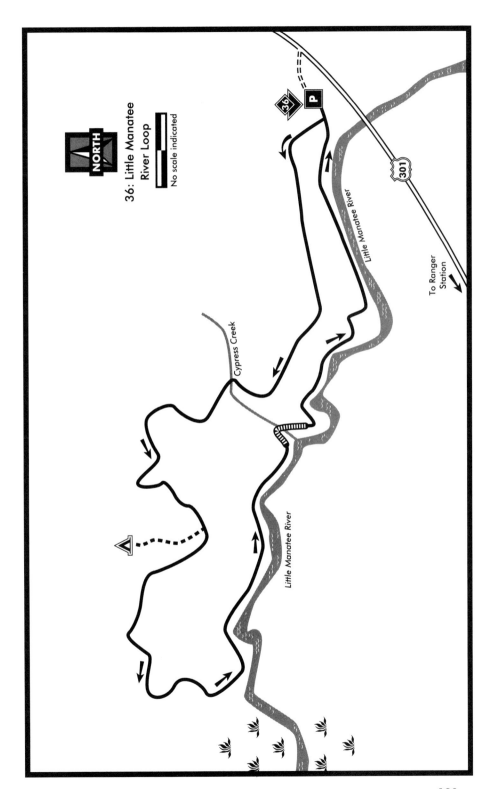

36: Little Manatee
River Loop

NORTH

No scale indicated

301

To Ranger
Station

Little Manatee River

Cypress Creek

Little Manatee River

This trail traverses a number of really lovely hardwood hammocks.

Soon you'll pass into an open field, and from there into an area of oaks that overhang the trail. When you reach the blackberry field, watch underfoot—on the day we hiked this trail, we saw a pair of quail with a brood of chicks here.

Continue into the pine flatwoods, where you'll see evidence of a recent fire. Beyond that is another hardwood hammock, then more pines that lead down to a crossing of Cypress Creek. This is not a natural creek, but a man-made one. The spoil material was dumped along the edges of the project, creating berms.

After you cross the creek you'll find yourself back in an oak hammock, which soon gives way to an open area

where sand pines once grew. Unlike most other pine species, which are exceedingly fire tolerant, sand pines are killed by fire.

After you cross an open sandy area, the trail enters another shady area as it approaches the turnoff to a campground. Stay on the main trail, though, to continue your hike. Before long you'll find the trail paralleling a fence line, which is the park boundary.

After a quarter mile or so the trail bears back to the left and passes through a scrub oak area. Just as the trail bears to the left, look to the right for a large oak tree. The Florida Trail Association calls this the "Lunch Tree"; it's where members stop for lunch when they have a maintenance day on the trail.

After the Lunch Tree you'll traverse an open, scrubby area, but soon the trail drops down into a swamp bottom. Here you'll begin walking one of two long boardwalks on the trail.

Soon the trail reaches the river and turns back to the east to follow its course. As you again approach Cypress Creek you'll find another long board-walk through a wet area.

Past the Cypress Creek crossing, the trail continues to follow the Little Manatee River. The trail turns away from the river for a short stretch, then rejoins it past another couple of small bridges. Pass through a hardwood area along the river until you reach bridge No. 3, which crosses a ravine.

Beyond the ravine the habitat becomes more open until you enter an overgrown field with no trees. Beyond the field, near bridge No. 2, you'll pass a concrete boat ramp on your right. A short stretch of oaks and old pines leads you back to the trailhead.

McGough Nature Park Loop

IN BRIEF

This combination nature/walking trail is well suited to families with young children who are just starting to hike.

DIRECTIONS

Take Interstate 275 (the Howard Frankland Bridge) across the bay and exit at the Ulmerton Road Exit. Follow Ulmerton Road (Highway 688) west until you reach the intersection with Highway 686. Remain on Ulmerton Road toward Indian Rocks Beach. Follow Ulmerton as it swings south at 119th Street and becomes Walsingham Road. Stay on Walsingham Road until you reach 146th Street North. Turn right on 146th Street and watch for the park entrance immediately on the left. Park in the parking lot and walk west to reach the nature center and trail.

DESCRIPTION

Inside the nature center you can learn quite a lot about the area you're going to see. Once you've picked up a trail guide, go out the back door to find the trailhead.

As soon as you enter the trailhead, the trail turns to the left, enters a woodland, and passes under a stand of wild grapes before it reaches a T. If you go to the left, you'll reach a water fountain, another set of rest rooms, and a bench. However, go right then turn right again

AT-A-GLANCE INFORMATION

Length:
0.9 miles

Configuration:
Loop

Difficulty:
Easy

Scenery:
Mixture of habitats and water

Exposure:
About half exposed and half shaded

Traffic:
Fairly busy

Trail surface:
Combination of paved and sand

Hiking time:
30 to 45 minutes

Season:
All year

Access:
No permits or fees necessary

Maps:
A park and trail map is available at the nature center office

Facilities:
Rest rooms and a water fountain are located in the nature center.

Special comments:
Marked interpretive stations correspond to a trail booklet available at the nature center.

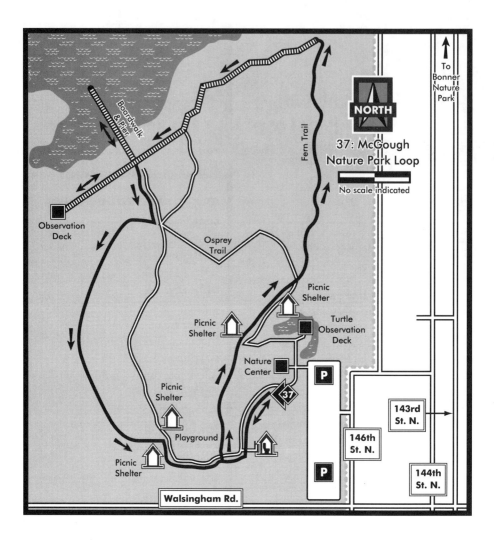

almost immediately. You'll step onto a shell trail that bypasses the park's main picnic area and playground. At the end of the shell trail, proceed straight ahead past two picnic areas.

Proceed through the picnic area and on through a quiet and wooded section of trail. As the trail curves to the left, a sign invites you to take another sand trail to the right, along the Fern Trail and to the boardwalk. Before you turn right, however, look around—to your left is a large birdhouse or nesting box.

Turn right onto the Fern Trail, pass the bench where you can sit under the trees and enjoy the quiet, and proceed into the woods. This portion of the trail is shaded and is surprisingly quiet to be in the heart of a bustling city. A short distance into the trail, there's a bench on the left and a water station as well.

At the end of the Fern Trail, turn left onto the boardwalk toward the pier. The boardwalk takes you through what once was a native swamp, but which now has many exotic species in it. Park officials

124

have indicated that they're going to undertake some clearing of the exotic species in the near future.

As you walk, watch on the right for a stand of native palmettos under oaks. This area is fairly open and sunny and can be hot. As you traverse this trail you'll see a short left-hand spur going off the boardwalk. However, proceed straight ahead for a short distance until you reach a cross boardwalk; here, turn right to go out onto the pier. This section of the boardwalk takes you out to the mangrove swamp and into the Intracoastal Waterway, where you can observe a small bay surrounded by mangroves. Here the water is quite shallow, so that you can look down and see fish and turtles. In the mangrove swamp itself you can see little crabs on the bottom, especially at low tide. This also is a good area to look for large wading birds such as egrets and herons.

Return down this spur to the main boardwalk and turn right to go to the observation deck. A good breeze blows across the shaded observation deck much of the time, making it a good place to stop and rest.

Return from the observation deck down the main part of the boardwalk and back to the cross boardwalk. This time turn right, away from the pier, and exit the boardwalk onto the paved trail once again. After a short walk through pines, you'll come to a four-way intersection. Turn right onto the shell trail and proceed into a woodland area. This trail passes by Walsingham Road once again on its way around the park. Watch

The main trail takes you through a small woodland and to the Fern Trail.

in this area for gopher tortoises feeding on the edges of the trail.

As the trail turns to the left and away from Walsingham Road, you'll see the main playground and picnic area once again. Rejoin the main paved trail through the park and turn right to return to the nature center. On your way past the playground, watch on the left for the butterfly garden, which contains flowering species that butterflies, such as the monarch, enjoy. Just past the butterfly garden, turn left on the main trail and return to the nature center.

McKay Bay Wildlife Park Trail

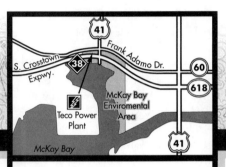

IN BRIEF

This surprising wildlife refuge and nature trail located off US Highway 60 (Frank Adamo Drive), in Tampa's industrial center offers hikers an in-town wildlife experience.

DIRECTIONS

From downtown Tampa, take Highway 60 east to the TECO power plant access road. Turn right and go under the Crosstown Expressway. The park is on the left, next to the power plant.

DESCRIPTION

The hardest thing about this trail is realizing that it's located in the middle of Tampa's industrial area. Situated next door to one of the city's large power generation plants, and one of only a very few refuse-burning power plants in the state, the park and trail act as a buffer for, and in some ways as a symbiotic partner to, the power plant. The plant provides an environment that allows wildlife and vegetation to flourish—expect to encounter wading birds such as large flocks of flamingos—while the park softens the harsh industrial nature of the area.

From the parking lot, take the trail to the right. Here, sabal palms and saw palmetto border the trail, with native Florida wildflowers providing color along the way. The small islands of plants also are

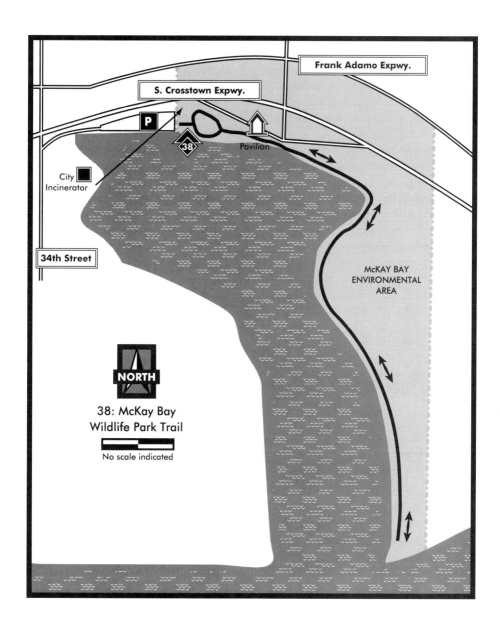

NORTH

38: McKay Bay
Wildlife Park Trail

No scale indicated

home to box turtles and birds. The city has provided bird houses and turtle boxes that will get the attention of young and old hikers alike. In this area also you may catch a rare sight of the threatened Florida scrub jay. Follow this short trail to the pavilion, which serves as the park's scenic overlook, and is the

jumping-off point to the longer out-and-back trail along the shore of McKay Bay. Stop at the pavilion and spend some time watching for butterflies in the garden there, where a number of butterfly attracting plants are cultivated.

This pavilion also serves as an over-look for this portion of the trail. From here, you can see the back of McKay Bay, where you can watch ospreys dive for fish. In the spring, you may see them feed their chicks in either a massive nest located in one of the taller trees, or the man-made nesting platforms provided by the electric company.

This pavilion also serves as the trailhead for the longer trail that follows the shore of McKay Bay. Although this trail is about eight feet wide and could be an outstanding urban footpath that would stand up to heavy traffic, this trail is seldom used and is overgrown with long grass. As a result, this area is a good place to see a number of species of snakes. We recommend you wear shoes at least as stout as chukkas to help protect your feet.

As you hike, you'll pass by a number of mangroves, typical of the habitat of low-energy beaches in this part of Florida. At low tide you'll see oyster beds in the water, also typical of this area.

Watch carefully for wildlife, both on the shore and in the water. This bay is filled with bird life; you often can see pelicans diving for fish and hear and see ospreys fishing. On rare occasions, particularly in the winter, you might even see a bald eagle. Around the edge of the bay, look for wading birds, including egrets and herons, as well as wood storks from time to time. And surprise! In the winter, you may even see flocks of flamingos and roseate spoonbills.

The wildlife in the water is almost as varied. Watch for manatees, dolphins, rays, and schools of redfish and snook. You may even see small blackfin sharks chasing schools of baitfish.

Follow the trail until you reach the marker at the end. Then return along the bay to the pavilion and back to the parking lot for the entire 1.5-mile hike.

NEARBY ATTRACTIONS

McKay Bay is two miles east of the Channelside District, a redeveloping area with high-end shops, a movie theater, and fine dining. The Florida Aquarium also is located here. Two miles northwest is the famous Centro Ybor, another area of shops, restaurants, and entertainment that takes its name from Tampa's past as the cigar capital of the world.

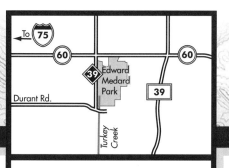

Medard Park Trail

IN BRIEF
This hike follows a short section of the network of hiking/horse trails that sprawl through Edward Medard Park.

DIRECTIONS
From Tampa, take the Crosstown Expressway to its eastern end, then take the left-hand fork toward Ocala on Interstate 75. When you get on the entrance ramp to Interstate 75, stay in the right-hand lane and exit onto State Road 60, turning right (east). Stay on SR 60 for 9.5 miles to South Turkey Creek Road; turn right. Follow Turkey Creek Road for one mile until you see the entrance to Edward Medard Park on the left.

Turn into the park, and take the main road through the park until you come to a sign indicating that the office and campground are to the right and the horse unloading area to the left. Turn left to the horse unloading area, then make an immediate right turn. Follow the road until you cross the trail (it's obvious), and park in the grassy area beyond it.

DESCRIPTION
Edward Medard Park is one of Hillsborough County's most popular parks, comprising 1,284 acres. The park's main attraction is the 700-acre reservoir used for swimming, fishing, and boating. This reclaimed phosphate area was dedicated

AT-A-GLANCE INFORMATION
Length:
About 2.5 miles
Configuration:
Out and back
Difficulty:
Moderate
Scenery:
A variety of central Florida habitats
Exposure:
Mostly shaded
Traffic:
Busy on weekends
Trail Surface:
Shell and sand
Hiking Time:
1.5 hours
Season:
All year
Access:
A $1 donation is requested
Maps:
A park map is available at the campground office, but the trails aren't shown on it.
Facilities:
None at the trailhead, but rest rooms are available in the park.

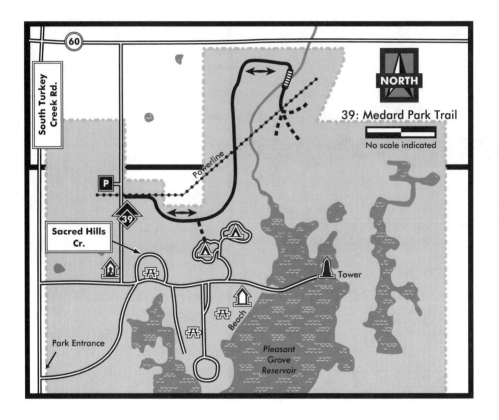

North

39: Medard Park Trail

No scale indicated

South Turkey Creek Rd.

60

Powerline

P

39

Sacred Hills Cr.

Tower

Park Entrance

Beach

Pleasant Grove Reservoir

as a park in 1972, and is the product of a land reclamation project with the American Cyanamid Company, the Alafia River Basin Board of the Southwest Florida Water Management District, and Hillsborough County.

Walk back down the road from the parking area, and make a left turn onto the trail. As you're walking, watch the weedy area to your left, which goes around the corner from the parking area and borders the trail for a short distance. This weedy area contains blackberries, several legumes, Spanish needles, lantana, and a number of other wildflower species that are very attractive to butterflies.

At this point, the trail follows the right of way of a high-voltage power line, and is very open. To the right of the trail, the land slopes down into a ravine where

you'll see some old oaks. Both sides of the trail had many wildflowers blooming when we hiked it in late September.

As you walk, you can see into private property that's primarily farmland, and if you listen, you'll hear roosters crowing. The trail goes almost to the edge of the private property, then swings to the right and parallels the fence. At the same time, it leaves the powerline and goes into the trees at the edge of the park. Then the trail turns back to the left at the corner of the private property and continues to roughly parallel the fence line inside the park. Look to the right and you'll be able to see into a ravine, where a little stream flows. On the left, you may see a few cows or goats on the private property you're passing.

Before long, you'll pass very close to the top of one of the camping circles. At this point, you can take a short spur to the right and follow a boardwalk right into the camping area, where rest rooms are available.

At the next corner, a horse trail goes to the right into the woods. There are a lot of oaks here, and the area is fairly wet; following a rain, you'll probably have to dodge puddles. If you hike this trail after several days of rain, you'll probably find it quite sloppy in places.

If you're given to exploring, you'll see some side trails off to the right that you can take. However, the main trail continues more or less north, and comes out of the edge of the woods when it reaches the powerline right of way again. Cross the right of way, and you'll be back in the woods in a hammocky area, where the trail meanders through some pretty hardwoods and palmettos. Before long you'll be close to SR 60, behind a residential area but close enough to the road to hear some of the traffic.

Cross the first boardwalk over a little creek, and look at the difference between the construction of most boardwalks, and this boardwalk for horses. This one has little steps on it so the horses' hooves won't slip.

In this area you'll pass several wet swampy areas, where you'll see a lot of nice ferns. Then as the habitat starts to dry out, the trail passes between two very nice oaks. The trail makes a rather sharp right turn and moves away from SR 60, then crosses another boardwalk that bridges a fairly substantial stream. Follow the trail to the right again, as it almost doubles back on itself and passes into a more open, drier area.

Notice that you're walking through a grove of sweet gums, common in north Florida but unusual here—this is the only hike in this book where you'll see a substantial number of sweet gums.

In another hundred yards or so, the trail emerges from the trees back onto the powerline right of way, perhaps half a mile from where it previously crossed. At this point, the trail branches and goes off in three directions through the trees. We elected to turn around at this point and return to where we began for a 2.5-mile hike. However, if you're adventurous and have lots of time, there are literally miles of unmapped trails throughout the area that are open for hiking at your leisure.

NEARBY ATTRACTIONS

This well-developed county park is open for many recreational activities. A family camping area provides 40 sites, available on a first-come, first-served basis. Swimming is allowed at designated beaches in the reservoir, and the reservoir is open for boating and fishing. Three picnic areas have tables, shelters, grills, and rest rooms. Playgrounds in the park contain play equipment and horseshoe pits. At Burnt Stump you'll find a dock that's open for fishing.

Morris Bridge Main Trail

IN BRIEF

Part of the Wilderness Parks Complex, this trail wander across lazy Hillsborough River, through open grassland and pine/palmetto forest, and offers abundant opportunities for bird enthusiasts.

DIRECTIONS

From Interstate 75 north of Tampa, exit onto Fletcher Avenue and head east about two miles until it becomes Morris Bridge Road. Follow the road as it winds its way into and through Morris Bridge Park. Watch for the "Morris Bridge Park" sign and parking area on the left side of the road. The trailhead is about 50 feet beyond.

DESCRIPTION

The trail this hike follows is part of the Wilderness Parks trails complex, and you could easily connect with the Flatwoods Hike (see pp. 77–82) to extend your outing. This particular trail is very popular with mountain bikers, primarily because of its hard-packed surface, so keep an eye out for them. However, it's still a great longer hike that's very family friendly.

To begin the hike, cross the Hillsborough River, using the small bridge, and take a moment to look over the side and into the water below. You'll probably see a mini-game of survival between minnows and larger predator fish. On the

AT-A-GLANCE INFORMATION

Length:
5.6 miles

Configuration:
Out and back.

Difficulty:
Flat and easy

Scenery:
Nice views of Hillsborough River

Exposure:
Shaded throughout

Traffic:
Busy; bikers often use the trail

Trail surface:
Hard-packed shell and sand

Hiking time:
4.5 hours

Season:
All year

Access:
No fees or permits required; $1 donation requested

Maps:
Trail Guide for Hikers and Bikers on the Wilderness Park Off Road Trails available from Hillsborough County Department of Park and Recreation

Facilities:
Rest rooms at the trailhead only

Special comments: Rest rooms aren't always open; when closed, use facilities at nearby Flatwoods Park.

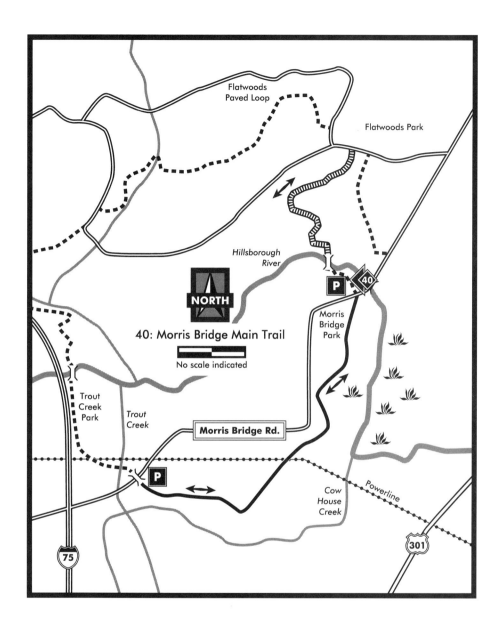

40: Morris Bridge Main Trail

No scale indicated

banks of the river you're likely to see small alligators.

After you cross the bridge, begin your hike by taking what the park bills as a mini-hike for kids. Here, a boardwalk turns slowly away from the river and offers a good view of a true Florida swamp without the hiker having to get wet. Cypress knees are abundant, and

this area is a home for all kinds of birds and wildlife. You're likely to see ospreys overhead, and watch for wading birds such as ibises and wood storks. On both occasions we were on the trail we saw alligators in the six- to seven-foot range.

Return down the boardwalk to the trailhead and step onto the Morris Bridge Main Trail; spend the first quarter mile hiking under a dense canopy of oaks. Watch for the reddish-orange flower petals that fall from the vines climbing among the tree limbs overhead. On the day we hiked this trail we saw hummingbirds above us feeding on the red trumpet-shaped flowers.

The trail is straight and flat for the next quarter mile or so. The terrain begins to open up as you come to a gradual turn that brings you to within 20 yards of Morris Bridge Road. A stand of pine with an understory of palmetto dominates the next half mile.

As the trail turns away from the road you'll approach and pass under a high-voltage power line. In this area the habitat is more of a grassland with a few pines and a lot of saw palmetto. Like most similar habitat it's a good place to see snakes and gopher tortoises. When we were there, we also saw several red-tailed hawks sitting in the treetops.

In this area, be sure to look at the bases of some of the saw palmettos, where you may be able to see some small black berries. These berries are the source of the food supplement of the same name you find in dietary stores. Be careful; this is prime habitat for venomous snakes.

The trail takes a turn away from the power line, and as you get farther away from it you'll see even more wildlife. On the day we were there, we saw turkey and black vultures riding the thermals above us. We also noted that they had a roost to the left of the trail where there were between 30 and 50 birds in the trees. Most bird-watchers may not think of vultures as being the most exciting birds in the world to watch, but they're a necessary part of a wild ecosystem.

The trail takes a sharp, nearly V-shaped bend as it begins its turn toward the end of the trail. About a mile after the sharp bend, the trail ends at another parking lot. From there, you can cross Morris Bridge Road and connect to some of the other trails in Trout Creek Park, or you can return the way you came for the full 5.6 mile hike.

NEARBY ATTRACTIONS

You can combine other trails in Wilderness Park and Flatwoods Park to extend your hike. When you are through hiking, use the canoe launch available in Morris Bridge Park. There's also a wonderful indoor flea market off Morris Bridge Road as you head west. Canoe Escape is across the street from the flea market; they use the Morris Bridge Park as a pickup point for their Hillsborough River outings.

Morris Bridge Primitive Trail

IN BRIEF

This short out-and-back trail, located within the Hillsborough County Wilderness Park Complex, runs beside the Hillsborough River, offering the hiker a true taste of wilderness with great views of bankside oaks and occasional canoeists.

DIRECTIONS

Take Interstate 75 north to the Fletcher Avenue exit. Turn east on Fletcher and follow it as it turns north and becomes Morris Bridge Road. Follow the road as it winds its way into and through Morris Bridge Park. Watch for the "Morris Bridge Park" sign and gravel parking area on the left side of the road. You may also park on the right side of the road, where you will find a trail map posted.

DESCRIPTION

This trail is described as primitive for a reason. Because it lies so close to the Hillsborough River, it is a tough trail: portions of the trail are covered with protruding roots and vines, so footing can be difficult. We recommend you wear boots with good ankle support.

Leaving the trailhead behind, you'll find the first of several cleared bank areas used by anglers. If you're wearing polarized sunglasses, look into the water for fish. During the spring of the year, this is a prime bedding area for panfish, so you

AT-A-GLANCE INFORMATION

Length:
3.8 miles

Configuration:
Out and back

Difficulty:
Flat, but the primitive nature of the trail adds difficulty

Scenery:
Nice view of the river and surrounding area

Exposure:
Mostly shaded

Traffic:
Secluded

Trail surface:
Packed dirt and roots

Hiking time:
2 to 2.5 hours

Season:
All year

Access:
No fees or permits

Maps:
None available

Facilities:
Located across Morris Bridge Road in the main park near the canoe launch area.

Special comments:
There is a spot for fishing on the trail.

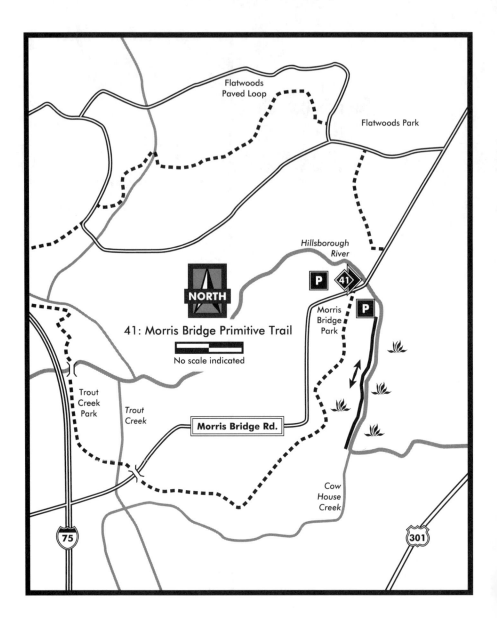

Flatwoods
Paved Loop

Flatwoods Park

Hillsborough
River

NORTH

41: Morris Bridge Primitive Trail

No scale indicated

Morris
Bridge
Park

Trout
Creek
Park

Trout
Creek

Morris Bridge Rd.

Cow
House
Creek

75

301

may see adult fish guarding their beds. Be aware that alligators live here, and that alligators in high-use areas may be habituated to humans.

Just past the fishing area, head south against the flow of the river. Note that during wet weather, you may have to step over and around standing water in a number of places.

On the trail, overstory trees include oaks and small palms, with an understory of ferns and palmettos. In this area, feral hogs have rooted up the ground looking for grubs, acorns, and whatever else they can find to eat.

As you continue along the trail, you'll come to a large oak tree that's grown out over the water. This tree is used as swimming and fishing spot, but if you're not comfortable swimming with alligators, then this isn't the place for you (we would not do it, and we certainly would not recommend that you do).

Past the stand of oaks, you'll enter a cypress swamp. Watch for the cypress knees, some of which are quite tall. The trail eventually leaves the river behind.

The trail continues in almost a straight line for the rest of the hike, so you can spend time observing both the trailside and the far riverbank as well. On the day I did this hike with friends, we spied a large oak on the opposite bank that had almost fallen into the water. At the base of its massive root system, we saw a den of raccoons peering out as if they were looking for a handout from passing canoeists. A little farther along, we saw another group of raccoons fishing in the river. It was a real treat, so be alert for wildlife you may see on the other side of the river in this area.

The return trip provides a totally different perspective on the river from the trip out. The soft earth along the riverbank shows the tracks of small game. Deer and feral hog tracks lead to the edge of the water, making this a prime place to find animal sign.

The river is so close that if you take two or three steps to the side you'll be wading in it. One experience we found novel is that people coming down the river in canoes and kayaks spoke to us, which is something we haven't often experienced. This is a unique trail, made even more peaceful by the slow roll of the river.

NEARBY ATTRACTIONS

The Big Top Fleamarket is about two miles west on Morris Bridge Road, and the Canoe Escape is across the street from the Fleamarket. The University of South Florida is five miles west, as is the Museum of Science and Industry.

Otter Loop

IN BRIEF

This short nature trail traverses several typical central Florida coastal habitats. It's most suitable for families with young children who are just learning to hike.

DIRECTIONS

Take either Dale Mabry or Memorial Highway north to Hillsborough Avenue. Turn west on Hillsborough Avenue and follow it west to Double Branch Road. Turn left on Double Branch Road and follow it almost to the end where you will see the entrance to Upper Tampa Bay Regional Park on the right. Turn right and follow the main road through the park until you pass the nature center. Just beyond it, park at the entrance to the family picnic area. Walk into the picnic area, turn left on the sidewalk and go past two picnic pavilions, a rest room, and the entrance to the third picnic pavilion. Just past that entrance, an unmarked sidewalk goes to the right. Take the sidewalk, which will lead you to the trailhead of the Otter Loop.

DESCRIPTION

Upper Tampa Bay Regional Park is a 596-acre peninsula bordered on the east by Double Branch Creek and on the west and south by Old Tampa Bay. Archaeological evidence indicates that the area was inhabited long before the arrival of European explorers in the sixteenth century.

AT-A-GLANCE INFORMATION

Length:
1.4 miles

Configuration:
Loop

Difficulty:
Easy

Scenery:
Typical central Florida coastal habitats

Exposure:
Mostly exposed

Traffic:
Some traffic on weekends

Trail surface:
Boardwalk and sand

Hiking time:
40 minutes

Season:
All year

Access:
No permits necessary, but a $1 fee is necessary to enter the park.

Maps:
Available at the nature center

Facilities:
Rest rooms and a water fountain are located at the trailhead.

Special comments:
You can combine this trail with the Bobcat to create a hike with a total length of 1.25 miles.

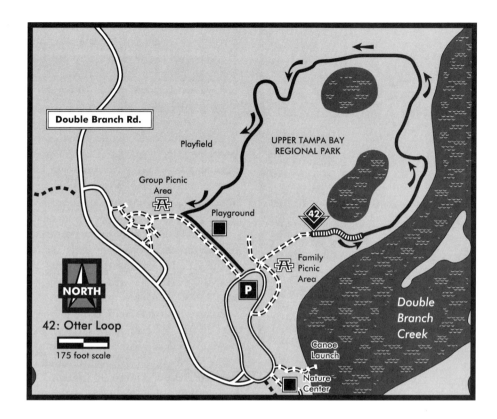

The park contains a diversity of habitats that result from subtle interactions between moisture and salinity. The area is quite flat, with a peak elevation of six feet. As a result, much of the park floods several times a year during periods of high tides. The rest of the park is dominated by pine flatwoods, although there are hardwood hammocks growing around a number of small ponds.

Because of the environmentally sensitive nature of the park, there's little development, with only a nature center, a few picnic shelters, and a centrally located playground. Other than that, this park is pretty much the way the Native Americans left it five centuries ago.

The Otter Loop begins as a boardwalk that takes you across an open prairie into a pine flatwoods area. Look to the right,

where you can see part of Double Branch Creek. Here, an interpretive sign at the trailhead illuminates the salt marsh habitat you're viewing.

Follow the trail as it winds through the trees at the edge of the prairie, where you're still overlooking the creek. This trail is kept well mowed so that it's easy to walk. However, the area is prime rattlesnake habitat, so watch where you put your feet!

The pine flatwoods that you're walking through here are the most abundant habitat found in Florida, an open sunny pine forest with a low bushy understory of saw palmetto and wiregrass. In this plant community, periodic controlled burns are necessary to prevent hardwoods from taking over and eventually forming a hardwood hammock.

Plenty of sun on the Otter Loop

birds also are common here; if you listen carefully, at certain times of the year you can hear quite a few birds all around you. Other animals that you might see include marsh rabbits, as well as cotton rats and mice, all of which serve as food for the rattlesnakes here.

As you proceed along the trail, the land continues to rise slightly. You'll pass through a lot of pines and small oaks, but they're quite scattered, so at no point are you walking in a lot of shade. Consequently, this trail tends to be a hot walk.

Watch along the trail for the big stands of saw palmetto, which grow extensively in the park. This is the same saw palmetto whose berries are used in herbal supplements made for prostate disorders.

Follow the trail around to the playground area. Hike along the edge of the big open field and play area until you come to a footpath to the left through the trees. Take that footpath through to another little play area and turn right to go around the edge of it. When you reach the sidewalk, take it to the left and back around to the road that goes through the park. Turn left and follow the road back to where you parked, which is just around the little curve in the road.

NEARBY ATTRACTIONS
The nature center offers interpretive and environmental information about the park area. Several shelters provide a place for families or groups to have lunch in the shade, and a playground and an open field near them offer a site for recreation.

A little way around the loop, a bench invites you to sit where you can see Double Branch Creek winding by lazily. As the name of this trail implies, there are otters in this area. They're quite shy and stay well hidden, so you're not likely to see them. However, if you walk quietly and look closely you may get lucky and see some along the creek.

Just after you pass the bench, the trail swings inland under an oak tree and into a more upland habitat, although the trail continues to be quite exposed. This is a good place to watch for birds of prey, including eagles and ospreys. Song-

Pam Callahan Nature Preserve Trail

IN BRIEF

This quiet, 96-acre site remains virtually undiscovered even though it's right in town. Located next to a large apartment complex, this little trail is truly a hidden treasure.

DIRECTIONS

Take John F. Kennedy Boulevard (Highway 60) to the west, and follow it as it turns north toward the Veterans Expressway. When you reach the turnoff where Highway 60 goes to the left and the Veterans Expressway goes straight, follow the Veterans Expressway straight ahead. From the Expressway, take exit 2B, which is Independence Parkway. Follow Independence Parkway past the golf course until it intersects with Memorial Highway. Turn left on Memorial Highway and follow it a short distance until you see the Audubon Apartments on your left. At the Audubon Village Apartments turn around and go back the other direction less than half a block. The entrance to Pam Callahan is on the right. It's not well marked, and the entrance is nothing more than a steel gate. Pull off the road and park in front of the gate.

DESCRIPTION

This little hike is truly a hidden treasure. Located next to a large apartment complex, it has yet to be discovered by the public. In the several times we've been

AT-A-GLANCE INFORMATION

Length:
1.4 miles
Configuration:
Out and back
Difficulty:
Easy
Scenery:
Wetlands and woods
Exposure:
Fairly exposed, but some shade
Traffic:
Virtually deserted
Trail surface:
Grass
Hiking time:
About 20 minutes
Season:
All year
Access:
No fees or permits
Maps:
No published map
Facilities:
None
Special comments:
Look for commemorative plaque at the end of the maintained trail.

141

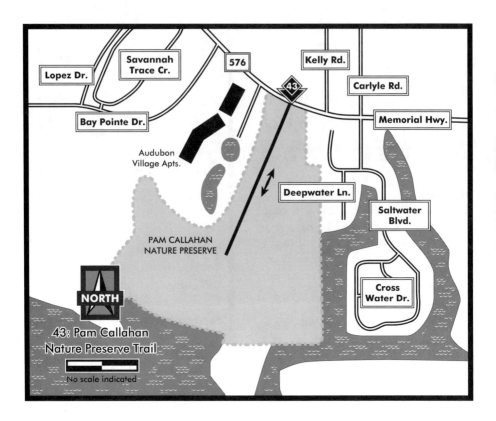

Savannah Trace Cr.

Lopez Dr.

576

Kelly Rd.

Carlyle Rd.

Bay Pointe Dr.

Memorial Hwy.

Audubon
Village Apts.

Deepwater Ln.

Saltwater
Blvd.

PAM CALLAHAN
NATURE PRESERVE

NORTH

Cross
Water Dr.

43: Pam Callahan
Nature Preserve Trail

No scale indicated

there, we have never encountered anyone else on the trail.

The maintained trail (which really is just a grassy path mowed from time to time) travels about 0.7 miles until it stops at a large rock and plaque that commemorates the woman for whom the site is named. However, if you're adventurous and well shod (as in a stout pair of boots), you can continue beyond the end of the trail into the wetland, which has a sourish smell. This area is not maintained, and there has been some dumping of trash. You'll want to watch for snakes and poison ivy, so watch where you put your feet. However, you'll find a hidden wild place with a lot of interesting plants; and this is a great place for butterfly watchers.

Walking in this area is more difficult than on a maintained trail, with lots of sticks and stems. The presence of fiddler crabs indicates that during high-water periods this area is wet. To reach the trailhead, just walk around the gate and start down the trail. This is a straight in and out that first takes you through a little mixed woodland with mostly oaks in the overstory and a palmetto understory. Shortly after you start the trail you'll see a narrow path to the right that takes you over to the apartment complex, but you'll also see that it's closed off with a chain.

Continue on, and briefly you'll see another narrow path to the left. This path doesn't go anywhere except to what looks like a maintenance area. If you look around you'll see a lot of exotic plants, including Brazilian pepper.

The trail borders a seasonal stream on the right at this point, then passes through a wet area. You'll notice a lot of willows and other native wetland species, and then as the land rises just a bit you'll begin to see pine trees.

As you walk, listen. You'll hear a good bit of birdsong here. And even though you can hear the airport nearby, this area is surprisingly quiet; although near a main highway, once you get away from the gate, you could be miles from town.

Another opening into the apartment complex appears on your right, and an increase in willows and other wetland species indicates a slight drop in elevation. Further on, you'll pass a seasonal pond, on the right, that during drought is bone dry. However, the presence of vegetation such as cattails and other aquatic species indicates that during wetter weather there's standing water there.

As you venture farther along the trail it's hard to believe that you're in the middle of an urban area because everything is so quiet. At the end of the trail you'll find a large granite rock with a plaque that reads: "The Pam Callahan Nature Preserve, in tribute to and in memory of Pamela A. Callahan, 1947–1993. Pam loved all aspects of nature and had a special feeling for these wetlands. She spearheaded a community effort to prevent this site from becoming another dense development. She fought for almost three years and never gave up despite difficult odds. She proved to the skeptics that you "can fight city hall" and win. Her success in stopping the developer allowed this land to remain pristine and available for ELAPP (Environmental Lands Acquisition and Protection Program) purchase. We as well as future generations owe her a debt of gratitude. Pam did not live to see her dream become a reality, but now her name is linked to this land. Thanks, Pam, from a grateful community. Dedicated January 22, 1996."

If you feel adventurous, you can continue to explore beyond this point. Otherwise, return to the gate for the 0.7 mile distance.

Philippe Park Trail

Enterprise Rd.

Old Tampa Bay

611 Philippe→ Pkwy.

44 Philippe Park

Bayshore Ave.

590 Main St.

To Courtney Campbell Causeway

IN BRIEF

Follow the converted route of the old Philippe Parkway that parallels the shoreline of Old Tampa Bay, passing by a gorgeous oak hammock, the gravesite of the man who introduced grapefruit to Florida, and a Native American mound.

DIRECTIONS

From Tampa, take Courtney Campbell Causeway across Old Tampa Bay and turn right at the first traffic light after the causeway ends, which is Bayshore Boulevard. Follow Bayshore north, as it becomes Philippe Parkway, for about four miles. The entrance to the park is on the right, just after the intersection of Philippe Parkway with Enterprise Road, and is somewhat hidden until you are right on top of it. After you enter the park, turn right on the main road and take it to the parking area at the end near the footbridge that goes across to the Bayshore Linear Greenway Recreation Trail.

DESCRIPTION

This trail is actually the old Philippe Parkway. Be aware that you'll be sharing the trail with bicycles and cars. If you want to make a longer hike, combine this hike with the Bayshore Linear Greenway Recreation Trail south of the park, which also connects with the Clearwater East–West Trail. This is a well-developed county park with many

AT-A-GLANCE INFORMATION

Length:
2.2 miles

Configuration:
Out and back

Difficulty:
A little more grade than most trails in the area, but easy

Scenery:
A stunning live oak hammock, a Tocobagan Indian mound, and Odet Philippe's gravesite

Exposure:
About half shaded and half open

Traffic:
Busy on weekends

Trail surface:
Paved

Hiking time:
45 minutes

Season:
All year

Access:
No permits or fees, but if the park fills officials will close the gate to more visitors

Maps:
Area map and a site map are available from the park office.

Facilities:
Rest rooms and water fountains located at a number of pavilions throughout Philippe Park

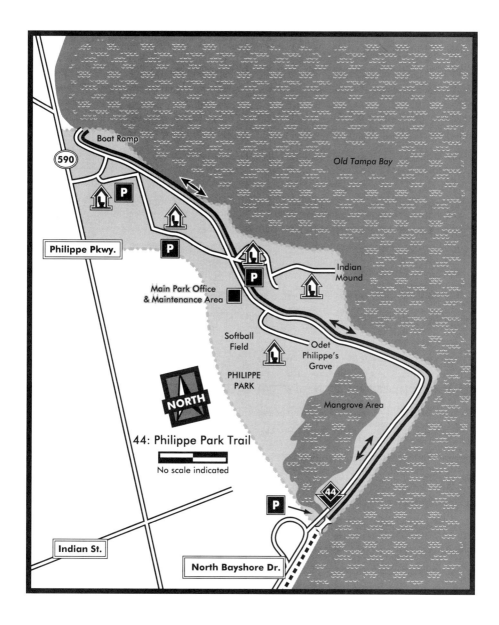

590

Boat Ramp

Old Tampa Bay

Philippe Pkwy.

P

Main Park Office
& Maintenance Area

Indian
Mound

Odet
Philippe's
Grave

Softball
Field

PHILIPPE
PARK

Mangrove Area

NORTH

44: Philippe Park Trail

No scale indicated

P

44

Indian St.

North Bayshore Dr.

amenities, including playgrounds and
picnic areas for families.

From the parking lot, retrace the
path you took in your car when you
came in; you'll pass a mangrove area on
the left. After a short distance, you'll
arrive at a parking and picnic area on
the right, where you'll be able to see
Old Tampa Bay. At low tide, this is a

good place to watch for wading birds.
Across Old Tampa Bay, a power generat-
ing station is visible; towers for high-
voltage lines march straight to Philippe
Park, across it, and beyond. In this area
the habitat is typical central Florida
shoreline, with wax myrtle, sabal
palms and some pines, as well as more
mangroves.

At the 0.25-mile post, the trail takes a left-hand bend, with another little parking area on the right amid the first few live oaks. This section of trail provides a good view of the north part of Old Tampa Bay, but heed the signs: there's no swimming here. During low tide, this is another good place for bird-watching on the sand flats. The live oaks foreshadow the habitat you're about to enter.

A little farther on, as the trail starts to rise, you'll pass through a thicket of sabal palms on the right and a few large live oaks on the left. A large plaque here gives some history of the park, as well as directions to the Indian mound and to Odet Philippe's gravesite. Philippe was a native of France who served under Napoleon. He settled on a plantation here in 1842 and grew the first grape-fruit in Florida. His grave is across the trail, and is accessible. At the base of the plaque, don't miss the coontie plants, native Florida cycads. To reach the Indian mound, turn right into the small parking area just past the plaque; the mound is behind the parking area.

The trail continues to rise and curve to the left. Beginning at the half-mile point there are picnic pavilions and open areas for recreation on both sides of the trail. As you come up the rise, you enter a spectacular live oak hammock, con-taining literally hundreds of huge oak trees. The trail is heavily canopied throughout the hammock, making it a stunning hike. In the understory you'll see a number of other native species, including American beautyberry.

As the trail starts back down, you leave the big live oaks and go into the same kind of mixed palmetto and oak habitat the trail passed through earlier. At this point, which is at the 0.75-mile point of the trail, there's a playground on the left with swings and other equipment for families with small children. This area also gives you another good view of Old Tampa Bay on the right. At this point in the trail there are a number of native hickory trees, as well as planted palms and other ornamental species.

As you continue along the trail, you'll pass an information center on the left. At the one-mile mark you pass the entrance to the park where you came in. Continue into the boat launch area, walk around the traffic loop, and return the way you came for the full 2.2 miles.

NEARBY ATTRACTIONS
Playgrounds, picnic pavilions, and a boat launch ramp are located within the park; the pavilions can be reserved for group use. Odet Philippe's gravesite and an Indian mound also are in the park, near the midpoint of the trail.

Picnic Island Loop

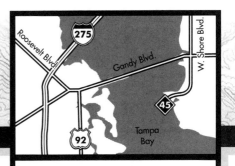

IN BRIEF

Although this is a short hike, it has an interesting challenge: the hike follows the shoreline of a mangrove swamp, creating a potentially wet experience. It's a great hike for families with children who are past the paved trail stage and who are ready for an adventure.

DIRECTIONS

Go south on West Shore Boulevard past Gandy Boulevard to where West Shore makes a right-hand turn and becomes Commerce Street. Follow Commerce Street through the industrial district until Commerce makes a left-hand turn and dead ends. Just before the dead end, take a right turn at the small sign that reads "Picnic Island Park." Turn left just before you go under the pipeline overpass, where a large sign indicates the entrance to the park.

Once inside the park, go past the fishing pier, boat ramp, and sailboat launching area. When you reach a **T** in the road, make a right turn and go around the parking area to the back of the area. You'll find rest rooms and a water fountain at the west end of the parking area.

DESCRIPTION

This hike begins just as you leave the parking area. Walk east to the edge of the woods, and follow the woods south past the picnic pavilions all the way to the beach. When you reach the water, you'll

AT-A-GLANCE INFORMATION

Length:
0.4 mile

Configuration:
Loop

Difficulty:
Moderate

Scenery:
Beach and mangroves

Exposure:
Mostly exposed with some shade

Traffic:
Moderately busy on weekends

Trail surface:
Sand and mud

Hiking time:
25 minutes

Season:
All year

Access:
No permits or fees needed

Maps:
No trail map is published.

Facilities:
Rest rooms at the parking lot

Special comments:
We strongly suggest that you hike from an hour before low tide to an hour after low tide; even then, expect to have wet feet. If you try to take it when the tide is high, you'll get more than your feet wet.

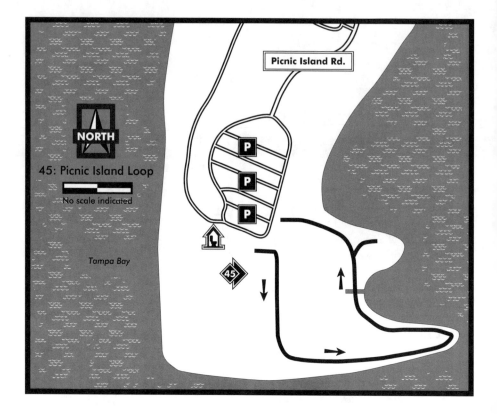

NORTH

45: Picnic Island Loop

No scale indicated

Tampa Bay

Picnic Island Rd.

45

see a sign that reads, "Please stay out—
the park's future depends on your coop-
eration."

Turn left at the sign and enter the
mangroves (the sign refers to the little
lagoon here, not to the mangrove
swamp). At this point, there's not a
defined trail; you'll find only a couple of
footpaths that lead east through the
mangroves. Find your way through the
mangroves until you reach the beach,
and follow the beach to the east.

This is an excellent place for beach-
combing—on one of our trips there, we
found a flamingo feather above the high
tide mark. It's also a wonderful beach to
see many species of small wading birds.

Proceed along the beach, past the
grasses and the mangroves until you
reach the end of the little point of land

that juts out into Tampa Bay. Here, the
beach almost doubles back on itself. Follow the beach into the lagoon as the
shoreline curves around to the right.

About halfway around the lagoon,
you'll see that you can't follow the beach
any further. This entire area is good fiddler crab habitat, and if you watch your
feet, you'll see hundreds of them scurry-
ing away into their burrows.

When you reach the end of the beach,
turn left into the grass and follow the
footpath there. The path will take you
across a little canal that has a varying
amount of water in it, depending on the
tide and the wind. Cross the canal and
continue up the slough and into the
mangroves. You'll see a lot of fiddler
crabs here as well. As you proceed, you'll
see a spur to the right that takes you

among the mangroves for a short distance, but it's a dead end. Continue on the main trail as it rises and dries, and you'll come out at the edge of the parking area where you left your vehicle.

NEARBY ATTRACTIONS
Picnic Island County Park contains a boat ramp, fishing pier, playground and picnic pavilions. It's a great all-around recreation area.

Pinellas Trail Expansion

IN BRIEF

This extension of the Pinellas Trail follows East Lake Road from John Chesnut Sr. Park to Keystone Road.

DIRECTIONS

From Tampa, take the Courtney Campbell Causeway across Old Tampa Bay to McMullen Booth Road. Take McMullen Booth Road north about 9.3 miles (it changes to East Lake Road near the park). Park in John Chesnut Sr. Park, on the left. The Pinellas Trail Expansion starts outside the park gate and goes north to Keystone Road.

DESCRIPTION

The Pinellas Trail is a 47-mile corridor that links parks, coastal areas, and residential neighborhoods in Pinellas County. Some portions of the trail traverse heavily used urban areas. This section, the Pinellas Trail Expansion, is discontinuous from the main trail at this time, although plans call for linking this portion of the trail with the main one. This hike begins just outside John Chesnut Sr. Park, on the west side of East Lake Road, at a sign that indicates the south end of the trail. Almost immediately, the trail crosses Sandy Point Road at a traffic light. Just after the crossing, you'll pass a convenience store and a small pizza restaurant where you can stop for water or soft drinks.

Shortly after you pass the convenience store, the trail drops down from the

AT-A-GLANCE INFORMATION

Length:
8.2 miles

Configuration:
Out and back

Difficulty:
Flat, easy

Scenery:
Urban but pleasant

Exposure:
Mostly open

Traffic:
Moderately busy

Trail surface:
Paved

Hiking time:
4 to 5 hours

Season:
All year

Access:
No permits or fees

Maps:
No map of this portion of the Pinellas Trail is yet published.

Facilities:
Because this trail is in an urban area, there are several convenience stores and other places to stop for a drink or visit the rest room.

Special comments:
Signs indicate each end of the trail.

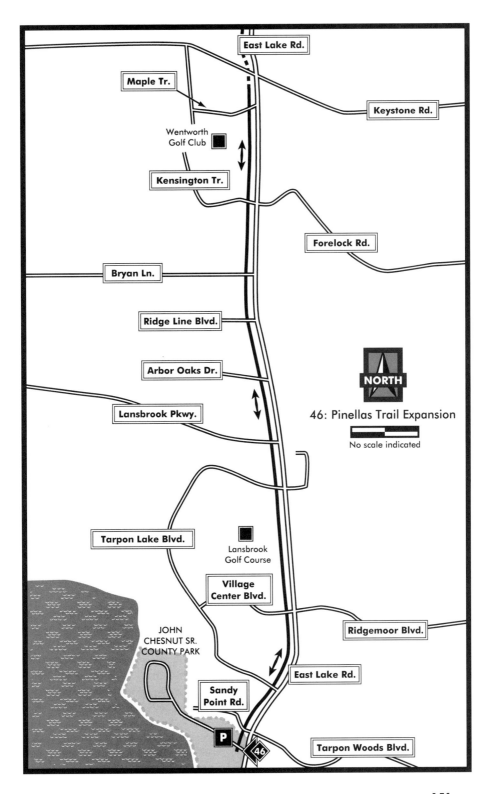

Maple Tr.

East Lake Rd.

Keystone Rd.

Wentworth
Golf Club

Kensington Tr.

Forelock Rd.

Bryan Ln.

Ridge Line Blvd.

Arbor Oaks Dr.

NORTH

46: Pinellas Trail Expansion

No scale indicated

Lansbrook Pkwy.

Tarpon Lake Blvd.

Lansbrook
Golf Course

Village
Center Blvd.

Ridgemoor Blvd.

JOHN
CHESNUT SR.
COUNTY PARK

East Lake Rd.

Sandy
Point Rd.

P

46

Tarpon Woods Blvd.

height of East Lake Road and passes between a wooden fence and a high shoulder, which provides a buffer between the trail and the traffic. The trail continues in this fashion almost to Tarpon Lake Boulevard, where it comes back up to the level of the road, so that you're between East Lake Road and a brick wall that borders a residential area.

A short distance past the crossing for Tarpon Lake Boulevard, you'll come to the Lutheran Church of the Resurrection, which is at the intersection of East Lake Road and Village Center Boulevard. There's a traffic light here, so you can make the crossing easily and safely. If you need to stop for a while, you also can cross East Lake Road at this intersection, and get to several fast food places and a convenience store on the other side.

Continue north, however, and you'll pass a woodland area where the trail swings a bit farther away from the road. The trail continues past Lansbrook Golf Course and crosses a small street, and then passes another wooded area of some size. Before long, you'll enter an upscale residential area, where the shoulder of the road has been very attractively landscaped, making this section a hike to look for pines, oaks, bottlebrush trees, and magnolias, as well as some other ornamental species. Also, at this point, look across the road; there's quite a bit of undeveloped land here, so that you're actually passing through green space amid this urban area.

As you continue, you'll pass the entrance to Lansbrook Parkway, where you'll see a fountain in a small lake and formal landscaping. Cross Cypress Woods Boulevard at the light, and you'll pass a lake with a fountain in it. The entire area is very parklike and pleasing, and gives way to more landscaping on the shoulder, similar to that found along the golf course. Here, the community has made a successful attempt to protect the remnants of a live oak hammock, saving several very large oaks between the trail and the residential area and incorporating them into the planned landscaping.

After you cross Arbor Oaks Drive, you'll pass another residential community, and then a little man-made wetland. Just past this area there's new construction taking place, where another planned community, Northfield at Lansbrook, is underway.

Continue across Ridgeline Boulevard; here, there's another convenience store. The next short section of the trail is more developed and not as pleasant as the area you've just been through, as you pass Oak Crest Preschool, East Lake Baptist Church, and the Meadow Ridge subdivision. After you cross Bryan Lane and pass a bit more construction, you're in a more rural area, where the trail runs past a stable and some woods. As you pass one more golf community, you're in a woodland that borders the golf course. Just beyond the woodland is another stable, and another residential area, before the trail ends at the edge of more woods. From this point, return the way you came for the full 8.2-mile hike.

NEARBY ATTRACTIONS

At the south end of the trail, John Chestnut Sr. Park offers picnic facilities, a boat ramp, short hiking trails, and a fishing pier.

Pioneer Park to Vinoy Park Greenway

IN BRIEF

This is one of two inner-city hikes in this book. Don't let its location right in St. Petersburg discourage you; this hike is delightful on a pretty day. By taking a short spur from the loop at the top, you can connect this hike with the Vinoy Park–to–Flora Wylie Park Greenway hike.

DIRECTIONS

From anywhere in Tampa, take Interstate 275 south across the bay to St. Petersburg. Follow I-275 south past I-375 and Tropicana Field. Take the next exit, I-175, exit 9. Follow I-175 to the end, where it becomes Fifth Avenue South. As you pass Second Street South and the University of South Florida at St. Petersburg campus, get in the left lane. Turn left on First Street South, go past Al Lang Stadium (Florida Power Park), proceed to Central Avenue, and turn right on Central Avenue. Cross Beach Drive, and, in the next block, parallel park on the right.

DESCRIPTION

Although this is a very urban hike, it's interesting and relaxing. The waterfront has a European feel to it, in part because this hike falls in the shadow of the Vinoy Renaissance Resort. You'll encounter people on bicycles and in-line skates, as well as mothers with strollers. In the yacht basin of the Vinoy, expect to find

AT-A-GLANCE INFORMATION

Length:
2.1 miles

Configuration:
Out and back with a loop and an optional spur

Difficulty:
Easy

Scenery:
Waterfront and parks

Exposure:
Mostly exposed

Traffic:
Busy on weekends

Trail Surface:
Sidewalk

Hiking time:
About an hour with the spur

Season:
All year

Access:
No permits, fees, or even parking meters

Maps:
No trail map published

Facilities:
Rest rooms at one location; water fountains in the parks

Special comments:
Site of many concert activities, including the Tampa Bay Blues Festival

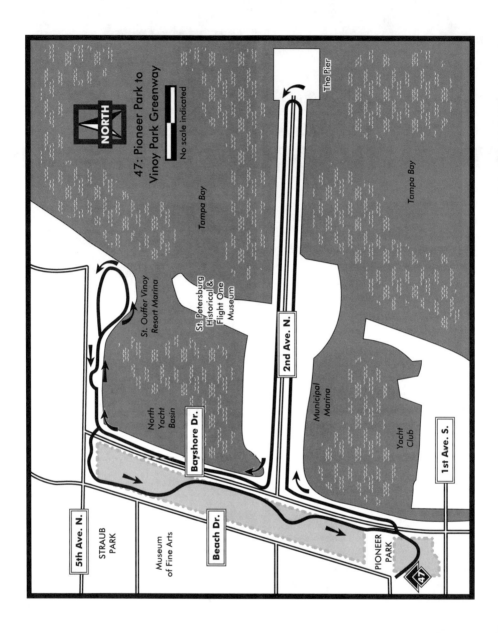

47: Pioneer Park to Vinoy Park Greenway

NORTH

No scale indicated

The Pier

Tampa Bay

Tampa Bay

St. Outfer Vinoy Resort Marina

St. Petersburg Historical & Flight One Museum

North Yacht Basin

Bayshore Dr.

2nd Ave. N.

Municipal Marina

1st Ave. S.

Yacht Club

5th Ave. N.

STRAUB PARK

Museum of Fine Arts

Beach Dr.

PIONEER PARK

47

everyday anglers shoulder to shoulder with guests of the upscale resort. On the day we took this hike, one of the things that struck us was how friendly everyone was. It may be in town, but it's a hike worth taking.

To reach the beginning of the trail, walk back along Central Avenue to the corner at Beach Drive. Here, turn left to enter Pioneer Park. Close your eyes and listen for a minute to the birdsong.

Proceed along the sidewalk to the center of the park, and find an obelisk with the following inscription: "Dedicated to the memory of the pioneer families and their families whose vision and leadership helped create St. Petersburg, Florida." Here in the center of the park there are benches; despite its urban nature, this is a peaceful place to sit.

Continue through the park, bearing to the left, until you reach the corner of Central Avenue and Bayshore Drive. Cross Bayshore Drive to the sidewalk on the other side, in the yacht basin. Turn left—north—and follow the sidewalk along the yacht basin until you reach Second Avenue North.

If you want to cut off 0.6 miles from the hike, go straight. Otherwise, turn right to hike east on Second Avenue North to The Pier. Follow the sidewalk along Second Avenue North until you reach The Pier. Visit The Pier if you wish, and then return west on the north side of Second Avenue North, passing the St. Petersburg Museum of History just before you reach Bayshore Drive. Turn right onto Bayshore Drive, and, on your right, you'll see a brick building; this is a "Comfort Station," with rest rooms inside.

Continue along Bayshore Drive, where the sidewalk runs through a greenway and along the seawall of the North Yacht Basin. People fish off the seawall, and a number of shaded benches provide a place where you can sit and look out over the harbor. As you walk, watch to the right for a good view of The Pier; this also is a good place to look for wading birds and pelicans.

When you reach the corner of Fifth Avenue North, turn right and continue along the north side of the marina. You'll find more anglers here; those who know what they're doing catch some nice sheephead.

A number of signs in the area warn boaters that this is a no-wake zone because of the presence of West Indian

Manatees in the area. Keep a watch for these gentle creatures—if you see them, they're worth stopping to watch.

Continue through the marina until you reach Vinoy Park. Follow the side-walk to the right, and then turn right again. This is a peaceful place to sit and watch the water, and it offers a great view of The Pier. Follow this loop around and through Vinoy Park; note the rather odd sculpture in the middle of the loop. We couldn't find any explanation of what it is, so just use your imagination! At the top of the loop, a sidewalk links this hike to the Vinoy Park–to–Flora Wylie Park Greenway hike (see pp. 180–182).

Follow the loop until it rejoins the sidewalk where you entered Vinoy Park. Return along the marina—the Vinoy Renaissance Resort is across the street—until you reach Bayshore Drive. Cross Bayshore Drive to Straub Park.

As soon as you enter Straub Park, bear left and then right, where you'll find a small arboretum covered with bougainvillea. Under the arboretum are several benches where you can sit and gaze down the length of Straub Park.

Just beyond the arboretum is a water fountain. Past the water fountain bear to the left, which will take you into the main part of the park. Throughout the park you'll find reproductions of a number of sculptures. Although there are no recreation facilities in this park, there's lots of green space, and it's a lovely place to pass a quiet afternoon.

Walk through the oaks in the center of the park, bearing to the left to return to the Bayshore Drive side of the park. Once you reach Bayshore Drive again, continue south. Watch to your right—you'll pass another nice oak hammock, this one with a water fountain where you can stop for a drink.

As you proceed, you'll pass the Museum of Fine Arts on your right. Cross Second Avenue North again, continuing south. When we hiked, the sidewalk was damaged due to construction.

Just after you cross Second Avenue North again, bear to the right and you'll find two granite benches and a placard, as well as a water fountain. The placard reads, "Straub Park, dedicated in honor of William L. Straub, on March 7, 1939, by the St. Petersburg City Council. As editor of the *St. Petersburg Times* from 1901 to 1939, he worked many years to preserve the waterfront for the beautification of the city and the enjoyment of the general public." In our opinion, he did a good job—this is a city park at its best.

Instead of returning to the street, follow the sidewalk to the interior of the park. You'll pass a magnificent old oak in the center of the park; listen here for birdsong. Also in the interior of the park is a decorative fountain. When we were there it was turned off, which may have been because of the persistent drought in Florida.

Proceed past the fountain, bear to the right, and arrive at the main sidewalk. Pass the St. Petersburg Yacht Club and cross Central Avenue to Pioneer Park to return to your car.

NEARBY ATTRACTIONS

There's plenty to do in this area! At the end of the optional spur you'll find The Pier, which is a five-story inverted pyramid containing shops, a museum, restaurants, an aquarium, live music, and boat docks. A trolley runs through the historic district and back and forth to The Pier.

Besides The Pier, this area contains many other points of interest. Museums and galleries include the Florida International Museum, the Glass Canvas Gallery, the Museum of Fine Arts, the Salvador Dali Museum, and the St. Petersburg Museum of History.

Rhodine Road Loop

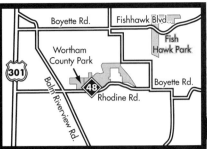

IN BRIEF

Be prepared for a difficult but rewarding journey as you hike through a portion of this primitive, 600-acre tract of land located adjacent to Stephen J. Wortham County Park. In addition to the main trail, there are plenty of opportunities to explore on your own.

DIRECTIONS

Take either Interstate 4 or the Cross-town Expressway east to I-75, and follow I-75 south from Tampa to US Highway 301. Take US 301 to the intersection where Balm Riverview Road forks to the left; follow Balm Riverview Road to Rhodine Road. Turn left on Rhodine Road, follow it two miles past the entrance to Stephen J. Wortham County Park, and watch for the entrance to the Rhodine Road ELAPP site on the left.

DESCRIPTION

If you're looking for a trail that will challenge your hiking and observation skills, this hike through an ELAPP site next to Stephen J. Wortham County Park is a good one for you. This 600-acre site opened in 1991 and has been developed as an environmentally pro-tected public access site. The trail is a big contrast to the trails in Stephen J. Wortham Park next door, which is quite well developed; rest rooms and other facilities are available there. The county does not offer any facilities or improved

AT-A-GLANCE INFORMATION

Length:
4 miles

Configuration:
Loop

Difficulty:
Flat, but lack of maintenance adds difficulty

Scenery:
Typical Florida oak hammocks, pal-metto groves, and pines

Exposure:
Open for the most part with a few shaded areas

Traffic:
Very little.

Trail surface:
Sandy in some areas; hard-packed in others

Hiking time:
3 to 3.5 hours

Season:
All year

Access:
No fees or permits

Maps:
None.

Facilities:
None

Special comments:
Boots recommended

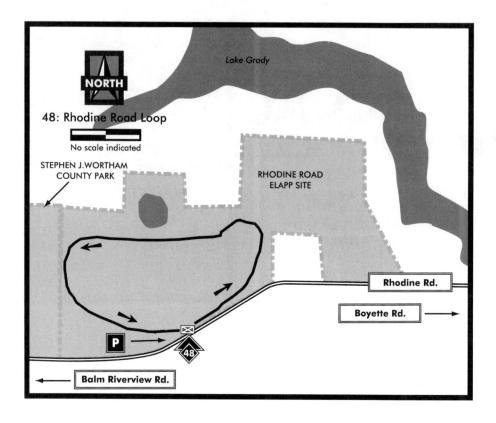

48: Rhodine Road Loop

No scale indicated

trail on this site—in other words, what you see is what you get. That's what makes it such a great hike for someone with experience in the outdoors. The trail has pleasant wooded scenery, but be prepared for a difficult journey. We strongly suggest you wear boots with good ankle support because of the primitive nature of and the lack of maintenance on the trail.

This site is open to hikers during daylight hours only, with access via a walkthrough point on Rhodine Road. This trail also can be used by horseback riders who can access the Rhodine Road ELAPP site through the horse trails that originate in Stephen J. Wortham Park next door.

Although we've followed the most clearly defined trail on the site, there's

certainly room to wander here, especially if you follow some of the paths that cattle from the ranch next door have created. We advise carrying plenty of water on this trail, and if you're inclined to go exploring off the trail, a compass or GPS unit would certainly be helpful.

Your first introduction to this site lets you know right up front that it's going to be challenging. As you enter the trailhead from Rhodine Road, you begin by crossing a patch of sandy ground so soft that it's hard on your feet and calves. To your right, watch for a stand of old citrus trees abandoned years ago by a former property owner. The trees still produce fruit, and a lot of animals use it as a source of quick snacks. Spend a little time here looking for animal sign. Tracks and other sign tell you that hogs, raccoons, and a number of other species frequent the area.

The rough trail continues for the next mile or so through small stands of southern yellow pine and palmetto. The pines lay down a thick carpet of needles, making the walking here a little easier. In many places you'll see that the palmettos have been stripped of their fronds by horses and straying cattle from a farm that borders the property. Park officials have accepted the fact that cattle have been straying over property lines for a hundred years or more in central Florida, so don't be surprised if you come across a stray steer or two.

Quite a bit of the trail is poorly defined, so it may be necessary for you to push back the overgrowth to expose the trail. Do not cut back any plants, as park personnel do enforce the no-cutting rule.

As you proceed along the trail, you'll eventually emerge from the jungle you're in and find yourself paralleling the trail on Stephen J. Wortham Park next door. This section of the trail provides easier walking. Here, overhanging oaks with their flowing strands of Spanish moss canopy the trail, providing a pleasant counterpoint to the tangle of undergrowth that characterizes the Rhodine Road trail. In a number of places, horses have cropped the Spanish moss; to those of us who are accustomed to seeing it

hanging in long strands from the trees, this gives the trail a sort of eerie manicured look.

As you leave the Wortham Park trail and plunge back into the Rhodine Road thicket of brush, you'll find that the second half of the Rhodine Road trail is wild and unkempt, but also full of wild surprises. You'll find wild mulberry bushes along the trail, and when you come to the meadows, stop and watch for a while. On the day we hiked this trail, we watched mice ducking and hiding from a pair of red-tailed hawks that were hunting there.

This grassy area is also home to bobwhite quail. We encountered a female quail that fluttered away as if she were injured and unable to fly, a classic behavior of quail when they try to draw predators away from their young.

At the end of this trail, you'll be worn out, and you'll know you've had a good hike. For someone who has experience in the outdoors and is comfortable in primitive situations, this is a good way to spend the day.

NEARBY ATTRACTIONS
Stephen J. Wortham Park, a well developed county park, is next door to the west. Rhodine Road ELAPP site is very close to the Alafia River and its smaller feeder streams with several full-facility parks within a five-mile radius.

Sawgrass Lake Park Trail

IN BRIEF

The environmental education park through which this hike explores was created by Pinellas County Parks Department, Pinellas County School Board, and the Southwest Florida Water Management District. The three short connected trails explore the area surrounding 400-acre Sawgrass Lake.

DIRECTIONS

From Tampa, take the Gandy Bridge west to Interstate 275, then go south on Interstate 275. Exit on 54th Avenue North and turn left (east). Go to the third light, which is 16th Street North, turn left (north). Go to 62nd Avenue North and turn left (west). Go back under I-275 and turn right at the first light, which is 25th Street North. The sign here is the only one you'll see for the park. Proceed through the housing development called Fairview Estates. Twenty-fifth Street dead-ends at Sawgrass Lake Park. Enter and park near the Environmental Center.

DESCRIPTION

Sawgrass Lake trails are designed primarily as nature trails. However, combining all the loops makes a two-mile walk for adults wanting a light hike, and an excellent hike for families with small children. Although this trail is right in the heart of Pinellas County, and hikers can hear the traffic on I-275, the park has

AT-A-GLANCE INFORMATION

Length:
2 miles (combined length)

Configuration:
Connected and stacked loops

Difficulty:
Very easy

Scenery:
Variety of Florida wetland habitats

Exposure:
Mostly shaded; paved portion somewhat more exposed

Traffic:
Moderately busy

Trail surface:
Combination of boardwalk, packed sand and pavement

Hiking time:
45 minutes

Season:
All year

Access:
No fees or permits

Maps:
A trail map, arboretum map, and environmental self-guide are available at the John A. Anderson Environmental Education Center.

Facilities:
Rest rooms and water fountains are located at the Environmental Education Center.

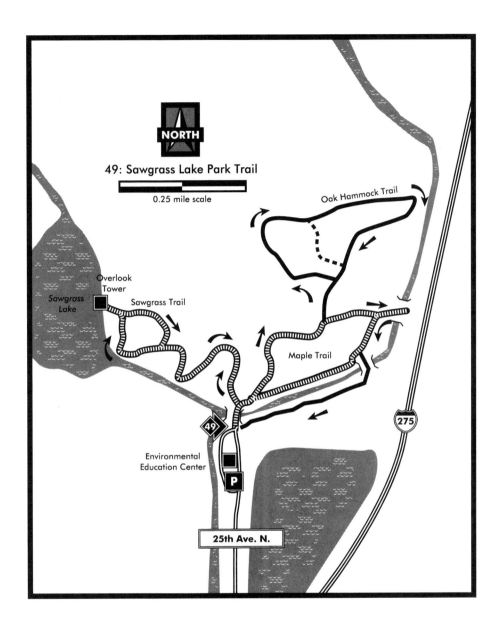

49: Sawgrass Lake Park Trail

0.25 mile scale

Oak Hammock Trail

Overlook
Tower

Sawgrass Trail

Sawgrass
Lake

Maple Trail

275

49

Environmental
Education Center

P

25th Ave. N.

the feel of deep woods. Wildlife visible on this hike includes alligators, many species of butterflies, white ibis, roseate spoonbills, skimmers, wading birds, and several species of large fish in the canal.

Enter the trails via a boardwalk north of the Environmental Education Center. The boardwalk crosses one of four canals that feed Sawgrass Lake Park. These

canals collect runoff from the area to prevent flooding during heavy rains; eventually this collected water enters Tampa Bay.

Just after you cross the canal, take the right fork onto the Maple Trail, which also will lead you to the Oak Hammock Trail. The Maple Trail is an entirely elevated boardwalk, which passes

The boardwalk takes you through swampy area that isn't accessible at ground level.

through wetlands. These wetlands are home to many species of ferns. In this area, also look for a number of hydric hardwood species, including maples and willows, as well as (unfortunately) some exotics such as Chinese tallow, air potato vines, and Brazilian pepper.

Along the trail, you'll find a number of covered benches where you can sit and read, or simply enjoy the birdlife of the trail. Just past the second bench, look for the wonderful large laurel oaks, which look very much like the live oaks around the Environmental Education Center, but which are an entirely different species.

When you come to the first shelter that spans the entire boardwalk, take the left fork, which will lead you to the Oak Hammock Trail; when you reach this trailhead, turn left again. The boardwalk ends just after you enter the trail; this area is a bit higher, and does not flood as readily. The plant species also are more

upland, although there are still many ferns in this area.

As you continue along the Oak Hammock trail another short stretch of boardwalk takes you through a wet area. After you leave the boardwalk, you must make a decision: take the right fork for a shortcut back to the trailhead, or take the left fork for the entire trail? The right fork is a very short stretch through an oak/palmetto thicket back to the trailhead. Take the left fork, and the trail skirts the thicket and takes you through a more upland area with many hardwoods and just a few palmettos. As you walk, you'll see a picnic pavilion on your right. Continue around the trail and you'll enter a fairly substantial stand of citrus trees gone wild; these trees bear fruit during the winter, though they are of indeterminate origin and variety. Past the citrus stand, the trail brings you right to the pavilion you saw earlier; this is the only section of the trail that's paved with bricks. Throughout this area, there are numerous benches where you can sit and rest. Just before you return to the trailhead, there's another stand of citrus.

When you return to the Oak Hammock trailhead and the main trail, this time take the left fork instead of returning up the right one. This portion of the boardwalk passes through another wet area with many ferns, citrus and oaks. As you continue along this boardwalk, a spur to the left takes you back out to the canal, where you can see the floodgate that controls the water level. It's a bit noisy here due to the proximity to I-275, but this also is a good place to look for wading birds, including anhingas, herons, egrets, gallinules, and coots. At this point you can exit the boardwalk and turn right to follow a maintenance road to the arboretum.

However, if you return up the spur to the main trail and turn left, you'll go past one more covered shelter with benches, cross over the canal again, and exit the boardwalk onto the path that borders the arboretum. This section of the trail is the best for butterfly watching; 37 species have been collected in this park.

This portion of the trail is paved, and follows the canal back to the Environmental Education Center. This entire stretch of trail is a good place to look for wading birds and other aquatic species, including alligators and turtles.

When you reach the Center, you will be outside the main trail, so you'll have to re-enter the trailhead as you did before. This time take the left fork onto the Sawgrass Trail to the Overlook Tower.

This area also has a lot of ferns, including some species that are so big

they're almost surreal. The boardwalk is elevated about four feet here, and some of the fronds of the larger ferns are so tall that they're over the heads of people on the boardwalk.

Along this portion of the trail there's one covered shelter that is actually out in the canal; this is another excellent spot for bird and wildlife watching. Continue along the boardwalk until you reach a fork—this is a loop, so either way you go, you'll reach the Overlook Tower. If you take the left fork, start looking for epiphytes in the trees, as well as a number of small birds during the winter. A lot of the epiphytes in this stretch of trail are of a good size, not just the little fist-sized species common throughout the Florida peninsula. Some of them are as much as three feet across, although they're easier to see in the winter when the leaves are off the trees.

When you reach the spur that leads to the tower, you'll get a spectacular view of the lake, including many bird and reptile species. Return down the spur that took you to the tower and turn left. You'll pass through another area of hydric hardwoods, complete with more large epiphytes. Don't just look at eye-level for these plants; look up as well for some outstanding large specimens. Continue around the loop and back to the trailhead and Environmental Education Center for the full 2-mile hike.

NEARBY ATTRACTIONS

At the trailhead is the John A. Anderson Environmental Education Center. On the south side of the Maple Trail is an arboretum run by the Environmental Education Center; a map is available at the Center.

Taylor Park Nature Trail

IN BRIEF

This measured hiking trail around the perimeter of John S. Taylor Lake provides a pretty and quiet hike in a small county park.

DIRECTIONS

From Tampa, take the Howard Frankland Bridge (Interstate 275) across Old Tampa Bay. Exit onto Ulmerton Road and follow Ulmerton Road west for nine miles until you reach New Ridge Road. Turn right on New Ridge Road and go north one mile to Eighth Avenue Southeast. Turn left on Eighth Avenue. The park entrance will be on your left. The trail begins at the footbridge beyond the first parking area and across the road. Just to the east of the trailhead and south of the parking area is an access point for the Pinellas Trail.

DESCRIPTION

When you reach the trailhead, which is marked with a "Measured Mile" sign, don't cross the footbridge onto the island, but turn south along the edge of the little lagoon. As you continue south, the trail passes between the lake and a grove of palm trees. Past the palms, a large stand of pines provides a shady area, where you can sit on a bench, overlooking the lake.

This is another lake where no swimming is allowed—watch for a while and

AT-A-GLANCE INFORMATION

Length:
2 miles

Configuration:
Out and back

Difficulty:
Flat, easy

Scenery:
Very pleasant lakeside woods

Exposure:
Mixture of open and shaded

Traffic:
Moderately busy

Trail surface:
Some grass, some paved, some shell

Hiking time:
45 to 60 minutes

Season:
All year

Access:
No permits or fees

Maps:
Available at the park office.

Facilities:
Water and rest rooms are available at the pavilions in the park.

Special comments:
The beginning and end of the measured mile are marked by signs, and where the hiking trail crosses a fitness trail, the various stations are labeled.

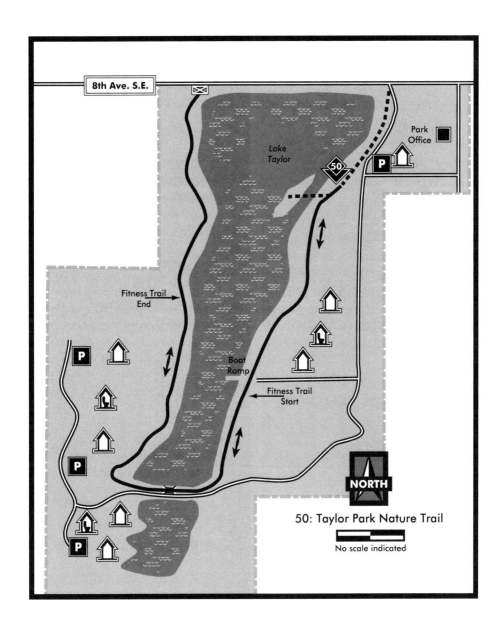

Lake
Taylor

Park
Office

50

P

Fitness Trail
End

P

Boat
Ramp

Fitness Trail
Start

P

NORTH

P

P

50: Taylor Park Nature Trail

No scale indicated

you'll see why, as several large alligators float by with only their nostrils and eyes showing. This also is a good area for bird-watching, where you may see wading birds and several species of ducks.

As you continue south and leave this first stand of pines, you'll cross a boat launch area and enter another pine grove to the south. Beginning in this area and continuing around the lake, the hiking trail runs concurrent with a fitness trail.

At the end of this stand of pines the trail turns right onto the grass between the road and the palms at the end of the lake. Follow the edge of the lake and the trail will take you across a small paved bridge and back onto the grass on the other side of the lake.

On this side of the lake, the first section of trail is sidewalk, which gives way to packed gravel. The gravel portion of the trail continues to parallel the edge of the lake, passing through ornamental palms planted among the pines. Here, there are benches that overlook the lake. This is a very good place to bird-watch. To the left of the trail, away from the lake, you'll see picnic tables, pavilions and a small playground. As you continue north along the edge of the lake you'll see several small stands of native cypress trees before you reach the end of the measured mile.

At the end of the measured mile, you have two options. You can exit the park through a small gate and follow the sidewalk east back to the park entrance for a hike only slightly more than one mile. To take the full two-mile hike, however, turn around and follow the trail back to the beginning of the measured mile on the other side of the lake.

NEARBY ATTRACTIONS

John S. Taylor County Park contains a number of picnic tables and pavilions for day use by groups and families, as well as a couple of small playgrounds for children.

In addition, the Pinellas Trail passes along the edge of the park, making this one of the places that hikers can get on and off that trail.

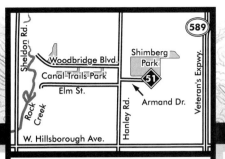

Town and Country Greenway

IN BRIEF

Good planning has turned this storm-water retention area into a short but peaceful greenway trail that's good for butterfly watchers most of the year.

DIRECTIONS

From Dale Mabry Highway, turn west on West Hillsborough Avenue. Drive about 3.5 miles, past Tampa International Airport on the left and under the Veteran's Expressway, until you reach Hanley Road. Turn right on Hanley Road and go one mile to Armand Drive. Turn right on Armand Drive, go one block and turn right again on Baseball Avenue. This takes you into Shimberg Park, which is a youth sports complex at the east end of the trail. Park between the sports complex and the trailhead.

DESCRIPTION

Tampa Bay is full of greenspace surprises, and this paved trail through a stormwater retention greenway between two residential areas is one of them.

At the trailhead, several benches surround a small butterfly garden with shade provided by sabal palms. Look for monarch butterflies and the host plants that typically attract them—pentas and milkweed plants.

The shoulders of the trail are regularly mowed so the greenway has a parklike feel, and the county has done some basic landscaping. However, the vegetation on

AT-A-GLANCE INFORMATION

Length:
2.4 miles

Configuration:
Out and back

Difficulty:
Easy

Scenery:
Park-like greenbelt

Exposure:
No shade; exposed

Traffic:
Moderately busy on weekends

Trail surface:
Paved

Hiking time:
30 to 45 minutes

Season:
All year

Access:
No permits or fees

Maps:
The Upper Tampa Bay Trail, Town and Country Trail, published in the Hillsborough County Parks and Recreation brochure

Facilities:
There are rest rooms and water fountains in Shimberg Park at the trailhead. Also, there's a water station in the first section of the trail, and a water fountain near the end of the trail.

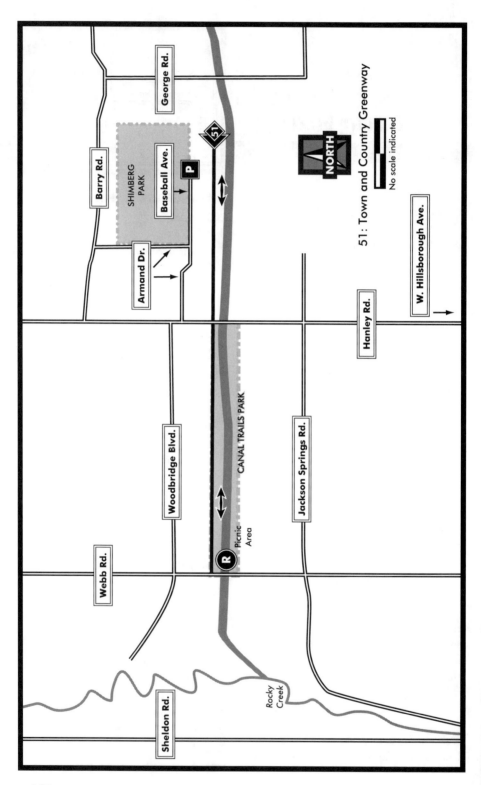

51: Town and Country Greenway

NORTH

No scale indicated

the trail is mostly a combination of native species and some common exotics that have gone wild. Take care not to get too far off the trail, as there is a deep ditch on the south side.

The first part of the trail parallels the Shimberg complex, so it can be noisy and fairly busy while games are taking place. The water station is along this stretch of the trail. Parents with small children frequently use this portion of the trail to teach them to ride bicycles.

Vegetation here is a mixture of native and exotic species on the shoulder of the drainage ditch, including several that are attractive to butterflies. Look here for white peacocks, buckeyes, sulphurs, blues, skippers, and other small butterflies that like grassy fields.

When you reach four-lane Hanley Road, you'll find a walk light at the crossing. The light can take a while to change, but when it does, you'll have adequate time to cross.

Once you get across, the greenway narrows as you hike between two residential areas. Here, the vegetation changes somewhat; on the fence to your right are ornamental plants from people's back yards, and there's lantana along the side of the ditch on your left. The butterfly population changes also, with a number of species coming to the lantana—look for large sulphurs and Gulf fritillaries in addition to the same species you saw earlier. As you continue along the trail the greenway widens again. From here to the end of the trail, look for maypops, the wild passionflower native to North America. Although they die back during the cool months, maypops throughout this part of the trail contribute to the butterfly population—maypops are the host plant for the Gulf fritillary.

A passion flower (maypop) along the greenway.

As you continue along the trail, you'll come to several benches under sabal palms where you can sit and rest, as well as a water fountain. And at the very end of the trail, a pavilion with a picnic table provides shade for hikers who have carried lunch with them. From there, walk back the length of the trail for the full 2.4 miles to return to your car.

Plans call for extending the trail both to the east and to the west in the next few years. This is a multi-use trail, with bicycles, dogs, and in-line skates allowed.

NEARBY ATTRACTIONS
The Shimberg Park Complex shares a parking lot with the trail. Shimberg has baseball and soccer fields, as well as a food concession when the fields are in use for organized games.

Trout Creek Trail

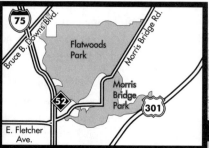

IN BRIEF
Part of the Wilderness Park system that includes Flatwoods Park and Morris Bridge, Trout Creek is the centerpiece of an Army Corps of Engineers project in the area. This area includes a series of three trails, each beginning at earthen levees constructed by the Corps

DIRECTIONS
Take Interstate 75 north from Tampa to the Fletcher Avenue exit, and then turn left (east). Follow the winding road to the Trout Creek/Four River Basins Park entrance. Park just off the road, past the second bridge, to access the trail. The trail begins at the park entrance.

DESCRIPTION
To reach the trailhead, go down the east side of the bridge embankment. Here, the levee has reduced this once wide-flowing creek to a trickle of its former self.

The first 100 yards of the trail runs right beside the creek, and the now-exposed creek bottom is a treasure trove of artifacts and tracks. As you walk, a look in the creekbed shows a cross-section of people who have used the river. Junk on the bottom runs the gamut, from watches probably lost by some angler casting his watch as well as his bait, to a variety of lures. Park rangers talk about finding lures from as long ago as the early 1940s that today are worth

AT-A-GLANCE INFORMATION
Length:
2 miles
Configuration:
Out and back
Difficulty:
Flat throughout
Scenery:
Pleasant woodlands
Exposure:
Shaded, with some open sections
Traffic:
Lightly used
Trail surface:
Hard packed sand and shell
Hiking Time:
1 to 1.5 hours.
Season:
All year
Access:
No fees or permits required; requested donation of $1
Maps:
Trail Guide for Hikers and Bikers on the Wilderness Park Off Road Trails available from Hillsborough County Department of Park and Recreation
Facilities:
None
Special comments:
A canoe launch area is available.

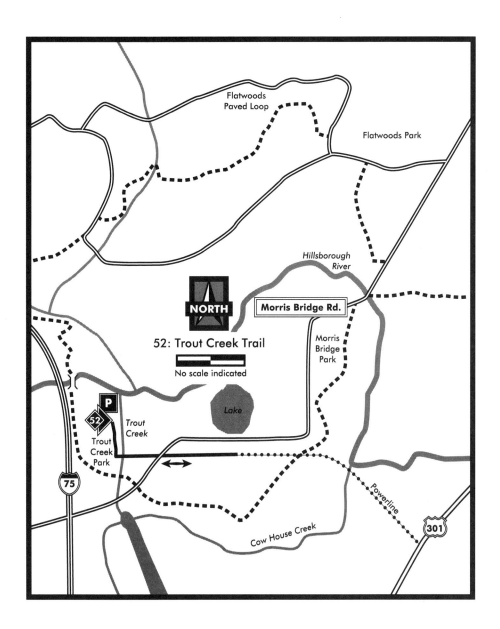

Flatwoods
Paved Loop

Flatwoods Park

Hillsborough
River

NORTH

Morris Bridge Rd.

Morris
Bridge
Park

52: Trout Creek Trail

No scale indicated

P

52

Trout
Creek

Lake

Trout
Creek
Park

75

Powerline

Cow House Creek

301

up to $500. On the day we took this hike, the other thing we found was money. When the spillway gates are opened, water from the Hillsborough River brings with it coins lost by boaters and swimmers. We even found several quarters that were solid silver.

On the right side of the trail, a tree line follows the length of the trail. For the first half-mile, most of the trees are cypress, in a remnant wetland habitat left from when the river ran free. There are a lot of wildlife viewing opportunities here. Watch for an active osprey nest high in a towering cypress tree that died long ago but is still standing by the riverbed. Look closely in the sand and you'll see deer and hog tracks going from the wet cypress swamp to the river. The tracks of other, smaller species of wildlife are evident as well.

As you continue along the trail, the dominant tree species changes from cypress to pine, with an understory of saw palmetto. This is prime rattlesnake habitat, and with the proximity of the water, moccasins are a possibility here—watch your feet.

Near the base of the palmettos, watch for the pale yellow bloom spikes in the spring and the berries in the fall and winter. Important as wildlife food, these berries also are the source of the saw palmetto nutritional supplement. Be careful if you reach down to see the berries; the saw palmetto lives up to its name with small sharp teeth at the base of the frond.

At its turnaround point, the trail runs to within 100 yards or so of the lake created by the levee, but doesn't quite reach the lake itself. As you start your return trip, you'll find that your perspective on the trail and creek are different. On the far bank of the creek, tall grasses march into more upland plants. While we were hiking a number of doves burst out of the tall grass.

Once you reach the trailhead again, cross the road and look down into the riverbed. The force of the water coming over the spillway has formed deep pockets where you may be able to see some good-sized fish. You can walk right up to the pools without spooking these fish that are well educated in the ways of anglers; they ignore any lure or bait you might be tempted to offer them.

NEARBY ATTRACTIONS
Trout Creek Park is about five miles east of both the University of South Florida and Busch Gardens.

Upper Tampa Bay Trail

587 589
Gunn Hwy.
Sheldon Rd.
Veteran Expressway
Anderson Rd.
587
589
Wilsky Rd.
Linebaugh Rd.

IN BRIEF

Among trail aficionados this greenspace trail, which snakes between a major highway and a semi-rural suburb of Tampa, is widely regarded as Tampa's best urban trail.

DIRECTIONS

Take Dale Mabry Highway to Linebaugh Road and take Linebaugh west to Wilsky Road 3.7 miles. Turn right on Wilsky Road and go 0.2 miles to the parking area on the left.

DESCRIPTION

This multi-use trail is open to hikers, bicyclists, and skaters. No horses are permitted on the trail.

This trail is a work in progress, with several extensions planned. The current trail, which is Phase I, runs from Linebaugh Road to Erlich Road, a distance of 2.8 miles (including the short spur to the south of the trailhead). A bridge over Gunn Highway is planned for construction during 2002. Phase II, which is scheduled for completion in late 2001, will start on the south side of Rocky Creek and run south and west 4 miles to Hillsborough Avenue. Phase III will extend the trail north from its present end to Peterson Road another 1.3 miles, and should be finished in the near future. Phase IV will continue north from Phase III, and will connect with the Upper Tampa Bay Trail to the

AT-A-GLANCE INFORMATION

Length:
5.6 miles

Configuration:
Out and back with a short spur

Difficulty:
Easy

Scenery:
Variety of wetland habitats, bridge over Rocky Creek

Exposure:
Mixture of shaded and exposed stretches

Traffic:
Moderately busy on weekends

Trail surface:
Paved

Hiking time:
2 hours

Season:
All year

Access:
No fees or permits

Maps:
Upper Tampa Bay Trail, Town and Country Trail, published in brochure by Hillsborough County Parks and Recreation

Facilities:
A portable john is in the parking lot. Water at the trailhead, on the south side of Gunn Highway, and just south at Erlich Road.

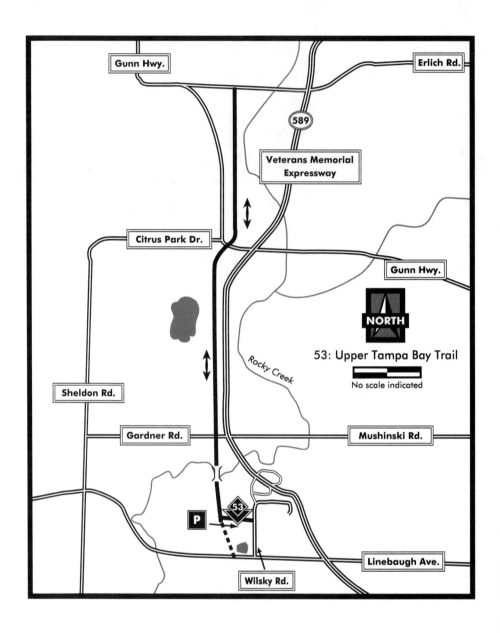

53: Upper Tampa Bay Trail

No scale indicated

proposed Suncoast Parkway Trail, which will be a paved trail from Hillsborough County all the way to Hernando County to the north.

A short paved trailhead leads past a lovely conservation easement lake to the main trail. This lake is not open for fishing or swimming.

When you reach the main trail, turn left (south) to take the short spur to Linebaugh Road. The scenery on the right is bland, since it's the backside of a golf driving range; a huge net keeps golf balls from flying onto the trail and hitting hikers. As you near the end of the spur, however, there is another conserva-

The Upper Tampa Bay Trail is a great place for families with small children.

tion easement area on the left. This is a little swamp, complete with a number of native Florida wetland species. During the very dry weather of 2000, the wetland pretty much dried up, but during normal wet seasons you should be able to see many wildflowers in this area.

Also along the sides of this spur, look for some of the common grassland butterfly species, including the white peacock, buckeye, and small sulphurs and blues. Although this trail is not the most consistent area for butterfly watching, sections of the trail have significant butterfly populations.

Turn north and return to the trailhead, then continue north past the lake, now on your right. At the corner of the trailhead and the main trail is one of a number of benches where hikers can sit and rest. Just north of the trailhead is the first of several interpretive signs, covering such topics as thunderstorms and lightning, recycling, pollution, spider webs, and live oaks.

A short distance north of the lake, an elevated plank bridge with fenced sides crosses Rocky Creek. The vegetation here is primarily wetland plants; if you look closely you can see a variety of species represented, such as willows and sweet bays.

Just beyond the creek, the trail passes between a semi-rural area with small farms and animals on the left, and the Veteran's Memorial Expressway on the right. Expect some farm-type noises and smells in this area. In the middle of this semi-rural area the trail crosses Gardner Street, where traffic does not stop at the trail crossing; there is no crossing light here, so take care. At the crossing is a list of wildlife, birds and reptiles that reputedly inhabit the area. In multiple trips to this trail, I've seen only one small water snake.

However, a short distance north of the Gardner Street crossing, the trail traverses an area with a generous population of zebra longwings, Florida's state butterfly.

Also through this portion of the trail, watch the grassy area on the right for butterflies that prefer open areas, and the lantana and other wildflowers on the left for other species of butterflies as well.

As the trail continues north, the Veteran's Expressway swings away from the trail and the scenery becomes more wooded, with another small suburb on the left. As you near the crossing at Gunn Highway, there's a McDonald's on the left across a dead-end street; this street, which is Citrus Park Lane, also provides a parking area in the middle of the trail.

Gunn Highway is a major (six-lane) highway, but a good crossing light provides safe passage. The section of the trail from Gunn Highway north to Erlich Road is new, having just opened in late 2000. For a short distance the trail parallels Gunn Highway, which makes a sharp right turn just after the trail crosses it, but soon Gunn Highway begins to swing away to the west, away from the trail. In this first section of trail you'll pass a fairly run-down residential area on the right; fortunately, the scenery improves.

Beyond Gunn Highway there are two more street crossings. The first is Edgemere Road, which is a small residential street with no need for a crossing light. The trail then enters another nice little wooded area before it crosses Manhattan Road, which is big enough to warrant a crossing light but still not a major intersection. Across Gunn Highway from the trail, you can see a small sheriff's department substation, which you can reach by crossing the highway if you should need help there. Beyond Manhattan, a lovely oak hammock woods on the right becomes a wooded wetland at a small creek crossing and a mixed oak and pine woodland as you continue north. Then you're back in the woods, as Gunn Highway continues to swing away from the trail.

In the next short stretch of trail are three more crossings, but these are driveways, where a few houses have been built "in the woods" right in this major metropolitan area. At its current end at Erlich Road, the trail emerges from the woods again and runs along the back side of a little strip of offices; the last water station is located here. Looking north across Erlich Road, you can see where the trail extension will enter the woods again. Return south down the length of the trail to the parking area for the full 5.6-mile hike.

Vance Vogel Park Loop

IN BRIEF

This under-used, rustic trail lies next to Little Bullfrog Creek in southern Hills-borough County, inside Vance Vogel Park.

DIRECTIONS

Take Interstate 75 south to the Big Bend exit, about 15 miles south of the inter-section of I-75 and I-4. Turn left (east) and go under I-75. Take the next left onto Bullfrog Creek Road. The park entrance is approximately one mile on the right. Take the park road south as it winds between the sports fields and park south of the picnic pavilions. You'll find two trailheads there; this description is of the right-hand trail.

DESCRIPTION

This trail is barely known and greatly under-utilized. It's located on the perimeter of a family park used primari-ly for baseball, soccer, and football leagues, and most people who come to the park never realize that hiking trails are there as well. Located beside Little Bullfrog Creek, the trail follows the tan-nin-stained creek for the first quarter mile of this rather difficult hike. The trail is overgrown by tall grasses, which requires some bushwhacking. However, the trail is lush and heavily shaded by the canopy of oaks and tall sable palms. Park rangers have said that if more people begin to use these trails, they'll step up

AT-A-GLANCE INFORMATION

Length:
1.5 miles

Configuration:
Loop

Difficulty:
Moderate

Scenery:
Dense grass and canopy oaks

Exposure:
Mostly shaded by oaks

Traffic:
Hardly ever used

Trail Surface:
Sand and grass

Hiking Time:
1 to 1.5 hours

Season:
Open year round

Access:
No permits or fees

Maps:
No map published

Facilities:
Rest rooms, concessions, and picnic area located near the soccer fields in the main part of the park

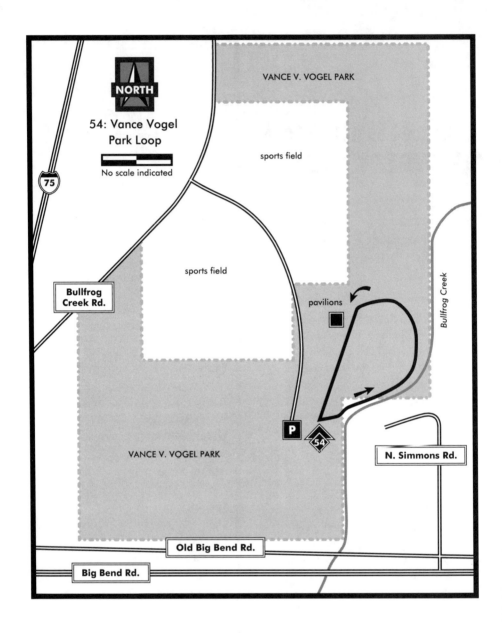

NORTH

54: Vance Vogel
Park Loop

No scale indicated

VANCE V. VOGEL PARK

sports field

sports field

pavilions

Bullfrog
Creek Rd.

VANCE V. VOGEL PARK

Bullfrog Creek

P

54

N. Simmons Rd.

Old Big Bend Rd.

Big Bend Rd.

their trail maintenance program. This is a short hike that families with older children will enjoy.

As you walk along Little Bullfrog Creek, take a moment to peer into the small creek and watch what seems to be a never-ending supply of small fish. Pay attention to where you put your feet, though. Narrow little streams like these are favored hangouts for dark-brown cottonmouth moccasins, which can be quite aggressive. But don't assume that every snake you see here is venomous; several very attractive species of water snakes like to lie along branches that overhang the water, and are quite harmless.

This area also is a good place to look for other wildlife. On the day we hiked, we surprised a family of raccoons who, despite our presence, kept their attention on the task of catching small fish.

As you continue along the trail, watch overhead for a lovely canopy of oaks, draped with Spanish moss. Here you'll see many squirrel nests. Since the trail is so seldom used, the squirrels seem to ignore anyone on the trail below them. Some of these squirrel nests are quite large, as wide as three feet. If you'll watch in the trees about 200 yards in from the trailhead, you may be able to find the nest; squirrels tend to use the same nests year after year.

As you reach the top of the trail's crescent, watch for animal tracks in the sand. On the day we were there, we saw deer tracks, as well as raccoon and possibly opossum tracks.

On the back side of the trail, you'll begin to see tall pines mixed with oaks, typical of many Florida habitats. Historically, these pines were slashed at an angle so they would ooze sap into a ceramic pot; the sap was used commercially for turpentine and other products. Today, they're primarily used for pulpwood and dimension (construction) lumber.

When you come out of the woods at the end of the trail, you'll see picnic pavilions in front of you. Turn left and walk along the grass by the treeline to return to the parking area and to your vehicle.

Vinoy Park to Flora Wylie Park Greenway

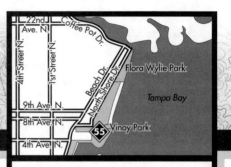

IN BRIEF

This greenway follows the shoreline of Tampa Bay on the St. Petersburg side of the bay from Vinoy Park to Flora Wylie Park and beyond. This is one of two inner-city hikes in this book. Don't let its location discourage you; this hike is delightful on a pretty day.

DIRECTIONS

From anywhere in Tampa, take Interstate 275 south, across the bay to St. Petersburg. Follow I-275 south to I-375, which is the Tropicana Field exit. Take I-375 east until it becomes 4th Avenue North. Take 4th Avenue North until it dead ends at Beach Drive. Turn left on Beach Drive, take it one block to 5th Avenue North, and turn right. When you reach the end of 5th Avenue North follow it to the left as it becomes Bay Shore Drive North. A right turn will take you into the parking lot for Vinoy Park. Walk to the southwest corner of the parking lot to find where this hike begins.

DESCRIPTION

Although this is a very urban hike, it's still quite interesting and relaxing. The waterfront has a European feel to it, in part because this hike is in the shadow of the Vinoy Renaissance Resort. You'll encounter people on bicycles and in-line skates, as well as mothers with strollers. It

AT-A-GLANCE INFORMATION:

Length:
2.5 miles

Configuration:
Out and back

Difficulty:
Easy, except for a detour around some temporary construction

Scenery:
Seaside and an arboretum

Exposure:
Exposed

Traffic:
Busy on weekends

Trail Surface:
Paved

Hiking Time:
1 to 1.5 hours

Season:
All year

Access:
No fees or permits needed

Maps:
None

Facilities:
Rest rooms in some of the parks along the route

Special comments:
By continuing south after you've completed the "back" portion of the out-and-back, you can connect this hike with the Pioneer Park to Vinoy Park Greenway hike.

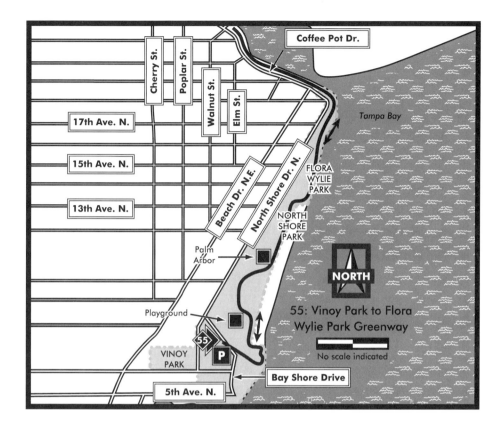

55: Vinoy Park to Flora Wylie Park Greenway

No scale indicated

may be in town, but it's a hike worth taking.

Take the diagonal sidewalk that points straight toward The Pier (The Pier is across the inlet that forms the North Yacht Basin). This is the most spectacular view you'll get of The Pier from anywhere along the waterfront.

When you reach the end of this sidewalk, bear to the left to follow this hike north. In the little triangle formed by these sidewalks coming together you'll find a spot to sit and watch the the sailboats coming into the yacht basin.

Proceed north along the waterfront and through several nice clumps of sable palms, the state tree of Florida. This area is rather busy with families sitting on benches or on the grass, and anglers fish-

ing off the seawall. The scene here reminded us quite a bit of George Seurat's 1884 painting, "A Sunday on La Grande Jatte."

Follow the greenway past the trees and to the beach, where the sidewalk takes a turn to the left. This area is popular with anglers, and you'll see people in the water with both rods and reels, and cast nets.

Here the sidewalk passes between the beach and a little playground, and detours away from the waterfront and around the North Shore Park city pool, although it stays inside the park. Turn right again to start back toward the waterfront, but before you get there, look to your left and you'll see the entrance to the Gizella Kopsick Palm

Arboretum. This is a neat place to take a little side hike—the arboretum contains many species of palms and cycads from all over the world.

At this point, you'll have to use your judgment about which way to go, depending on the state of construction in North Shore Park. Normally you would exit the arboretum through the same gate through which you entered, pick up the sidewalk, and continue east until you reach the waterfront once again. However, at the time we took this hike, there was quite a bit of construction going on east and north of the palm arboretum, making the waterfront impassable at that point. So we exited the palm arboretum at its northwest corner and took the sidewalk that runs along the west side of North Shore Park until we had passed the construction and could safely return to the waterfront.

Either route you follow will take you past Elva Rouse Park, where you will find rest rooms, and then into Flora Wylie Park. Once you return to the waterfront you'll again pass anglers, and see benches where you can rest and look out over the water. This section of the waterfront is not nearly as busy as the southern end.

At the north end of Flora Wylie Park, whether you've been able to get back down onto the waterfront or have elected to stay on the west side of the parks, you'll find yourself on a little ribbon of a greenway that continues along the waterfront through some small oaks. This area, along Coffee Pot Drive, reminded me a bit of a similar waterfront in Maputo, Mozambique, that was originally built by the Portuguese.

Follow the waterfront around and under the oaks and palms until you reach the bridge that links to the Stouffer Vinoy Golf Club. We elected to turn around here and go back, because a sign on the sidewalk on the west side of the bridge indicated construction ahead; however, a street map of St. Petersburg shows that the waterfront continues around Coffee Pot Bayou all the way to Coffee Pot Park.

NEARBY ATTRACTIONS

There's a lot to do in this part of St. Petersburg. South of the greenway is The Pier, which you'll see just as you begin your hike. The Pier is a five-story inverted pyramid containing shops, a museum, restaurants, an aquarium, live music and boat docks. A trolley runs through the historic district and back and forth to The Pier.

Museums and galleries include the Florida International Museum, the Glass Canvas Gallery, the Museum of Fine Arts, the Salvador Dali Museum, and the St. Petersburg Museum of History. And don't miss the Vinoy Renaissance Resort, which you'll see to the south and west of where your hike begins.

Along the way you'll pass the Gizella Kopsick Palm Arboretum, a short side hike we definitely recommend that you take.

Violet Cury
Nature Preserve Loop

IN BRIEF

Not far from downtown Tampa, this primitive, 160-acre nature preserve provides an excellent hike for those wanting a near-wilderness ramble.

DIRECTIONS

From anywhere in Tampa, get on Interstate 275 going north. Get off at the Bearss Avenue exit and go right (east). Turn left (north) on US 41 (Nebraska Avenue) and go to Sinclair Hills Road. Turn right on Sinclair Hills Road and watch for the entrance to Violet Cury Nature Preserve on the left side of the road.

DESCRIPTION

Although Violet Cury Nature Preserve is located in an urban area, it's definitely not a typical urban trail. This 160-acre nature preserve was created in October of 1995, but no attempt has been made to develop it. It's a tough and very primitive trail; this is not a good hike for families with small children. But for anyone who wants a wilderness experience that's close to town, it's a great place to spend the morning or the day. Because it is so rarely visited, it will likely retain its wildland nature.

The trailhead is 30 yards north of the only picnic table on the site. Note, however, that you can pick up the trail at a number of openings in many places on the preserve. People using the preserve

AT-A-GLANCE INFORMATION

Length:
About 2 miles

Configuration:
Loop

Difficulty:
Experienced hikers who appreciate a challenge will like this trail

Scenery:
Hardwood hammocks and flatwoods

Exposure:
Some shaded portions, but mostly open

Hiking Time:
2.5 hours

Access:
No permits or fees necessary

Maps:
No trail map is printed.

Facilities:
None

Special comments:
Wear lightweight hiking boots with ankle support, and bring insect repellent and water with you.

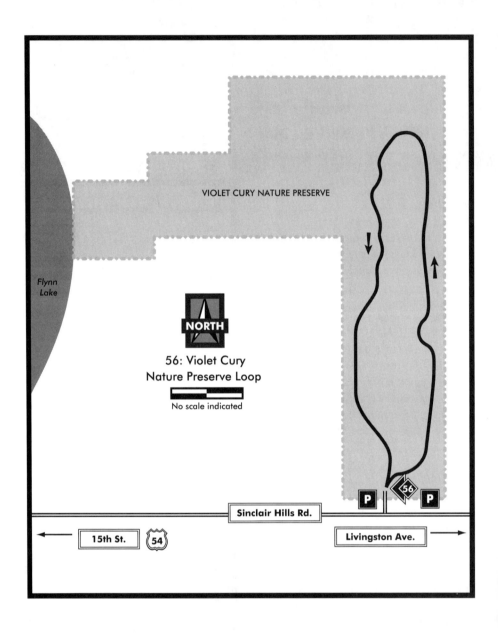

VIOLET CURY NATURE PRESERVE

Flynn Lake

NORTH

56: Violet Cury
Nature Preserve Loop

No scale indicated

56

P   56   P

Sinclair Hills Rd.

15th St.   54

Livingston Ave.

have created these unofficial entrances to the trail, each of which enters the path that serves as the main trail. Also note that since the area isn't maintained by the county on a regular basis, the trail is overgrown.

When we hiked here, we entered near the picnic table, and headed east through a thick undergrowth of high grass into a grove of large oaks. These oaks tower over the trail; look up into them and you'll see several large squirrel nests high overhead. At this point, the trail's surface is soft sand, which makes footing difficult.

For the first quarter mile, the trail continues through the stand of oaks.

Then the habitat changes, and becomes a pine flatwoods. As we walked into the flatwoods, we spooked a flock of doves feeding in the grass. They fluttered ahead of us, seeming to leapfrog over one another along the trail. They flew only 20 yards or so at a time before they took cover, only to break that cover a few minutes later as we again approached.

The trail continues through the flatwoods habitat for three-quarters of a mile or so, and at various points along the trail wild mulberries grow. There's also evidence of small animals feeding on the fruit. Armadillos seem to really love this section of the trail. We did this hike in the late afternoon and saw several of the little armored creatures. Since they don't see or hear well, we were able to sneak up quite close to a couple of them before they knew we were there. Then they froze, jumped straight up into the air, and scurried off like the Mad Hatter of *Alice in Wonderland* who was so afraid he was going to be late.

The trail leaves the flatwoods habitat and passes into an area of scrub oaks and saw palmetto interspersed with tall pines. Several of the tall pines appear to have been struck by lightning, and in the very top of one is a very large osprey nest. On the afternoon we hiked, a magnificent bird was perched on the limb beside to the nest, and seemed completely indifferent to our presence.

Walsingham Park Trail

IN BRIEF
This multi-use trail is a quiet hike through a county park that's peaceful even on weekends.

DIRECTIONS
From Tampa, take Gandy Bridge west to Pinellas County and follow Gandy Boulevard as it becomes Park Boulevard at US Highway 19. From US 19, go 6.3 miles west on Park Boulevard to its intersection with Seminole Boulevard (Alternate US 19). Turn right (north) and go 1.8 miles to the intersection of Seminole Boulevard and 102nd Avenue. Turn (west) left onto 102nd Avenue and go 1.75 miles. The entrance to Walsingham Park will be on the right. Follow the main road through the park all the way to the back parking lot to find the trailhead. Besides the trailhead, there are a number of access points to this trail, including one near the park entrance on 102nd Avenue. In addition, this park is very close to the Pinellas Trail, and hikers can park here during the day to access the portion of the trail nearby.

DESCRIPTION
This trail begins at the north parking area, where you'll find rest rooms and a water fountain right at the trailhead. Start east on the trail as it follows the north shore of the lake. This is a lovely area, with native Florida water plants visible in the shallow water of the lake, a

AT-A-GLANCE INFORMATION

Length:
2.75 miles

Configuration:
Out and back

Difficulty:
Mostly flat, with a few very mild slopes around the lake near the trailhead; easy

Scenery:
Pretty, with a nice view of the lake

Exposure:
Mixed shade and exposed

Traffic:
Quiet even on weekends

Trail surface:
Paved

Hiking time:
1 to 1.5 hours

Season:
Open all year

Access:
No fees or permits

Maps:
The location of the park is shown on the brochure, *Pinellas County Parks*. A park map is available at the office.

Facilities:
Rest rooms and a water fountain at the trailhead, as well as at several picnic areas along the trail

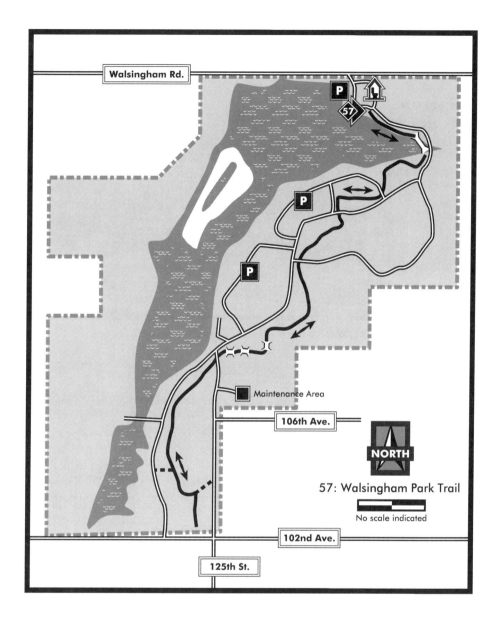

Walsingham Rd.

P

57

P

P

Maintenance Area

106th Ave.

NORTH

57: Walsingham Park Trail

No scale indicated

102nd Ave.

125th St.

big contrast to the saltwater habitats along some of the hikes in this book. This is a good area to watch for wading birds and ducks. Across the lake you can see picnic areas and playgrounds, which usually are busy on weekends.

After a short meander along the north shore, the trail turns to the south and crosses a bridge over the lake. Look into

the clear water, and you can see schools of small fish and an occasional bass or other large fish.

Just beyond the bridge, the trail passes through a short stretch of mixed pines and oaks as it starts to swing away from the lakeshore. At the quarter-mile post you pass one of the picnic areas you can see from across the lake, and then come

The first part of the trail follows the shoreline of Walsingham Reservoir.

to the first place where the trail crosses one of the park roads. At this intersection, as at all such intersections in the park, vegetation has been cleared away from the trail on both sides, providing good visibility for both vehicles and trail users.

After the crossing, the trail enters a mixed pine/oak woodland with a lot of palmettos in the understory, typical of central Florida. This section of the trail is surprisingly quiet. Listen carefully throughout the woods for birdsong. In this area, there are a number of footpaths leading into the woods from the main paved trail.

At the next crossing, there's an area where you can pick up shredded mulch, donated by Pinellas County. Just after this crossing, the trail re-enters the woods and passes the half-mile post. Just past the half-mile point, you'll see an example of a small Florida oak ham-

mock, as the trail passes through one edge of it.

Cross another side road, and you enter a drier habitat with a lot of oaks and an occasional sand pine thrown in. In this area you may see a few sandhill species, including gopher tortoises. Here, too, the oaks and other species are smaller, typical of the drier soils.

At the three-quarter mile post the woods start to deepen again, gradually giving way to larger pines. There's a truck crossing here, where a side road leads to a maintenance yard.

Shortly after that crossing, just before you come to a little bridge, look for a sign on the left indicating a protected mitigation area. Look carefully past the sign to see into a slough that's fairly well hidden by brush in front of it, but if you're lucky you may see some unusual wading birds here, including storks. The two small bridges just in front of you cross the slough, but because of the angle of the trail to the water you can't see into the slough from them.

Past the bridges, there's one more crossing, where a small road leads to the ranger's residence. Just beyond this crossing the trail passes the one-mile post and enters an open woodland with large pines and some landscaping, including planted maples, sweet gums, as well as ornamental species.

At the 1.25-mile marker, the trail branches. Take the right fork and you'll end up on the main road into the park in just 30 or 40 yards. Take the left fork to continue on the trail.

In a short distance, the trail branches again. This time the left fork takes you about 70 yards or so to the fence; the right fork keeps you on the main trail. Along the main trail you'll see southern magnolias on both sides of the trail, and on the left is a small pond where you

can sit in a swing and look out at the water. This pond is not open for fishing.

The trail ends at the park fence, where you can exit the park and make a left turn to access the Pinellas Trail. Return the way you came to complete the 2.75 mile hike.

NEARBY ATTRACTIONS

Walsingham Lake is a managed fish habitat area stocked by the Florida Fish and Wildlife Conservation Commission. Special fishing regulations are posted at the fishing pier near the trailhead and at the entrance to the park.

The Pinellas Trail office is located in Walsingham Park, near the trailhead. You can reach the Pinellas Trail by exiting the south end of the park trail and following the sidewalk east for several blocks until you cross the trail.

Several picnic areas with playgrounds are located in the park as well.

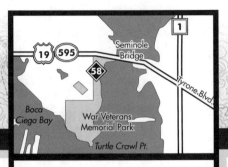

War Veterans Memorial Park Trail

IN BRIEF

This combination paved and shell trail traverses a number of nice oak hammock and upland pine habitats and passes a historic monument.

DIRECTIONS

Take Gandy Bridge west to Interstate 275, then take I-275 south to 38th Avenue North. Take 38th Avenue North west to Tyrone Boulevard, then turn right on Tyrone. In approximately one mile, you'll cross Seminole Bridge. The first left after the bridge will take you onto the road that leads into the park. Just before you actually enter the park, turn left into the boat ramp parking lot. To reach the trail, proceed out of the parking lot on foot and turn left on the road to enter the park.

DESCRIPTION

After you leave the parking lot and turn left, you'll pass the main gate of the park and enter an area with an oak hammock on the left and pines on the right. Before long the canopy opens up a bit; when you reach this point, start watching to the right, off in the woods, for two big dead pines. Ospreys frequently perch in these trees, making it a good place to see these wonderful predatory birds.

As you proceed, you enter a saltwater habitat typical for this area. On both sides of the road, saltwater sloughs con–

AT-A-GLANCE INFORMATION

Length:
2.5 miles

Configuration:
Extended loop

Difficulty:
Flat, easy

Scenery:
Some nice views of oak hammocks and pine uplands

Exposure:
Mixed shade and exposed

Traffic:
Moderately busy on weekends

Trail surface:
Paved road

Hiking time:
1 to 1.5 hours

Season:
All year

Access:
No fees or permits needed

Maps:
No trail map is published.

Facilities:
Rest rooms and water fountains can be found at several locations in the park near the picnic areas and boat ramp.

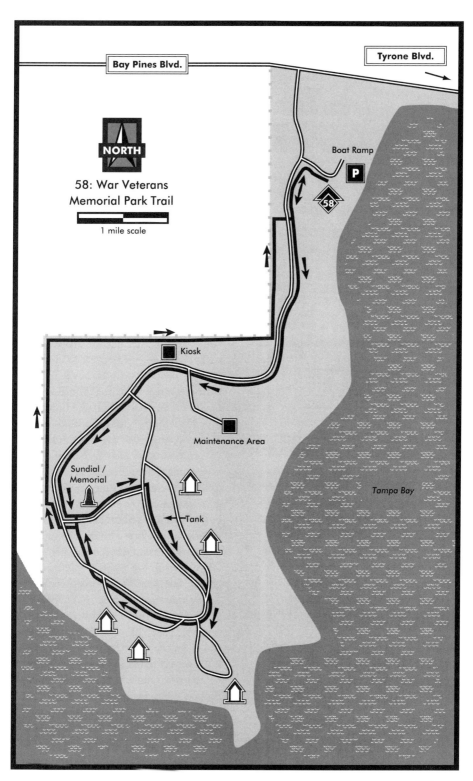

Bay Pines Blvd.

Tyrone Blvd.

NORTH

58: War Veterans
Memorial Park Trail

1 mile scale

Boat Ramp

P

58

Kiosk

Maintenance Area

Sundial /
Memorial

Tank

Tampa Bay

As the trail passes the cemetery, it traverses a lovely oak hammock.

tain mangroves and marsh areas, providing a home for a number of marine animals.

Before long, this wet area gives way to a stand of pines and mixed oaks over an understory of palmettos. As the road bends to the right this area continues, with the addition of a number of sabal palms. As you walk, listen; you may hear bells playing from the bell tower in Bay Pines National Cemetery, which is next door to War Veterans Memorial Park.

After a short distance, you'll come to a maintenance road that goes to the left; pass it, but watch to the right for an information kiosk where you can find out more about this park and its historical significance. There's also a half-mile marker in the woods on the left, but you'll have to look hard to find it.

As you proceed, you'll come to a fork in the road. Take the right side of the fork; the left side is a one-way exit from the park. Continue on through some smaller oaks and pines, and continue straight ahead as you pass one road to the right and another to the left.

The pines and sabal palms in this area show evidence of fire, which isn't surprising, considering that the parks department conducts controlled burns here. As a result the habitat is more open than in other parts of the park, and is more typical of Florida piney woods. Watch for an interpretive sign on the right side of the road that gives information about prescribed burns, what they are and how they are used.

Before long you'll be in an area that's a little wetter, where you'll see some larger oaks that are part of a hammock with a palmetto understory. Make a left turn on the road into the Sundial/memorial area of the trail. On the left, where the sundial is located, you can find a brief history of the park:

On November 1, 1966, the federal government returned 12 acres of surplus land south of Bay Pines Veteran's Administration Hospital to Pinellas County. Two years later, the board of county commissioners dedicated 86 acres as park land, and added another 34 acres in May 1971. Inside the sundial memorial are plaques honoring the US Coast Guard, the Navy, War Office, Marine Corps, and Air Force.

Another plaque reads: "Time will not dim a memory of a grateful nation for those who sacrificed so much to keep our country free."

This is a good area to look for butterflies on the pentas planted here. Across from the sundial is a large American flag and a plaque that says, "This public park is dedicated by the Pinellas County

Board of County Commissioners to the memory of those who honorably served in the Armed Forces of the United States of America and to all residents and guests of this country for their wholesome outdoor recreation, April 6, 1974."

Continue past the flagpole and the sundial, and when the road reaches a **T**, turn right. This leads you into the picnic and playground area. In a minute you'll pass a tank on display, with a sign that says, "For viewing only." This is a full-track combat tank with a 76-millimeter gun; an interpretive sign near the tank gives many pertinent statistics regarding the tank, including its cost of $87,941.

To the right of the trail in this area is a little pond that's partly hidden by the trees; here you'll find benches along the way where you can sit and overlook the pond. This entire area is open, with lots of oaks, pines, and sabal palms, as well as lots of mosquitoes!

Follow the main trail as it curves to the right and forms the top of the loop of the trail. Follow the loop around to the right, and stay on the main road. As you proceed on this side of the loop and out of the picnic area, look to the right for the end of the Meditation Trail, which leads to the sundial. Cross the road and make a right turn onto the Meditation Trail, where you'll find a water fountain just as you enter it. For the next 50 yards or so, you'll pass through a lovely oak hammock where there are picnic tables and benches. In this area watch for birdhouses, which were part of an Eagle Scout project. Judging by the amount of damage around the openings of the boxes, they appear to have been taken over by either flying squirrels or woodpeckers.

At the end of the Meditation Trail turn left, which will bring you back out onto the main road. When you reach the main road turn right, and then make an almost immediate left turn onto the pedestrian trail that goes into the woods. This shell trail takes you right to the edge of the park property. When you reach the fence turn right; however, you also can turn left to reach a little beach area where you can play volleyball or fish in the bay.

From that point the trail follows the fence line of the property, first taking you through some of the pine-oak mixed habitat you could see from the main road. Unlike the paved portion of this hike, the pedestrian trail is not open for bicycles, but you will encounter people walking dogs on leashes. Before long you'll be able to see the Bay Pines VA Hospital grounds and the cemetery through the fence. This portion of the trail also can have a lot of mosquitoes on it. There are a few fitness stations here with equipment, although there are no directions for using them. After a pleasant walk through the oak hammock, follow the trail as both it and the fence make a right-hand turn to follow the edge of the cemetery. Then the trail makes a left-hand turn and re-enters the woods. Watch on the right for mangroves and other saltwater species; this is one of the sloughs you passed by as you entered the park. Once you are in the saltwater area, watch carefully to the right. The pedestrian trail makes a right-hand turn, although the fence and a maintenance path continue straight ahead; if you don't watch carefully, you'll miss the turn.

Shortly after you make the turn to the right you'll reach the paved road once again. Turn left, pass through the park gate, and then turn right to enter the boat ramp area where you parked.

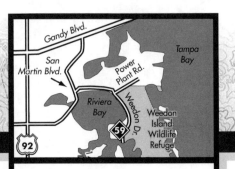

Weedon Island Preserve Trail

IN BRIEF

This nature trail and boardwalk provides a three-mile hike through mangrove marsh habitats.

DIRECTIONS

From Tampa, take Gandy Bridge west. Approximately 0.5 miles after you leave the causeway, turn left on San Martin Boulevard (just before Derby Lane Greyhound Track). Follow San Martin Boulevard south approximately 1.4 miles to Weedon Drive. Turn left on Weedon Drive, which will take you into the preserve. You will pass Power Plant Road and a maintenance area road on the left before coming to a parking area, also on the left, where you will see a sign indicating the boardwalk.

DESCRIPTION

About ten miles from downtown Tampa and five from St. Petersburg, Weedon Island Preserve is one of the most historically significant places you'll visit in the area. Not only is it home to several endangered species, it's one of the Southeast's most important Native American burial complexes. Since 1923, this 1,500-acre island has undergone extensive archaeological excavation. More than 250 skeletons have been uncovered, dating from 10,000 BC to AD 1,200. The entire island, from both an environmental and a historical perspective, is very carefully protected.

AT-A-GLANCE INFORMATION

Length:
3 miles

Configuration:
Two connected loops with spurs

Difficulty:
Flat, easy

Scenery:
Salt marsh and estuarine habitats

Exposure:
Mostly exposed, with some shady sections

Traffic:
Moderately busy on weekends

Trail surface:
Paved and boardwalk

Hiking time:
1 hour

Season:
All year

Access:
No permits or fees needed

Maps:
See brochure for Pinellas County Parks. No site map is published.

Facilities:
Rest room and telephone located at the end of the preserve road, next to the fishing pier and canoe launch area

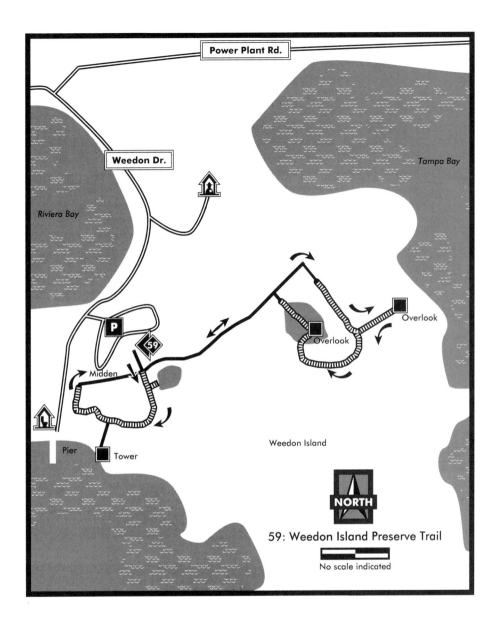

Power Plant Rd.

Weedon Dr.

Tampa Bay

Riviera Bay

P

59

Midden

Overlook

Overlook

Pier

Tower

Weedon Island

NORTH

59: Weedon Island Preserve Trail

No scale indicated

At the parking lot, look for the large rock with a plaque that provides a brief history of the area. Walk around the rock, and the entrance to the trail is visible. Cross the asphalt path and go straight ahead to take the Tower Trail boardwalk—the right-hand loop of the trail—through a mangrove marsh habitat. You'll then cross over a brackish slough that runs through the preserve; in the middle of the day, you can see dozens of little silver fish flashing in the sunlight. Watch for birds throughout the mangroves; wading birds such as ibises and herons are common, and it's not unusual to see wood storks, ospreys or even an occasional eagle soaring overhead. A little way through the loop, a

195

A gopher tortoise along the trail

left-hand spur leads to an overlook in a small brackish mangrove lake. Continue along the trail, and three quarters of the way around, you'll see another left-hand spur that will take you to the preserve's observation tower. Climb the three flights of stairs to the top of the tower for a spectacular view of all of Weedon Island Preserve and the surrounding area. To the south you can see St. Petersburg's downtown skyline, Florida Power's three smokestacks are to the west, and you can see the marshes of Tampa Bay to the east.

A short distance past the tower turnoff, the boardwalk gives way to asphalt, which leads back to the trailhead. In this section of the trail, watch on the left for a small interpretive exhibit, showing a cutaway into a Native American kitchen "midden"—a fancy name for an old trash heap that's a gold mine for archaeologists. Careful study of this midden has provided a great deal of

insight into the people who lived here. Also, along the entire asphalt section of the trail, watch for gopher tortoises; although they're rare in most places, they're quite common in the drier areas of Weedon Island Preserve.

Once you reach the trailhead, continue straight ahead onto the paved connector between the two loops. This section of the trail traverses a flatwoods area where you'll see native pines, sabal palms, and a small oak hammock; gopher tortoises continue to be common here.

When you reach the second loop, which is the Bay Trail, continue straight ahead to the shaded picnic area. Here, the trail turns back from asphalt into boardwalk. The slough you crossed earlier in the hike is big enough here to bring a canoe or johnboat up from the bay to the picnic area. Continue along the loop until you reach a spur trail going off to the left. This spur takes you to an overlook in a little estuary of Old

Tampa Bay. Look into the water and watch schools of mullet feeding, or watch them jumping all around the bayou. Return to the main trail and continue on around the loop. Although this area also is primarily mangrove habitat, there are a few higher spots with sweet bay, magnolias, live oaks, and one sabal palm for variety. Three-quarters of the way around the loop, the loop itself makes a left-hand turn. Go straight ahead, though, and you'll be on yet a third overlook into a brackish pond.

When you reach the end of the boardwalk, a short asphalt section will take you back to the map board where you began the loop. Turn left and follow the connector back to the trailhead and your car.

NEARBY ATTRACTIONS

A kayak and canoe rental livery is outside the main gate.

Once inside the preserve, look for a small parking area on the left just after you pass the entrance to the power plant; behind that parking area is Boy Scout Trail, which is a dirt bike trail about a mile long.

Inside the preserve, if you go all the way to the main road, you'll find a fishing pier and a canoe launch site where

The boardwalk passes through a lovely oak hammock before entering a mangrove area.

you can get onto a canoe trail in the preserve.

Outside the preserve, on Gandy Boulevard just west of San Martin Boulevard, is Derby Lane Greyhound Track.

Wortham County Park Loop

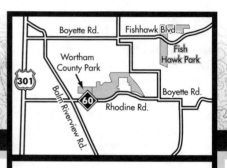

IN BRIEF

Compared to many of the county's other parks, Stephen J. Wortham County Park is not well known, but a number of multi-use trails, as well as a variety of other recreational facilities, make this an enjoyable place to spend an afternoon

DIRECTIONS

Take either Interstate 4 or the Crosstown Expressway to Interstate 75, and follow I-75 south from Tampa to US 301. Take US 301 south to the intersection where Balm Riverview Road forks left; follow it to Rhodine Road. Turn left on Rhodine Road and follow it two miles to the park entrance on the left.

This is one of several parks in the Tampa Bay area with an urban fishing pond that's regularly stocked by the Florida Fish and Wildlife Conservation Commission. This particular pond is wheelchair accessible; special regulations are posted at the fishing area.

DESCRIPTION

Although Stephen J. Wortham County Park adjoins the Rhodine Road ELAPP site, the two sites are stunningly different. The Rhodine Road ELAPP site is completely undeveloped, while Stephen J. Wortham County Park is a great park for families with children, with hiking and horse trails that mirror its overall personality. The park is well developed

AT-A-GLANCE INFORMATION

Length:
4 miles

Configuration:
Loop

Difficulty:
Flat, easy

Scenery:
Pleasant flora and fauna

Exposure:
Canopy in some areas, shady throughout

Traffic:
Quiet during the week; a good bit of horse traffic on weekends

Trail surface:
Sand and hard-packed dirt

Hiking time:
2.5 hours

Season:
All year

Access:
No fees or permits

Maps:
No trail map is published.

Facilities:
Rest rooms, picnic area, playground, wheelchair-accessible public fishing pond

Special comments:
The western entrance to the park is exclusively for the use of horseback riders.

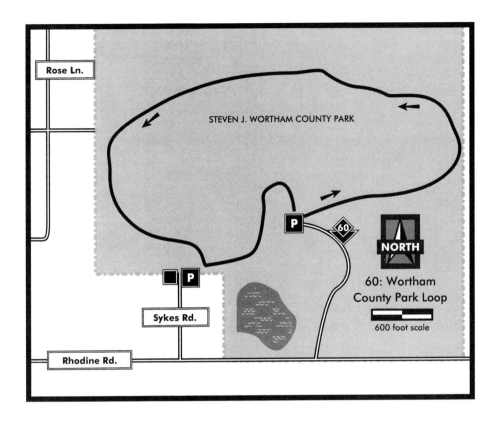

Rose Ln.

STEVEN J. WORTHAM COUNTY PARK

P

60

NORTH

60: Wortham
County Park Loop

600 foot scale

P

Sykes Rd.

Rhodine Rd.

with a children's playground, a well-kept picnic area, and a public fishing pond.

The trailhead is located on the side of the main picnic area. As the trail begins, you'll pass under a heavy oak canopy with Spanish moss draped over the low-hanging limbs. The horses that pass on the trail have cropped the hanging moss in many areas, which gives those sections a kind of shorn look. This is a good place to watch for songbirds, including woodpeckers. There are a lot of squirrels here as well, and they'll keep you amused with their antics and their acrobatic jumps from one tree to the next. The sandy trail is wide and can be used by hikers, mountain bikers, and horseback riders as well.

For about the first mile, a wide swath of ferns borders the trail, giving the area

a peaceful feel. The woodland here is a mixture of scrub oak and southern yellow pine.

As you continue along the loop, you'll pass through several stands of great oaks and pines, and then enter a large meadow of tall grass. This area is quite dry, and in keeping with that you'll see a number of prickly pear cacti, which are native to this part of Florida.

Approach this meadow slowly and you may come across a wild boar, as we did, eating the fruit of a cactus. He amused us, as his nose was covered with cactus thorns, and we wondered how he'd get them out. The prickly pear cactus fruit have a reputation for being quite good on the dinner table when properly prepared, but with the number

This boardwalk is the gateway to a hiking adventure.

of thorns on the plant, we weren't inclined to try it.

As you hike this section of trail, watch the tall dead oak in the far corner of the meadow. The tree contains a huge osprey nest, and if you're there when the nest is active you may see adults feeding youngsters. This isn't the only osprey nest you'll see in the park. Officials have placed nesting platforms on tall poles in other areas in the park, which is a common practice in central Florida. If you watch the sky while you hike, you may see one of these beautiful predators as it returns from hunting over the nearby Alafia River or one of its tributaries. It's a special treat to see one of these birds winging over the landscape with a fish grasped firmly in its talons, or watch it as it perches on a nesting platform while eating its catch.

The last section of the trail is hard-packed sand and passes through several thick stands of great oaks and pines with a dense understory. This last section runs close to the western perimeter of the park, and serves as the main entrance point for horseback riders. Take caution in this area—you need to be aware that these thousand pound animals are coming your way, and you also need to watch for the large "deposits" they leave in their wake—so watch where you step!

NEARBY ATTRACTIONS
Rhodine Road ELAPP site, which is almost completely undeveloped, is next door to the east. Stephen J. Wortham County Park is very close to the Alafia River and its smaller feeder streams, and there are several other full-facility parks within a five-mile radius

Appendices

What good is hiking without the chance to break in boots, try out a new kind of sock, or see how the latest piece of outdoor wicky-wacky works? If you're looking for gear, here's where to go in Tampa:

Adventure Outfitters
4315 El Prado Blvd. W.
Tampa, FL 33629
(813) 832-6669

Bill Jackson, Inc.
9501 US Highway 19 N.
Pinellas Park, FL 33782
(727) 576-4169

Champs Sports
Brandon Town Center Mall
Brandon, FL 33511
(813) 685-8514

Champs Sports
2149 University Square Mall
Tampa, FL 33612
(813) 979-9771

Champs Sports
6901 22nd Avenue N.
St. Petersburg, FL 33710
(727) 347-4996

Peter Glenn of Vermont
10330 N. Dale Mabry Highway
Tampa, FL 33618
(813) 960-2453

Sports Authority
4900 W Kennedy Blvd.
Tampa, FL 33609
(813) 282-1180

Sports Authority
4340 W Hillsborough Ave.
Tampa, FL 33614
(813) 875-2220

Sports Authority
1730 E. Fowler Ave.
Tampa, FL 33612
(813) 632-9091

Appendix B—Maps and Trail Information

A Mapsource
5712 W. Waters Ave.
(corner of Waters Ave. and Veteran's
Expressway)
Tampa, FL 33634
(813) 890-9595

A World Of Maps
6820 N. Florida Ave.
Tampa, FL 33604
(813) 237-1711

Florida Division of Forestry
Dept. of Agriculture
and Consumer Services
3125 Conner Blvd.
Tallahassee, FL 32399
(850) 488-4274

Florida Fish and Wildlife
Conservation Commission
620 South Meridian St.
Tallahassee, FL 32399
(850) 488-4676

Florida Park Service (State Parks)
Dept. of Environmental Protection
3900 Commonwealth Blvd.
Mail Station 535
Tallahassee, FL 32399
(850) 488-6131

Hillsborough County
Dept. of Parks and Recreation
1101 East River Cove
Tampa, FL 33604
(813) 975-2160

National Park Service
Southeast Regional Office
100 Alabama St. S.W.
1924 Building
Atlanta, GA 30303
(404) 562-3100

Office of Greenways and Trails
Dept. of Environmental Protection
3900 Commonwealth Blvd.
Mail Station 795
Tallahassee, FL 32399
(877) 822-5208

Pinellas County Parks Department
631 Chestnut St.
Clearwater, FL 34616
(727) 464-3347

Rails to Trails Conservancy
2545 Blairstone Pines Dr.
Tallahassee, FL 32301
(850) 942-2379

Southwest Florida Water
Management District (WMD lands)
2379 Broad St.
Brooksville, FL 34609
(800) 423-1476

US Fish and Wildlife Service
(National Wildlife Refuges)
1875 Century Blvd.
Suite 400
Atlanta, GA 30345
(404) 679-4000

Appendix C—Hiking Clubs

Florida Trail Association
5415 S.W. 13 St.
Gainesville, FL 32608
(800) 343-1882

Florida Trail Association–
Suncoast Chapter
906 Montana Ave.
Lutz, FL 33549
(813) 948-8821

Sierra Club–Florida Chapter
St. Petersburg, FL
(727) 824-8813

Sierra Club–Tampa Bay Group
P.O. Box 1948
Tampa, FL 33601
(813) 253-3555

Sierra Club–Suncoast Group
P.O.Box 16006
St. Petersburg, FL 33733

Wilderness Trekkers, Inc.
284 E. Long Creek Cove
Longwood, FL 32750

Index

Carolee Boyles

Carolee Boyles is the creative director for the Phalanx Media Group, a business communications and public relations firm headquartered in Tampa, Florida. She started writing about hunting and about women in the shooting sports 20 years ago, long before it became fashionable for women to go into the field. She's covered such diverse topics as fishing, hunting, environmental issues, wildlife management, and agriculture in magazines that include *Florida Sportsman, Florida Game & Fish, Rifle & Shotgun SportShooting, AllOutdoors.com, Women & Guns, American Hunter, American Forests,* and many others. Carolee holds a Bachelor's Degree in biology from Florida State University and earned a Master of Forest Resources and Conservation at the University of Florida. She's lived in Tampa with her son Chris for almost four years, and says working on this book has shown her how much green space can exist in a large urban area when a city, county, and state work together to preserve the natural areas that exist within their boundaries.